D0142159

PAUL CLAUDEL

WORLD DRAMATISTS
In the same series:

WORLD DRAMATISTS

C PAUL LAUDEL

BETTINA L. KNAPP

WITH PHOTOGRAPHS

FREDERICK UNGAR PUBLISHING CO.

NEW YORK

842
Kn

To my students
at Hunter College
and the Graduate Center
of the City University of New York

Copyright © 1982 by Frederick Ungar Publishing Co., Inc.
Printed in the United States of America
Design by Edith Fowler

Library of Congress Cataloging in Publication Data

Knapp, Bettina Liebowitz, 1926-
  Paul Claudel.

  (World dramatists)
  Bibliography: p.
  1. Claudel, Paul, 1868-1955—Dramatic works.
I. Title. II. Series.
PQ2605.L2Z699   842'.912   81-40465
ISBN 0-8044-2479-9   AACR2

CONTENTS

ACKNOWLEDGMENT

My deepest thanks go to Tobey Gitelle for having edited this manuscript.

CHRONOLOGY

1868   Birth of Paul Claudel on August 6th at Ville-neuve-sur-Fère-en-Tardenois. Baptised on Oct. 11th.

1870   Moves to Bar-le-Duc, where his father becomes the Director of Records.

1873   Enrolls at the Sisters of the Christian Doctrine school.

1875   Goes to the Lycée at Bar-le-Duc.

1882   Paris. Begins his studies at the Lycée Louis-le-Grand.

1884   Receives Baccalaureat.

1885   Completes his year of Philosophy. Begins a Licence in Law.

1886   Reads Rimbaud's *Illuminations*. December 25th "converts" at Notre-Dame de Paris.

1887   Attends Mallarmé's Tuesday gatherings. Writes his play, *The Sleeper (L'Endormie)*.

1889   Studies at the School of Political Science. Writes *Golden Head (Tête d'Or)*, revised in 1894. Jean-Louis Barrault directed *Golden Head* at the Odéon-Théâtre de France, 1959.

1890   Enrolls as a student at the School for Oriental Languages in Paris. Does not pursue his studies. Passes competitive examination required to study Foreign Service. Writes *The City (La Ville)*, revised in 1897. Produced at the Festival d'Art Dramatique at Avi-

1

gnon, 1955, by Jean Vilar and the Théâtre National Populaire.

1892–93   Writes *The Young Girl Violaine (La Jeune fille Violaine)*, revised in 1898. Produced at the Festival de Touraine, 1959; directed by Maurice Jacquemont. Writes *Fragment of a Drama (Fragment d'un drame)*. Begins his translation of Aeschylus' *Agamemnon*.

1893   Named Vice-Consul. Leaves for New York; then in Consulate in Boston. Writes *The Exchange (L'Echange)*. Produced at the Vieux-Colombier, 1914; directed by Jacques Copeau.

1894   Named Consul Suppléant in Shanghai.

1895   Remains in China until 1899. Returns to Paris via Palestine. Writes *Verses in Exile (Vers d'exile)*.

1896   Writes *Knowledge of the East (Connaissance de l'Est)*.

1900   Meets André Gide and Francis Jammes for the first time. Goes on a retreat at Solesmes and at Ligugé. Leaves for China on the Ernest-Simmons. Meets Rose, his great passion.

1903   Writes *Knowledge of Time (Connaissance du Temps)*.

1904   Completes *Co-Birth of the World and of Oneself (De la Co-Naissance au monde et de soi-même)*.

1905   Returns to Europe. Writes *Break of Noon (Partage de Midi)*. Produced at the Marigny Theatre, 1948, directed by Jean-Louis Barrault. Composes the poems "Ténèbres" and "Obsession."

1906   Marries Reine Sainte-Marie-Perrin. Returns to China. Writes "The Spirit and Water" and the second of his *Five Odes*.

1908   Writes *The Hostage (L'Otage)*, produced at the Théâtre de l'Oeuvre, 1914; directed by Lugné-Poë. Named Consul in Prague.

1911   Writes *The Tidings Brought to Mary (L'Annonce faite à Marie)*, produced at the Théâtre de l'Oeuvre, 1912; directed by Lugné-Poë. Named Consul at Frankfurt. Composes *The Cantata for Three Voices (Cantate à trois voix)*.

1913   Writes *Proteus*. Produced at the Foyer des Etudiants, 1937. Translates Aeschylus' *Choephori*, produced in Brussels in 1935, with music by Darius Milhaud.

Writes *Stale Bread (Le Pain dur)*, produced at Porrentruy, 1941; directed by Ludmilla Pitoëff. Takes his sister, Camille, to a mental hospital where she will remain until her death, 1942.

1914   Bordeaux. Minor official at the Ministry of War.

1915   Gives series of lectures in Switzerland and Italy. Writes *The Humiliated Father (Le Père humilié)*, produced at the Théâtre des Champs-Elysées, 1946; directed by Georges Le Roy.

1916   Rome. Translates Aeschylus' *Eumenides*.

1917   Leaves as Chargé d'Affaires for Rio de Janeiro. Travels in Brazil. Writes "Ballad," a play *The Bear and the Moon (L'Ours et la lune)*; a ballet, *Man and his Desire (L'Homme et son désir)*. *Man and his Desire* is created at the Théâtre des Champs-Elysées by the Swedish ballet, 1921; music by Darius Milhaud.

1919   Leaves for Denmark. Begins *The Satin Slipper (Le Soulier de Satin)* which will be completed in 1924, produced at the Comédie-Française, 1943; directed by Jean-Louis Barrault.

1921   Writes "My Voyage in Indochina."

1922   Tokyo. French Ambassador. Writes the mimodrama *The Woman and Her Shadow (La Femme et son ombre)*, produced at the Imperial Theatre in Tokyo, 1923.

1925   Returns to France. Lectures in Italy, England, Belgium, Switzerland. Writes *Hundred Phrases for a Fan (Cent Phrases pour Eventail)*. *Reflexions and Propositions on French Verse (Réflexions et propositions sur le vers français)*.

1926   *Occidental Ideograms (Idéogrammes Occidentaux)*.

1927   Named Ambassador to the United States of America. Writes *Under the Rampart in Athens (Sous le Rempart d' Athènes)*, produced at the Comédie-Française, 1929. Writes *The Diary of Christopher Columbus (Le Livre de Christophe Colomb)*, produced at the Berlin Opera, 1930; with music by Darius Milhaud; Au Grand Théâtre de Bordeaux, 1953; directed by Jean-Louis Barrault. Writes *Religion and Poetry (Religion and Poetry)*.

1928   Returns to Paris for the signing of the Briand-Kellog Pact.

1930   Washington, writes *Commentaries on the Apocalypse (Commentaire sur l'Apocalypse); Drama and Music (Le Drame et la musique)*.

1933   Named Ambassador to Brussels. Travels throughout Belgium and Holland. Writes an *Introduction to Dutch Painting (Introduction à la peinture hollandaise)*. Completes a dramatic oratorio, *Joan of Arc at the Stake (Jeanne d'Arc au Bûcher)*, produced in 1938 at Basel, Switzerland; music by Arthur Honegger.

1935   Retires to his home in Brangues during the summer months; in Paris in the winter.

1936   Lectures on French poetry and the Far East. Writes continuously: essays, poems, commentaries.

1938   Writes a morality play, *The Story of Toby and Sarah (L'Histoire de Tobie et de Sara)*, produced at the Festival d'Art dramatique at Avignon, 1947; directed by Maurice Cazeneuve.

1939   Attends coronation of Pope Pius XII. Made Doctor *honoris causa* in Cambridge. Writes *Spanish Painting (La Peinture espagnole)*.

1941   Meets with Jean-Louis Barrault concerning the staging of *Golden Head, The Satin Slipper, The Diary of Christopher Columbus*. Travels. Lectures.

1946   Elected to the French Academy.

1947   Writes *The Moon in Search of Itself (La Lune à la Recherche d'Elle-Même)*, a radiophonic extravaganza.

1950   Poetic matinée devoted to the works of Paul Claudel at the Vatican. Pius XII was present.

1951   Operation for cataracts.

1954   Goes to Aix-les-Bains for sciatica treatments.

1955   February 23 (Ash Wednesday) dies of a heart attack. National Funeral at Notre Dame in Paris. Buried at Brangues on September 4.

PROLOGUE

Claudel's theatre is sensual and erotic. The protagonists of his dramas are earth lusting for heaven, body obsessed with spirit, and darkness longing for light. Perpetual turmoil rages in the hearts and minds of Claudel's split and chaotic souls. Each in his own way seeks to liberate himself from egotistical and arrogant tendencies while, at the same time, attempting to acquire altruism, humility, and godliness. Claudel's creatures are pagans clothed in Catholic vestments; they are hedonists yearning to be ascetics.

Claudel's plays are unique among those of twentieth-century playwrights. Neither Naturalistic nor Realistic, Claudel veered away from the Becque, Bernstein, Bourdet, Hauptmann type of theatrical venture. His work also did not conform to boulevard standards as did those of Guitry and Deval. Claudel created his own genre: poetic, but unlike the Platonic essences issuing from Jean Giraudoux's theatre of ideas; religious, but endowed with far greater amplitude, depth, and vigor than the litanies of Henri Ghéon; symbolic, but reaching more deeply into the elemental world than Ibsen; tormented with sexual problems, but different from those plaguing Strindberg. If comparisons are to be made, one might liken Claudel's dramatic dirges and dithyrambs to the works of Racine and Aeschylus. They reach into the very core of human nature and flesh out its agonies. They deal with collective beings and collective problems; his theatre is archetypal in dimension.

Claudel's *Golden Head, The City, Break of Noon, The Satin Slipper, The Tidings Brought to Mary,* his *Trilogy, The Diary of Christopher Columbus,* plays under scrutiny in this volume, are all thesis dramas. They do not fly the banner of political ideology, as do Brecht's works, though they certainly express Claudel's propensity for monarchical forms of government. They do, however, emphasize his religious ideations: each in a different way, each pointing up a new reality for him, a fresh and glowing force in his life. Catholicism is the great *sine qua non* of his world, along with family, tradition, and order. Catholicism gave structure to his chaotic inner world: it rendered the fluid fixed; it controlled the uncontrollable; repressed and suppressed the unmanageable in his psyche, his incredibly *immense urge for life.* Claudel's existence, as well as his theatre, which is a transmutation of it, centered around the awakening of the flesh, the call of the flesh, the need for the flesh, the obsession with the flesh and its counterpole the punishment of the flesh, its flagellation, its annihilation. Ecstasy reached its culminating point, both existentially and artistically, when transcendence became humanized through the flesh.

Claudel's theatre is cosmic in dimension. It is also elemental in that earth, water, fire, and air each participates in a giant animistic embrace. The sun, the moon, constellations of all types, trees, flowers—each plays its part—taking on value in a perpetually evolving dynamic process which is the creative work. Claudel's theatre is global and Promethean in sweep. His protagonists, whether in *Golden Head, The Satin Slipper, Break of Noon, The Diary of Christopher Columbus,* travel from continent to continent:

Asia, Europe, America, Africa. They are explorers, discoverers who seek to possess the earth, the world, the cosmos. Voyages such as these are quests, viewed as initiatory devices leading man into deeper dimensions, into his own arcane realm, there to experience a spiritual, religious, and aesthetic discipline. The stage under Claudel's direction becomes a network of analogies, patterned and focusing on energetic particles which are his characters; it is a meeting place of needs, a juxtaposition of longings, an abrasion, raw nerves rubbing against each other, bloodying flesh, splintering bone, blending heavenly, earthly, and infernal textures.

Claudel's theatre is a Creation, a Feast in which Death and Transfiguration become the motivating factors.

"Watch ye and pray, lest ye enter into temptation. The spirit truly is ready, but the flesh is weak."

ST. MARK *14:38*

1. INTRODUCTION: "EVERYTHING WITH ME WAS INSTINCTUAL. . . ."

Paul Claudel was born on August 6, 1868, in the town of Villeneuve-sur-Fère-en-Tardenois in the Aisne region. His mother, Louise-Athenaïs Cerveaux, also came from a small hamlet near Notre-Dame de Liesse. Claudel claimed the Vosges, as well, as part of his ancestral heritage, since his father, Louis-Prosper, Conservator of Mortgages, hailed from this area. Claudel's forefathers stemmed from multiple classes: the peasantry, nobility, business and professional worlds, and the clergy.

Although Claudel's early years were spent moving about from one town to another, wherever his father's job took the family—Bar-le-Duc, Nogent-sur-Seine, Vassy—it was always to Villeneuve, where his mother's family had their home, that he returned on weekends and for holidays. On hot summer days, he loved to walk through the forests on the outskirts of this ancient town, enjoying the coolness of the trees and dwelling in the darkened solitude that such shade offered him. There, he feasted on the luxury of isolation. Musing, daydreaming, he allowed his imagination to make forays into formidable spheres, pleasurable as well as tormenting. He enjoyed sitting on the stately rocks which jutted from the soil here and there, running his hands across their harsh or smooth surfaces, experiencing their solidity and rigidity, their colorations attracting him in some strangely hypnotic way. Frequently, he stood still, looking about the flat and "austere" countryside, which he later said gave him access to infinite realms. The valleys seemed endless to him then; the plains surrounding Ville-neuve were like gigantic open spaces. Even at this early age, Claudel was filled with a desire to traverse the land-scape—to engage in a life of excitement and mystery—to go beyond the visible and cultivated world. Harshness marked this region, which shuddered with nearly continuously pounding winds and rains; at times, torrents drenched any-one who did not run for cover. "Nothing is more bitter, or more religious," he wrote, than Villeneuve. Its character is marked with duality: a "dramatic struggle" between serenity and a "terrible wind" which beats about violently, intransigently.[1] All is eroded by this powerful force; every-thing takes on its contours, Claudel suggested, even the Church which he compared to "a ship which sails into the sea"—leaning on its side as does a mast when flogged by tempestuous forces. Wind and ship, symbols dear to Claudel even then, would imprint themselves in his writ-ings: the former representing the spirit of God; the latter suggesting navigation, journeys, incursions into the un-known.

In 1881 Claudel's favorite sister, Camille, a talented sculptor, decided that she wanted to pursue her studies in Paris at the Colarossi atelier. Her passionate pleas, her enthusiasm for her art, convinced Mme. Claudel to yield to her desires. The family moved to Paris. The father re-mained behind, living wherever his job took him. His parents' separation, Claudel wrote, was a "catastrophe"; his whole "life was torn in two."[2]

His parents' separation led Claudel to an emotional up-heaval and an intellectual torment as well. Classes at the Lycée Louis-le-Grand in Paris were large; they included nearly forty students. In the country schools to which Claudel had been sent, classes numbered five or six students, and he was usually first in his group. Competition in Paris was acute. Claudel was no longer the head of his class, much to his parents' disappointment. Important, too, was the fact that he had been severed from the earth, that one force in life to which he had no trouble relating: trees, of particular importance to him, were increasingly described later in his plays, poems, or essays. He looked upon them as living beings, dynamic forces, creatures able to comfort him, whose sap strengthened him, whose branches rose to the heavens, yearning for spiritual comfort, and whose roots dug deep into the *prima materia*, earning for him the power he needed, the visceral experience which energized him. Unfortunately, in Paris he was greeted with masses of buildings, twisted and tortuous streets, and gray skies. People were impersonal; each attended to personal affairs, while steeped in centroverted existences. Claudel grew melancholy, dissatisfied, rebellious. He could not find himself. He had no one in whom he could confide. He searched, frenetically, for some answer; he longed to assuage his distress in something or someone.

The feelings of dread and a preoccupation with death, which had plagued Claudel since his earliest memories, seemed activated in Paris. Such attitudes may have stemmed in part from the fact that the country house in which he was born faced the village cemetery. Acute fear had been triggered in 1881 by the death of Claudel's grandfather, Athanase Cerveaux, from stomach cancer. He witnessed the acute agony, the harrowing pain. The image of this man in the throes of physical suffering never left him. Without the comfort of nature to ease his troubled soul, the

fear of death combined with feelings of "complete abandonment" overwhelmed the young Claudel in Paris. He
had no "guide," nor did he know to whom to turn. His
aloneness was complete.[3]

Endowed with a will of iron when it came to tasks in
which the intellect had to perform, Claudel concentrated
all of his energies upon his studies. He wanted to succeed
and would. At the age of fifteen, he decided to take the
Baccalaureat examination (1883). Although he received
first prize in French discourse and was awarded this honor
by the "great" Ernest Renan himself, he failed the Baccalaureat as a whole. Undaunted, he increased his study
time and passed it the following year. It was at this juncture,
too, that he found some compatible friends, young men of
promise with whom he could exchange ideas if not feelings:
Léon Daudet, Marcel Schob, and Romain Rolland. Despite the dialogue he enjoyed with them, it was insufficient
to quell the mounting furor in his soul.

Only when the family returned to Villeneuve, usually
once a week, did the young Claudel find temporary relief
from the turmoil. Then, he would write, assuaging his grief
and loneliness, pouring out the emotions and sensations
which had been constricted, drawing nourishment from
the vegetal world about him. Any place was good for writing: the house, barn, orchard, fields. Nature was his inspiration; the vast expanses were his catalysts.

Although Claudel's satire/farce, *The Sleeper* (*L'Endormie*, 1888) is naive, technically speaking, the germ of
his future characters lies embedded in this work. Duality
emerges within the *dramatis personae*, who are aggressive
and passive, solitary and gregarious, possessive and detached. Claudel's proclivity for images—the moon in all of
its mystery, the sun, strident in its glare, stars shimmering
from their celestial abode—is also evident. The poet is the
focal point of *The Sleeper*: the plot revolves around his

search for identity and definition. The world described in *The Sleeper* is strange; the sequences seem to emerge undaunted from the bleak world of fantasy and mystery. A poet falls in love with a beautiful girl, described as "impetuous" and "savage." He seeks to possess her; he is driven toward her by some outerworldly force. A mocking and hawking crowd follows as he makes his way toward the grotto where his beloved is supposedly asleep. He anticipates the ecstatic encounter awaiting him only to discover, to his horror, that the woman of his dreams has turned out to be a monstrous type, the kind of woman to whom the naive frequently fall victim. *The Sleeper* is not a great work. Rather, it is the outpouring of a lonely youth who seeks to relate to the outside world, to women in particular. Nascent, however, are the liquid emotions and ductile sensations which will flow through Claudel's future writings.

Neither Claudel's friends, nor certainly his parents, understood the depth of his despair. The pain was his alone, part of his secret inner world. He pursued his studies, nevertheless, throughout this tortuous period. He received a law degree, enrolled at the famous and prestigious Ecole des Sciences Politiques, and took it for granted that he would, eventually, work for the government, as had his father. He approached his studies in a meticulous, disciplined manner, but was uninvolved emotionally. He knew he had to succeed at something, that he had to earn a living. He also knew he had to leave his family. He was being stifled, submerged, isolated from society in the family cell which was his home. Mother, father, sisters, each had his or her own difficult personality, described by Claudel in later years as violent, and "not particularly agreeable."[4]

The intellectual atmosphere in Paris—the reign of Positivism, Naturalism, Scientism—also corroded his spirit. All these forces crushed his enthusiasm and hope for the future. Although he admired Auguste Burdeau, the positivist philosopher who was his teacher, Claudel had little respect for the objectivity, detachment, and calculated manner with which he approached life. The scientific determinism of Hippolyte Taine and the relativist, historical works of Ernest Renan did nothing to relieve his tormented soul. Claudel grew increasingly pessimistic; he was revolted by what he considered to be the facile answers offered by the scientists of his day, who claimed that all mysteries within nature would eventually be revealed to man. All problems would be solved. Claudel felt anger, rancor, when confronted by such generalizations. A *tabula rasa* had to be made by him. He would accept nothing: no answer, no certitude, no point of view. He called himself an "anarchist" during this period, and he was one, politically and socially. He read vociferously: Comte, Kant, Darwin, to mention only a few. He felt encumbered, dammed up, suffocated. He wanted fresh air, free thought, life, dynamism, excitement. He was fed up with the dry, cerebral conclusions offered him by the scientists. The microscope was insufficient to express an imagination in turmoil, the febrility of swelling emotions. A man of instinct, not of reason, Claudel found kinship in the music of Beethoven and Wagner; it nourished his soul: Aeschylus, Sophocles, Euripides, Seneca, and Shakespeare fired his being. Baudelaire incited him to create, to strive, but also to subdue his feelings.

Eighteen hundred eighty-six was a momentous year for Claudel. In May, he made what he considered an incredible discovery: Arthur Rimbaud's *The Illuminations*. This slim volume of poems was to become a "seminal" force in his life, having a shattering effect upon Claudel, because it opened up "the supernatural world" to him. Rimbaud, the Promethean, the Rebel, the adolescent who fought society and God, and himself, made Claudel aware of his own turmoil and dissatisfactions: the growing chaos within his psyche. In Rimbaud, Claudel found a blood brother, a fellow mystic, someone with whom he could relate on the profoundest level. Rimbaud's vibrancy activated his own feelings, offering a virtual transubstantiation. Rimbaud's poetry shook his circumscribed world to its very foundations. It cut, tore, bruised him. Claudel wrote that it freed him of "the hideous world of Taine, Renan, and the other nineteenth-century Molochs, from the imprisonment engendered by this horrible mechanical realm governed entirely by perfectly inflexible laws."[5]

The year 1886 was also of extreme importance because it brought Claudel the answer to his metaphysical anguish. During the Christmas Mass at Notre Dame Cathedral in Paris, he was so shaken by the experience of divinity that he was "converted" to the faith of his fathers, totally and completely.

> And it was at this moment that the event which dominated my whole life took place. In one instant my heart was touched and *I believed*. I believed with such adhesive force, with such powerful conviction, with such certitude, that an upheaval within my whole being occurred, and there was no place at all left for any kind of doubt.[6]

From that time on Claudel's faith never wavered.

A year later, 1887, Claudel began attending Stéphane Mallarmé's Tuesday gatherings in his apartment on rue de Rome. Around the Dean of Symbolist poets gathered such men as Maurice Maeterlinck, Henri de Regnier, René Ghil, Francis Vielé-Griffin, Villiers de l'Isle Adam, to mention only a few. Mallarmé encouraged Claudel to pursue his writing. He "approved" of his poem, "Chanson d'Automne," which the young writer subsequently destroyed. Claudel looked upon Mallarmé as a kind of God. From Mallarmé, Claudel learned to try to understand the quintessential value of words—their impact, logic, sensuality—as visual and intellectual instrumentalities, as solitary entities, and as connecting links within the poem's ensemble of dynamic forces.

At this time in Claudel's development, the drama seemed the most expressive of creative forms, allowing him to quell the antagonism breeding within him and to expel it in palpable creatures. "My dramas were really never more than complicated contraptions, so to speak, designed to flesh out an inner conversation,"[7] Claudel wrote to his friend, the poet Francis Jammes. *Golden Head (Tête d'Or,* 1889) was just that. The protagonist was a conqueror, a rebellious, active being who rejected the status quo, fomented divisiveness, and aroused fresh ideas and ideals. A projection of Claudel, Golden Head sought to discover the world, to participate in its dynamism; he also opened up "supernatural" domains. Along with Golden Head's conquests, his domination of kings, kingdoms, and armies which swelled the battlefields reaching out as far as the Caucasus, there was the image of the woman. Readers are introduced to a dual being: earth woman considered sensual and lustful, a veritable *magna mater*; and the spiritual ideal, the soul woman, the Gnostic Sophia, the Virgin Mary who lures the protagonist into her aerial domain. Caught in a maze of contradictory desires, he dies at the end, amid his guilt and spiritual yearnings. Maurice Maeterlinck compared Claudel's hero to a "demiurge," to Lautréamont's protagonist, Maldoror. He felt, while reading *Golden Head*, that a "Leviathan" inhabited his room. Octave Mirbeau considered it "violent" and "incoherent," a work filled with "passion," the breadth and scope of a great writer. André Gide spoke of its publication as, as powerful an event as an "exploding bomb." Jules Renard labeled Claudel a "genius."[8]

Claudel supplemented his readings. The Greek classics, always; now, Dante and Virgil would be added, the latter being "at the center of everything." Then came the discovery of the incredible Dostoevski: *Crime and Punishment*, whose characters reveal "the angel in the slumbering brute"; the first two-hundred pages of *The Idiot* likened by Claudel to the "crescendos of Beethoven" masterpieces.[9] Philosophical and liturgical tomes were also absorbed, analyzed, dissected, and imbibed, among them, Aristotle's *Metaphysics*, which Claudel stated "rid him of Kantism" once and for all. Claudel would read the Bible and Patristic literature throughout his life and comment upon them frequently. The "Meditations on the Gospel" by Bossuet were admired for their style as well as their religious orientation, as were the passionate outbursts of Saint Theresa of Avila.

The City (*La Ville,* 1890), a dramatic presentation set in the Sodom and Gomorrah atmosphere in which Claudel felt "plunged" at the time, was next. In this drama between man and society, the city—a product of modern civilization—emerges as a monstrous force, crushing and lacerating an individual, bringing him to stagnation. The poet/protagonist, who feels incarcerated within this destructive entity, struggles to discover new values amid a disintegrating bourgeois; it is a soul-less proletariat whose powers are misguided, whose desires misfire and serve to obliterate creativity. Claudel's descriptions are brutal, his expressions rough-hewn, his epithets, sequences of explosive cacophanies. The reader feels the visceral power of the poet as he breathes life into language, as he roots out feelings of asphyxiation, destroying the dark and fungal desires of archaic being. Claudel's subliminal realm pulsates, burns, as his all-engulfing appetite for freedom is ejaculated in verbal clusters. Claudel's city is destroyed in the end: constrictions vanish as the life-sapping enclave is reduced to rubble.[10]

That Claudel felt stifled in Paris, and particularly within

the family, was an understatement. Distance. Reserve. Control. These were the disciplines that kept his psyche intact. Unconsciously, he understood that his disruptive and ebullient nature needed strong and solid structure to prevent it from shattering. Enclosing oneself within a fortress made for solitude, encouraged introversion, secrecy, and cut ties with the outer world. Human contacts and relationships, except on the most superficial levels, were difficult for Claudel. An inability to integrate the chaotic forces within him encouraged an already intransigent nature to underscore incipient aggressive characteristics and incited outspoken and hostile attitudes. André Gide called Claudel a "congealed cyclone."[11]

"Above all else, I wanted to give myself air. I had to leave, absolutely, and see the world."[12] Claudel was adamant. Travel was his only salvation at this time. He prepared and passed the examinations required to obtain a diplomatic post. The "itinerant" nature of this kind of work had allure for him. Many difficulties, nevertheless, would await Claudel in his chosen profession; but then, with his rugged, brusque, frequently hostile and irascible personality, any work involving others would present problems. Tenderness was unknown to him; understanding was considered a weakness, an emotion to be subdued. Strength, power, force, energy, discipline, and conquest were his bywords.

These characteristics are evident in his next play *Fragment of a Drama* (*Fragment d'un drame*, 1892), a work in which his protagonist tries to adapt to various situations, attempting to understand life, its despair, struggle, and need for compassion. Again, the feminine principle appears in all of her sensuality and seductivity. Just as the poet/protagonist is about to yield, believing the woman's promise of joy in "conjugal" life, he turns away, repulsed, and leaves her to follow his own "long, painful, subterranean" route.[13]

That Claudel shied from women, rejecting and fearing them, while being inextricably bound to them, was not surprising. His father, although highly imaginative, had always been austere and never showed emotion. As for his mother, she never kissed her children, remaining distant, always reserved, controlled. Claudel wrote in his *Notebooks* about his mother with amazement: "How could this woman whose character spelled modesty and simplicity above all else, have had children such as my sister Camille and me."[14]

Claudel entered the foreign service, the start of a brilliant career. He was sent as Consul to the United States (1893–94), and there wrote *The Exchange* (*L'Echange*). Yet, powerful feelings of nostalgia and melancholia encroached upon him again. He had never realized how utterly isolated he would be in a new land, a different culture; nor did he feel more at home in France where he returned the following year. Uncomfortable, out of place, he knew he would have to break away again—choose another land—and become a world traveler. What he had learned in the United States, however, was important: depression is a crippling emotion to which he must never yield, and it should be transmuted into his writings. Feelings would become food for his future plays and poems.

Although *The Exchange* is perhaps Claudel's poorest play, revolving around adultery, materialism, and death, it did subsume themes to which he would again return. Claudel had been caught in the same trap that Georges Duhamel and Jean-Paul Sartre would be in later years. A brief journey to the United States had allowed these French writers to consider themselves experts in appraising the new world, materially as well as spiritually. "The enslavement in which I found myself in America was very painful, and I depicted myself in the traits of a lively young man who sells his woman to recover his freedom . . . it is I who am depicted in all these characters, the actress, the husband, the abandoned wife, the young savage and the calculating merchant."[15] In *The Exchange*, the characters are poorly delineated, the ideas superficial and banal; yet, the undercurrent of fire and flame for which Claudel would become renowned, was alive and radiated within his language.

China (1895–1900) was to be Claudel's next port of call. In the early stages of his stay in the Orient, he felt even more displaced than he had in the United States. Everything was so totally different: mores, language, religion, and psyche. To Mallarmé he wrote:

> China is an ancient land, vertiginous, inextricable. Life has not been struck by this modern evil. . . . It proliferates, dense, naïve, disorderly, emerging from the deepest instinctual resources and tradition. I feel only horror for modern civilization and I have always felt estranged from it.[16]

Visions of past eras, different races, and a mysterious culture—the antitheses of what Claudel had known—were opening up to him. Interestingly enough, the disorientation he now felt caused Claudel to carefully increase his readings of religious works, thereby counterbalancing the fear that he would lose his painstakingly absorbed Catholic values.

Claudel's psyche—no matter what the precautions taken—was split: each side worked against the other. Despite his longing for structure and security, peace of mind and serenity, he needed the excitement, tension, and searing experiences of new worlds. Curious, ever alert, he was a man who sought adventure. His heart and body were titillated at the thought of freedom; his muscles flexed with each new encounter. He was also a poet whose soul was corroded with guilt, and whose terror at losing his equilibrium was all-encompassing. Although he made the effort to open his mind to foreign ways and to accept the spiritual offerings of other peoples and lands, he completely rejected Buddhism at this time. In *Knowledge of the East* (*Connaissance de l'Est*, 1895–1900), his prejudices and intolerance were evident. These characteristics would be modified over the course of years, but would never leave him. For Claudel, Buddhism was a religion of "idolators,"a "pagan blasphemy"; it taught a "monstrous communion," based on a "Nothingness" which he viewed as "Satanic."[17] Furthermore, Claudel abjured all that was not Catholic and anyone assailing his sacred credo: "Whoever attacks the Church is like someone who strikes my father and mother"; such people are "personal enemies of Christ."[18] His inability to tolerate such insults, seemingly, was caused by insufficient security in his religious belief. He could not exercise the necessary detachment to live in harmony with other ideations.

In China Claudel clung most powerfully to Western thought: scholastic reasoning and logic gave him the solidity and emotional support which he craved. It was in China that he pursued his readings of Aristotle and Saint Thomas Aquinas. The *Summa* allowed him to review human knowledge; it permitted him to see clearly into the divisions and similarities existing between reason and faith and why these two forces were complementary to each other, allowing the hierophant to experience God as the *fons et origo* of all truth. From Thomas Aquinas, Claudel learned to think clearly and objectively, to use the power of observation, and to examine his faith. He gleaned an understanding of the religious universe that Aquinas had developed in his writings, with divinity as its center, and a structured cosmogony radiating all around. Claudel described the *Summa* as a kind of "grammar," a way of "listening" to things which "speak" to him.[19] Only later was Claudel introduced to the analogical way of thinking through the lessons of Saint Bonaventura which, requiring an intuitive approach, brought the irrational world into focus. Both attitudes toward life and aesthetics would be used by Claudel in his writings, infusing them with the power of luxuriating in fresh dimensions.

Knowledge of the East, an "intimate diary," "interior itinerary," and an "adaptation" to life, has been characterized as a way of understanding and accepting spiritual realities and fitting these into an eruptive and dynamic personality. Claudel never felt, then or thereafter, that religion included "ideas of immense enjoyment or sensibility." He had "converted" to Catholicism, he wrote, "for reasons of obedience and interest, to know what was expected of me, but I never had the idea that I would take pleasure in God, experience intense joy or any kind of pleasure." Claudel's Catholicism was looked upon as an *engagement*, an "obligation," a "loyalty," in the English sense of the word.[20]

During Claudel's stay in China he wrote *Verses in Exile (Vers d'Exile*, 1895), expressing feelings of disquietude and isolation, and a play, *The Young Girl Violaine (La Jeune fille Violaine*, 1892–1900). It was the forerunner of his most popular dramatic producton, *The Tidings Brought to Mary (L'Annonce faite à Marie*, 1910–11), a religious mystery in which the spirit of sacrifice becomes the dominant theme, a means of gaining access to heaven. *Rest on the Seventh Day (Le Repos du septième jour*, 1896–97), a complex theological drama, sets out to isolate the notion of Evil. The play takes place in China, where the cult of the dead enjoys such an important role. Claudel understood this view most acutely, since he had always been plagued with the notion of death. In *Rest on the Seventh Day*, "a transitional" work according to its author, the dead invade the domain of the living, with the result that the living can neither eat, drink, nor sleep, so possessed are they by those hovering, invisible forces.

Claudel returned to France in 1900. He had made up his mind to enter the Church. He wanted to "sacrifice" his worldly condition to God: life for spirit, sensuality for sublimity. Claudel went on a retreat to Solesmes, then entered the Benedictine monastery of Ligugé. In September of that year he experienced a religious crisis which he expressed in "Muses," the first of his celebrated Odes. Some scholars have looked upon this poem as a kind of farewell to literature. Claudel's religious rapture, however, was to be short-lived because his spiritual director believed the poet unsuited for monastic life. His great "sacrifice," unacceptable to the Church fathers, was, perhaps, overly filled with pride, and feelings of spiritual superiority and arrogance. Claudel was compelled to return to the world. The pain of his Fall, which he compared to Adam's, tore him asunder. It was "a rejection pure and simple," preordained by God, he thought; it was "a peremptory *no* . . . not accompanied with any explanation."[21]

Similar to Adam, Claudel would have to experience conflict, the disorder of daily existence, even sin. God had placed these temptations before man to test his faith. The Portuguese proverb, "God writes straight with crooked lines,"[22] would certainly apply to him. Important, also, in Claudel's religious philosophy were St. Augustine's words—*etiam peccata*—sins also serve in man's quest for redemption. It is through the experience of sin that the believer suffers real torture and can fight his base nature. In so doing, he ascends the hierarchy of spiritual values. Evil, which is a non-essence according to St. Thomas Aquinas, succeeded in spoiling human nature, but not in destroying it.[23] Claudel reasoned that sin becomes a virtual necessity if pardon is to be experienced, and that the absence of sin strengthened one's backbone and tested the will. Sacrifice of physical pleasure is a technique designed to increase ascetic endurance.

Claudel was sent back to China in 1901 where he remained until 1905. The political situation in China at this time was difficult and dangerous. The Boxer Rebellion (1900) with its secret society bent upon killing and/or deporting all foreigners who had virtually dismembered their land, was very active and laid siege to Peking. The uprising was supressed by joint European action.

It was on the ship, the *Ernest-Simmons*, returning Claudel to China that he met the beautiful Polish blond, Rose Vetch, a wife and mother. His passion for her was great and it was reciprocated. Despite the commandments of his religion and the fact that only months prior to this traumatic love affair, he had wanted to take the vows of chastity, the man of flesh was unleashed. Claudel's liaison, which included the birth of a child, lasted for several years. Few know the reasons for its conclusion. It has been suggested that Rose gave him up, weary with his bouts of remorse and élan toward God. Others believe he yielded to the advice of his superiors at Quay d'Orsay: they stated categorically that if he wanted to pursue a successful government career he would have to live a more conventional existence. Whatever the reason for his "break up," he expressed his grief in many poems including "Ténèbres" (1895).

I suffer, and the other suffers, and there is no road
Between her and me, no words nor hands between the
other and me.

Nothing but night common to us yet incommunicable,
Night in which no work is effected and the horrible
impracticable love.

I extended my ear, but I am alone, and terror engulfs
  me,
I hear the tone of her voice and her cry.

During this troubled period Claudel found an immensely understanding friend, Philippe Berthelot, who
occupied an important post in the Ministry of Foreign
Affairs in Paris at the time. His sympathy for Claudel, his
handling of his feelings, was described by Claudel as "incomparable." They remained lifelong friends.[24] Claudel's
grief and turmoil were transmuted into his great dramatic
work, *Break of Noon* (*Partage de midi*, 1905), a play which
he alluded to as a "deliverance," a work so personal, so
traumatic, that he refused to allow it to be staged until
1948, when Jean-Louis Barrault was awarded this singular
honor.

Break of Noon is the dramatization of Claudel's union
with Rose in all of its tempestuous and fulminating furor.
The vibrancy of the poetry and the authenticity of the
feelings are unparalleled in Claudel's works. *The Satin
Slipper* (*Le Soulier de satin*, 1919–24), which concludes
the Rose cycle for Claudel, is a play in which the notion
of denial, sublimation, and the joy of encountering and
sacrificing one's passion is uppermost. Written when
Claudel was in his early fifties, older and wiser, it is devoid
of the whirlwind passion, the frenetic tempo which is the
very fiber of *Break of Noon*. It is an intellectual construction resembling a baroque cathedral in which every area is
illuminated, as well as a global work in which Orient and
Occident, Africa, and the Americas participate. Influences
cohabit, each neatly etched into the fabric of the various
genres included in the play: tragedy, comedy, irony, burlesque, and more. What is lacking in this bulbous drama,
this gargantuan panoramic vision, is the fulgurating mur-
mur of the heart. The mind predominates. Structure is all-

important. Theology in its total syllogistic array is the focal point. Even poetry in its most sublime form is implicit in the dialogue; it is always placed in the right sequences, in clumps, tirades, dialogues. Yet, the mystery is dead, the feeling banished, and the melody, missing.

During the early 1900's Claudel was investigating the art of poetry, and he associated it with his metaphysical probings. Two essays are involved in what was to become one of his major works, *The Poetic Art*: "Knowledge of time" ("Connaissance du temps," 1903) and "Treatise on the Knowledge of the World and of Oneself" ("Traité de la co-naissance du monde et de soi-même, 1904). The first delves into the problems of being and time, viewed as networks, combinations, metaphors of values, harmonies, cacophonies, unisons of subdued and striated colors. All is linked in Claudel's monistic world: time in its linear or eschatological sphere is a parcel or particle of cyclical or mythical time. In the second essay, which includes the untranslatable word "co-naissance" which means co-birth as well as co-knowledge, Claudel penetrates the cosmos as one does a painting, fusing disparate objects, things and beings, into a solidified, yet fluid, mass, creating continuity and contiguity from dispersion. Claudel does not separate such human faculties as intelligence from the senses. For him they are one. Sensations may be experienced in a variety of ways: as continuously modified vibrations, taking on circularity of pattern, working in and out, to and from the center to the periphery, depending upon the artist's perpetually mobile reactions. Sensations are inner workings, likened by Claudel to "emissions of nervous fluid," which he then compares to a birth. An individual, particularly a creative one, never ceases to be born, reborn, in multiple creations "fulfilling the form attributed to him." For this reason Claudel affirms that "all knowl-

edge (*connaissance*) is a 'birth' (*naissance*), and that knowledge (*connaissance*) is a co-birth (*co-naissance*)." Words are
catalysts; each has a soul around which feelings cluster and
thoughts radiate.[25]

Claudel returned to Paris in 1905. Adaptation was again
difficult. "Modern civilization," Gide wrote about
Claudel, "spelled ruination, waste" for him.[26] Claudel
took the advice of his superiors in the government, consulted with his father confessor, and then married Reine
Sainte-Marie Perrin (1906). Three days after the wedding,
the couple left for Peking. Theirs was an ultra-conservative
Catholic household in which they eventually raised five
children.

In 1909 Claudel and his family returned to France, only
to leave for Prague six months later where he continued working on his trilogy: *The Hostage* (*L'Otage*, 1908), *Stale Bread*
(*Le Pain dur*, 1913), and *The Humiliated Father* (*Le Père
humilié*, 1916). These plays, which he described as "The
drama of the family and the earth,"[27] filled with bitterness,
hatred, cruelty, and lust for power, represent a world from
which love is banished. Claudel's affirmation that his protagonists are aspects of himself sheds light on his own soul
state. Solitude, isolation, restraint, discipline, the pain of
an existence based on extremes—passionate outpourings
and immense guilt feelings—were the mold he had chosen,
the structure he decided most suitable to his life's course.
To repress love is to arouse other facets of the personality,
such as, anger, hatred, dissatisfaction, hostility. Claudel
never really learned to relate to women: his view of them
ranged from lustful, feline, magnificently sensual *femme
fatale* to the saintly, spiritual, ethereal Marylike creature.
The oppressive disciplines, strictures, and theological view,
which he hoped would relieve his sorrow and enable him to
find balance, merely prolonged a functional antagonism

which corroded his existence. Such restraints, however, may have aided in the birth of his great dramatic works—his literary ejaculations. In a letter of explanation to André Gide, Claudel wrote: "The Christian does not live in the manner of an ancient sage, in a state of equilibrium, but in a state of conflict. All of his acts have consequences. He finds himself perpetually in a state of composition."[28]

The Cantata for Three Voices (1911), and a play, *Proteus* (1913), were written after his father's death at the age of eighty-seven, and following the painful incarceration of his sister, Camille. It was she, perhaps more than anyone else, for whom Claudel felt profound affection. She had displayed great talent as a sculptor when young, but her unrequited love for Auguste Rodin had sent her down the road to insanity. Camille remained institutionalized until her death in 1943. Such was her destiny.

Claudel was to pursue his country-hopping as well as his creative activities, one interspersed by the other. Drawn to the Greeks ever since his earliest days, he translated Aeschylus' *Choephorae* and *Eumenides* (1913). A stay in Germany, until the declaration of World War I, was followed by his departure for Rio de Janeiro, with Darius Milhaud as his secretary. There he wrote *The Bear and the Moon* (*L'Ours et la lune*, 1917), a charming playlet in which the Moon, a mediatrix, unites rather than disperses cosmic disparities. For Nijinsky, whom he considered the most extraordinary of artists, Claudel wrote a ballet, *Man and His Desire* (*L'Homme et son désir*, 1917). Nijinsky was an example of "a body dominated by the mind and the use of the animal by the soul." He called him a "God," a "great human creature in a state of lyrical being." When he walked, his steps resembled those of a tiger; "it was not the shifting of a dead weight from one foot to the other, but all the complex of muscles and nerves moving buoyantly, as a wing moves in the air, in a body which was not a mere trunk or a statue, but the perfect organ of power and movement."[29]

Claudel returned to France (1919) only to leave for Copenhagen (1919–21), then on to Tokyo (1921–25). Deeply immersed in Japanese culture, Claudel wrote "A Glance at the Japanese Soul" and "The Black Bird in the Rising Sun" ("Un Regard sur l'âme japonaise" and "L'oiseau noir dans le soleil levant," 1923), among many other works inspired by Japanese iconography, art, drama, and music. "Less intolerant" than in those early days when writing Knowledge of the East, his "metaphysical diatribes" were not as provocative; their virulence diminished.[30] Claudel's reactions had softened with the passage of years. Perhaps he felt his superiority less keenly, his security having gained in importance. He understood the ways of the Oriental now, and not only accepted them for what they were, but also understood some of their attributes. Intrigued by the mystery of Japanese art, its intensity, interiority, whether pictorial or literary, he commented on the works of Kano, Korin, Hokusai, and others; also on the haiku poems of Basho, which inspired him after having left the shores of Japan to write A Hundred Phrases for Fans (Cent Phrases pour éventail, 1941), in which he took paintbrush in hand and drew the characters described—the rose, the camellia, the moon, and other forms—both abstract and concrete, in a panoply of exquisite delineations. It was in Tokyo that Claudel's short play, The Woman and Her Shadow (La Femme et son ombre), was performed at the Imperial Theatre to the accompaniment of Japanese music (1922).

Claudel considered Noh drama "one of the highest forms of lyric and dramatic art." He was astounded by the intensity which emerged from the characters as they stood immobile on stage, underscoring attitudes and moods by a shift of the arm, a cry of despair, an eye movement. They were like clusters, networks of vibrations, which reached a peak of intensity in the singleness of their controlled gestures, their expressionless faces, their traumatic silences. Noh is a concentration of emotion, a distillation of plastic images. Bunraku, the Japanese puppet theatre, also fascinated Claudel. He described it as the work of a "collective soul." The puppet/protagonists severed earthly contact as they moved, gliding with ease in all dimensions. These wooden entities remained unfeeling; transpersonal forces, they wove their way about the stage oblivious to pain, divested of feeling, participating in the limitless world of dream. Bugaku, Japanese dance, was viewed by Claudel as something "inhuman," the interlocking of circuitous masked forces, as living Elements and Passions, colliding, bruising, or harmonizing with each other. Nothing was in vain in Japanese art: all was measured, distilled, decanted in infinitesimal tonalities.[31]

Claudel never ceased working. In 1927 he was made Ambassador to Washington: his days' activities consisted of meetings with various high dignitaries, lectures at universities (Yale, Princeton, Columbia, Chicago, and many more), where he was awarded honorary degrees. Essays, poems, playlets, notes on art, architecture, translations, and theological commentaries cascaded forth. The world for Claudel was still exciting. All was subject to change; therefore, everything glistened with beauty and novelty.

In *The Legend of Prakriti* (*La Légende de Prakriti*, 1932), Claudel wrote of the fluidity of emotions—his own to be sure—which prevented stagnation and enabled him to embrace unlimited spheres. Life was a composite of "swirling organic forces" similar to unformed blocks of consolidated movements."[32] The chameleonlike activities in which

Claudel indulged did not prevent him from reworking his own plays, much to the dismay of many of his theatrical directors, including Jean-Louis Barrault. Claudel was always ready to change his script, reinterpreting a role, altering an ending. He mentioned that there was always a fresh way of viewing a play, creating a backdrop, refurbishing a decor, blending sounds, detonating lights. In theatrical matters, Claudel was protean: glowing, evolving, changing, like constellated whirlwinds. Every possibility, every form was to be exploited by the artist, viewed, sensed, and absorbed in multiple means.

The world nourished Claudel: the universe was his inspiration, the earth his food, the ocean his sustenance. Secret affinities existed everywhere: in a tree, flower, word, image, rhythm, sonority. Writing in all genres—ballets, oratorios, operas, cantatas, films—was combined in what Claudel called "total theatre," of which *The Diary of Christopher Columbus (Le Livre de Christophe Colomb,* 1927), was an example. Claudel had always been impressed with Jacques Dalcroze's experimental theatre which blended music and movement, light and gesture, enabling the body to grow pliant and "to obey the soul."[33] In *The Diary of Christopher Columbus,* the mystery of matter and form were displayed in creatures grouped all about the stage, each unfolding its own secret realm in controlled and measured gestures. Darius Milhaud composed the music, conglomerates of stylized litanies shot through with wild and passionate outbursts of energetic tonalities; contrapuntal rhythms were projected onto sculptured forms which made their way on and off the stage. The page glowed, dilated; the moment was exciting.

All of Claudel's plays are thesis dramas. *The Diary of Christopher Columbus* was no exception. His liturgical outpourings in structured forms are numinous representations of rigid ideations, a carapace keeping a rebellious and titanic inner world from destroying itself. Had Claudel not possessed the outer garment, this cathedral-like edifice which he found in his religion, this unshakable foundation which gave his life cohesion, the swirling waters of his subliminal world would have torn him apart. "One undergoes terrible struggles and one needs an ever tensed energy to return to one's faith and to maintain oneself within it. The life of a Catholic is a scandal and a series of continual contradictions. Each conversation, each book, each journal is the negation of everything in which he believes, everything in which he believes and loves."[34] Claudel's writings were the manifestations of a veritable *war zone*.

In 1933 Claudel was made Ambassador to Brussels. His art criticisms *Introduction to Dutch Painting* are extraordinary in their perceptions, depth, and breadth of understanding, as well as in the excitement they engender. The same may be said of his essays on Jan Steen (1937), Jordaens (1936), Watteau (1939), Velasquez, Zurbarán, Goya, Ribera (1939), Rembrandt (1947) which were gathered together in *The Eye Listens* (*L'Oeil écoute*).

Joan of Arc at the Stake (*Jeanne d'Arc au bûcher*, 1934) with music by Honegger, and *Wisdom or the Parabole of the Feast* (*La Sagesse ou la Parabole du festin*, 1939) were created among many other works including essays, poems, and religious commentaries. Even after Claudel's retirement (1935) to Brangues (Isère) during the summer months, and Paris on rue Jean-Goujon in wintertime, his world was one of constant creativity. His pen never stilled. When he was not writing, he was traveling, lecturing. In 1946 Claudel was made a member of the French Academy.

On February 22, 1955, while reading, ironically enough, a book on Rimbaud, the poet who had had the greatest influence upon Claudel's creative life, he suffered

a heart attack. That evening the last rites were administered. Claudel told his family he wanted to be left alone. "I
am not afraid!" he said. He died peacefully during the
night.

On Claudel's work table, the Bible was opened on Chap-
ter XXX of the Book of Isaiah. Claudel had been commenting upon verses 32 and 33 during that afternoon, the fruit of
his labors to be included in a work in progress.

> And in every place where the grounded staff shall pass, which
> the Lord shall lay upon him, it shall be with tabrets and
> harps: and in battles of shaking will he fight with it.
>
> For Tophet is ordained of old; yea, for the king it is prepared;
> he hath made it deep and large: the pile thereof is fire and
> much wood; the breath of the Lord, like a stream of brim-
> stone, doth kindle it.

Even in death Claudel was not at peace with himself.
Tophet (or Hell), the fire and brimstone which had pursued
him throughout his life, kept gnawing at him to the end.
Now, however, the raw eruptive forces which cohabited
within his depths had been transformed into spectacular
monuments in his creative works—like baroque cathedrals,
each carved by hand from his flesh, their stones placed
amid mysterious shadows, shining, luminescent—with the
strength and power of eternity.

"For carnally minded is death; but to
the spiritually minded is life and peace."
EPISTLES OF PAUL 8:16

2. GOLDEN HEAD:
A BLOOD RITUAL

Golden Head (*Tête d'Or*, 1894) dramatically relates a
psychological and spiritual crisis. It is an eruption, a searing
and brutalizing transmutation of dormant characteristics
which lie buried or repressed within the author's subliminal
realm. These burst forth in clusters of firebrands, as unformed and deformed entities clothed in human proportions. As protagonists, they take on the stature of eternal
and mythical beings: archetypes. Each is an energy charge,
tormented and twisted as it cuts its way into the light of
consciousness, lusting for power and yearning for love.
Claudel's antagonists (protagonists) are divided: they seek
to experience aerial spheres, but instead are plunged into
mephitic depths. The blood rituals enacted in *Golden Head*
are brutal and blinding; murderous and moving; satanic
and godly—an Agave (dismemberment) and an Agape
(communion in divine love).

Golden Head was first published anonymously (100
copies) in 1890. A revised edition, the one upon which this
analysis is based, was brought out in 1894. When Claudel
wrote *Golden Head* he was experiencing the emotional

34

aftermath of his parents' separation. He was also in the process of rejecting the shackles which bound him to bourgeois family life. As yet, however, Claudel had not found anything to fill the void which his act of heroic divestiture had brought upon him. In 1886, however, he returned to the fold of his ancestors and became a devout Catholic. Claudel's religious struggle was far from over. An extremist, he longed to rise "above" the workaday world and to perform an *imitatio Christi*. His goal was to destroy the man of flesh within him, to scourge that part of himself he considered evil, degrading, and satanic, so that the pure and godly side of his being could reign supreme. The battle raged.

To reject one's earthly being in favor of what Plato called the divine part of man—the spirit—was tantamount to performing a psychological amputation, a murder, a dismemberment. It was a cutting away, an erosion of the human element, a cultivation of the inhuman and lofty factors. Claudel venerated what was "above" the normal: the saintly and fleshless. The schism grew broader: soma and psyche were at odds; each fought to gain supremacy; each vied for power. They acted as catalysts for Claudel who functioned in the world of contingencies—spurred on by these elemental forces—which fed him the excitement emerging from their heated struggle.

Thomas Aquinas' *Summa Theologica*, the Bible, and countless Patristic works nourished Claudel's spirit. Strict adherence to the Church's laws and doctrines became his soul food. The realm of instinct or the "animal" in him, however, was severed. It starved and remained outside the pale of understanding. When an animal is unfed it angers, it aggresses, it grips and snaps its jaws. The less attention given it, the more demanding it becomes. When fed, understood, and loved, it acts and reacts with warmth and gentleness. The split within Claudel's personality, as viewed in the creatures of his fantasy, reveals a painful imbalance: a man at odds with himself and with the world. Claudel was perpetually dissatified with his lot: sensuality gnawed at his vitals while the incorporeal imposed itself on his spirit. He longed to be a saint, but remained a sinner. Only the communion—the blood ritual—could bring order to his tormented soul, and then, only temporarily.

Golden Head was a solar hero. He could be described as the sun's earthly counterpart. In Claudel's words: "a sun which stuns and devours all shadow, a blinding splendor, so rigid it appears solid."[1] A conqueror and fire principle, Golden Head's drive for power was so great that it placed him beyond the human sphere in an extratemporal time scheme. He was swept along in Promethean style. His quest was energetic, exuberant, and replete with a passion for life. As he wandered about the earth in parallel course with the sun, he clashed and crushed his enemies, throbbing with orgiastic joy. During moments of repose and silence, however, he was haunted by a corrosive sense of guilt, caught up in visions of incorporeal spheres of divine beauty and spiritual perfection. Such intrusions—or irritants —impeded his archaic ways and anthropoid reactions. Comparable to a climactic happening, the interplay between earth/air and spirit/matter in Golden Head's being as expressed in Claudel's images, accelerated the drama's tempo and increased its suspense, while also grinding away and abrading the hero's flesh. Golden Head lived in two worlds—unappeased—each thirsting and hungering for the other.

The decor for *Golden Head* is spartan. Stark and sinewy, it takes on the hand-hewn quality of the medieval stone sculptures incised on the porticos and altars of the eleventh-century church Saint-Benoit-sur-Loire. The

Scene from Jean-Louis Barrault's production of *Golden Head* at L'Odéon-Théâtre de France. Golden Head (Alain Cuny) kills the king (Jean-Louis Barrault).
FRENCH CULTURAL SERVICES

single tree and earth mound in Part I, the roughly col-umned palace in Part II, and the seemingly limitless moun-tainous terrain in the concluding sequence, lend an im-pression of cosmic unidimensionality. No perspective, no nuances. The few stage objects (a tree, some stones) stand out like kratophanies (manifestations of power), underscoring the archetypal nature of the characters, their visceral ways, defiant encounters, and sordid/sublime relationships.

The names Claudel chose for his antagonists are indicative of their temperaments. *Simon Agnel*, known as Golden Head, the solar hero, is a name complex in its ramifications. Onomastically, Simon is associated with the French *semences* (seed), *semer* (to sow), and *semens*: fecundating and fructifying forces, referring to the verb *to conquer*. Simon, after Simon called Peter, one of the twelve disciples, denotes the character's spiritual yearnings. The Hebrew word *simon* means "to hear" or "to be heard" and reveals the hero's capacity to listen to his inner pulsations as well as to the swelling forces outside of himself.

Agnel brings to mind *Agni*, the Vedic fire God, a metaphor most suitable to Claudel's solar hero. *Agnel*, anagram for *angel*, reveals a longing for ascension or communion with deity. There are, however, many types of angels, each reflecting the protagonist's moods: guardian, revelatory, good, evil, and messengers of God who carry His sword as they confront and affront mortals. *Agnel* was also the name given to a gold coin used during the time of Saint Louis, the Crusader (1215–1270); it was stamped with the image of a lamb (*agneau*), the sacrificial animal, the spotless lamb of Christ.

Simon Agnel then is a composite figure: creator/destroyer, pacifist/warrior, the sacrificed/sacrificing. A primordial man, he acts and reacts spontaneously, fearlessly, unthinkingly and, therefore, automatically. Incapable of evaluation, his anthropoid psyche acts in consort with his seething passions. Unable to understand his motivations or torments, he is unaware of the power of these bulbous and ever-expanding tumescences living inchoate within his subliminal realm. He speaks his marvelous invocations to the sun and earth and powers that be, with Dionysian fervor. Words for him enclose a soul, breathe, and vibrate in atonal and tonal sonorities.[2] Similar to objects, they shatter and clatter, reflecting mood and emotion. In this manner, they participate in the giant happening which is the play. Simon Agnel is youth brandishing a sword: fighting, cutting, dismembering. Like Agave, Pentheus' mother who tore her son apart in a moment of religious frenzy, so Golden Head also separates and divides. He seeks wholeness and completion: he molds and fashions at the beginning; at the conclusion, the communal feast which man shares with divinity—an agape—is taken.

Cébès is Simon Agnel's shadow personality, that part of his being which remains weakly structured and unfulfilled. Cébès, unlike Golden Head, laments his fate, requests help, is tearful, identityless. He is also an *anima* (soul) figure: Golden Head's feminine aspect which lives through projection. Cébès' needs are neither understood by Simon Agnel, nor assimilated into the hero's personality. Like Kebes, the Greek philosopher and perhaps his namesake, author of the dialogue *Pinax (The Picture)*, an allegory which describes the condition of the soul before its union with the body, so Cébès also remains an external force, object and not subject. Cébès is a contemplator and not an initiator; he is negative and not positive.

I. *Tellus Mater Rejected:*
The Blood Ritual—Agave

Empty skies stretch into the distance over desolate and barren expanses of land. The end of winter is at hand; the earth, however, is still hard and unfriendly. Darkness imposes itself on the atmosphere, as does the chill of death.

Simon Agnel makes his way into the vacant world before him. He is carrying the corpse of a woman over his shoulder. He puts it down and then begins breaking the earth to make a trench in which he will place the body. As in ancient times, during vegetation cult rituals when the seed was implanted into the soil, there to be nurtured until it produced a living form, so Simon Agnel digs deeply into *tellus mater* in an effort to transform what is arid into a fertile condition.

Moments later he notices his old friend, Cébès, not far off. He hears him lament his fate; weak, hopeless, identity-less. Cébès' way in life is unclear; his course seems barred by insurmountable obstacles. The two men begin talking. We learn that Simon Agnel had loved and lived with the woman he was burying, that he had left her to travel, to see new lands, to cut through the confines of his circumscribed world. He returned to her just prior to her death. Feelings of tenderness enter into complicity with a seemingly hard and harsh attitude; guilt also intrudes, corroding his every move. He knows that had he not left home, the woman who had given herself to him completely would not have withered from neglect. Yet, he could not do otherwise. As the sun wanders about the earth, he, too, is a nomad at heart. He continues hacking at the hard crust of earth; he knows that just as the seed is plowed back into the humus, as winter recedes when oncoming spring takes over, darkness gives way to light, so he must bury—actually or symbolically—those forces which might impede his own growth. The woman, the female principle—the Eros personality—must be interred so that other facets of his being are allowed to germinate.

Simon Agnel tells Cébès how he had taken this woman, once happy and ardent, then left her to go his own way. He had to tear, rip out, shear this relationship in order to discover his own essence. His guilt is ferocious. He experiences that Empedoclean dichotomy, the love/hate within his own breast, which he projects around him. As he cuts into the earth and turns it over, he draws an analogy with his own life: uprooting staid principles, destroying pat answers. His youthful unchanneled energy (libido defined as both psychic and physical energy) flows forth as he explains his need for freedom, his hatred for strictures. He personifies plants, animals, and celestial worlds, and in so doing, kindles cosmic visions. Like the sun hero he is, energy bursts forth and flows from him; he sows light. The entire stage seems animated and agitated, thrust and torn by bolts of fire. "I nourished many dreams; I knew/Men and the things which now exist./I saw other paths, other cultures, other cities."

His dream of fulfillment could only be achieved in a masculine context. He had to bury the matriarchal force which this woman represented: she had to return to the ground, to decompose in earth. So would his servitude to that force end. Similar to Persephone, who entered the darkened regions of Pluto's kingdom (wealth, riches), so the woman would be plowed back into matter. The burial ritual takes on archetypal proportions; it becomes a cosmic impregnation, a seed placed in the blackness and richness of earth, there to be nourished.

Each time a hero forges ahead, breaks with a past, tearing the closeted asunder, guilt is the aftermath of the act. Infamous, sinful, ignominious, damned, the hero, Golden Head, is overcome with sharp and piercing pain. He no longer understands himself or recognizes his being. He has altered in consistency, divided in two; the man of action and the man of feeling become two personalities on stage: Simon Agnel and Cébès.

As a shadow figure, Cébès is that factor in Simon Agnel which he rejects, which cannot be assimilated into his psyche, and remains a split-off. Cébès denigrates himself

constantly by calling himself an "imbecile" and "ignorant." He fears the unknown, is terrified of the future. "I
know nothing and am capable of nothing. What can I say?
What can I do?" Cébès is depersonalized.

> What am I
> What am I doing? what do I expect?
> And I answer: I do not know! and deep within me I want
> To weep, or scream
> Or laugh, or leap and wave my arms!

Introverted, a seeming "nocturnal dream," Cébès sounds
out his depths attempting to discover the origin of his
disquietude. He cries out into the unresponsive night air,
his voice throbbing in parallel beats with the pulsing
rhythms of the universe. Identityless, directionless, action-
less, he describes his torments in terms of his hands, which
lie limp at his sides. Hands and legs are aggressive instruments which support the body and reach out into the world
at large. They direct and aid in the fulfillment of acts; they
imply control, particularly of sexual matters. Hands also
express an attitude of the psyche and mind; when raised,
they symbolize authority; when lowered or held close to the
body, they question.

Every so often Simon Agnel joins Cébès in a threnody of
deprecations. "I am vile," Simon iterates; each handful of
earth he casts into the pit as he covers the corpse is accompanied by an accusation against the "gluey earth"; and his
contemptible act sticks with him, like clods of dirt. Moments later, he stands back and assesses his work. Disconsolate, he looks at the corpse. She resembles a "queen who
wraps his bloody feet in her golden tresses!" He cries out
into the frigid night air, and the desolate countryside resounds with shrieks of despair. He has buried her face down,
"her mouth against the earth." There, in her womb/tomb,

she will decompose and recompose, carrying out her eternal procreative function, the life process.

Simon Agnel closes the gaping void, wipes it from his mind. He tramples the earth above the grave so that it appears untouched from above, invisible. The feminine element (the Eros principle) has been forced from his conscious world into the earth or the subliminal realm. The matriarchal order, as experienced by the earth/woman, is closed. The male forces will dominate henceforth, driving, flaming, and inflaming, as Simon Agnel walks the vigorous path of conquest.

Simon Agnel counters Cébès' sadness and fear; he banishes these lugubrious thoughts. Excitement sparks his blood; he tingles with new ideas, fresh views. Moments later, however, he stops to question: where shall he go now that his bonds and strictures have been cut? He stands at the threshold of a limitless existence. By the same token, he faces a gaping maw, a precipice, and emptiness fills his being, solitude engulfs him. To divest oneself of a past is tantamount to being *unborn*, rootless.

An old peasant pushing a wheelbarrow comes onto the stage. Simon Agnel recognizes him as the father of the woman whom he has just buried. Deaf, poor, decrepit, the senex figure scrounges about for food and wood as he seeks to prolong his useless existence. Half-mocking, and certainly with cruel intent, Simon Agnel asks him the whereabouts of his daughter. He does not know, he replies. She should be helping him, he suggests. He then meanders on into the void.

Simon Agnel is also a loner, somewhat of a pariah. Unwilling to comply with the laws of society, he stands beyond its protection, unwelcome, alienated. Divested of all material possessions except for the clothes on his back, severed from all human company, which is the lot of the hero as attested by Siegfried and Parsifal, so Simon Agnel must learn to fuel his own energies and feed his own future. Only in strength will his goals be accomplished.

Claudel chooses the stone as a symbol of strength: "I shall sit on a stone and will find myself sufficiently rich," Simon Agnel says. The stone is hard, durable, and not subject to the laws of birth and decay to the same degree as is the flower. The stone is the antithesis of dust and sand, which represent psychic infirmity. The stone is also the foundation of religious feeling, the *Beth-El*, or House of God. In Genesis we read: "And this stone which I have set for a pillar, shall be God's House (28:22). After the crucifixion of Christ, Peter said: "This is the stone which was set at nought of you builders, which is become the head of the corner" (Acts 4:11), later to be understood as the cornerstone of the Christian Church. The stone counters Simon's feelings of emptiness and annihilation. It infuses him with strength and sensations of durability, with confidence in his own worth. He stops to listen to his inner soundings, those incandescent forces within him which prod and activate "my own voice's word!" The word he hears is *logos*, spirit, which seems to have penetrated his very being, powerfully, intensely, completely. The spirit, which has donned the form of the word, speaks out to him as an inner voice, guiding him through what will become a harrowing and lonely path. Emerging from the very depths of his being, this inner voice dialogues with the outer man: God within him speaks.[3]

The blackness of night prevails as Simon Agnel undergoes this primordial experience. The frost of winter still congeals the world around him; brittle and iced thorns impede his march, tie him to the earth, to the very spot he seeks to leave: "The earth is melancholy." Yet, it is this very voice which prods him. Only in action does warmth exist; only then will hardness soften, rigidity become malleable.

The fresh flush of freedom forces Simon Agnel on his way. Not so quickly, however, since Cébès, the shadow figure, speaks out his anguish. Submerged in his undeveloped and formless personality, Cébès whimpers: "I am but a child!" He begs for warmth, evokes pity, and like an empty stalk of wheat, fragile and transparent, he is blown to and fro by the piercing and pitiless winter wind. Cébès compares himself to "a mad woman" who allows the wind to amuse itself with her hair and who enjoys the sensation of freshness and newness. Cébès is woman: the anima, Simon Agnel's unconscious image of the feminine principle. Passive, Cébès questions: who will understand his turmoil, strike down the impediments that prevent smooth access with the outer world of light, and allow communication between polarities: himself and God, conscious and unconscious, good and evil. The "yellow fire" which he seeks, that sulphuric masculine element, which he mentions in his plea to Simon Agnel, is that inner sun, that intuitive force buried like larvae in his debilitated being; it is hidden beneath the flesh-fabric of his being. It must be rescued, he cries out, for evolution to take place and harmony to exist.

Cébès, Simon Agnel's counterforce, confesses his discomfiture, expressing the frailty and vacillating nature of his ways: infirm, curved, spiralling. Strangely enough, his perpetual dirge acts as a catalyst for Simon Agnel. Impatient, Simon Agnel stands erect, and inflates his lungs with the fresh, crisp, night air, with fire and flame. He is ready to face the New Year. He feels renewed, drunk with desire and power: "O delirium which penetrates as a creator, producing the flower and the seed!" Simon's senses surge; a series of alliterations hammer out his ferocious needs: *b* as in *bouche* (mouth), *beurre* (butter), *bourgeon* (bud), *bloc* (block) are transliterations of his emotional response. He is ready to drink deeply of life: "Life's juices! strength and acquisition!" Oxygen aerates his blood, clears his thoughts, pulverizes notions of fear and constraint.

To go beyond what enslaves; stretch what has shrunk; leap over into a world outside of the known, spreading the harvest of creativity, is Simon Agnel's philosophy. The first step for youth, as well as for the artist/poet, is to sever ties with those forces which bind; to dismember what circumscribes: woman, home, responsibilities—and encourage experience to heighten and enlighten one's universe.

Simon walks over to a large tree. This ancient force and vital spirit, has been endowed with sacrality. In Claudel's play it becomes a hierophany. In the Garden of Eden, the tree held the "knowledge of good and evil" (Gen 2:9); in Deuteronomy it stood for life and growth: the "tree of the field is man's life" (20:19); in Matthew's Gospel it combines what is opposed: "Every tree which bringeth not forth good fruit is hewn down, and cast into the fire" (3:10). It is to the tree that sins must be confessed, wrote Peter: "Who his own self bare our sins in his own body on the tree, that we, being dead to sins, should live unto righteousness" (I Peter 2:3).

It is to the Tree that Simon Agnel pours out his heart: "O son of the Earth!" Unable to relate to humankind, Simon experiences unity with natural forces which he personifies, animates, and divinizes in an embrace of understanding. It is the tree which ministers to him and nourishes him. A positive senex force, the tree feeds him the milk of life. Its roots dig deeply into the earth. Its branches aspire toward heaven. Its trunk is solid and generates cyclical schemes. Three worlds are assembled in the Tree: the earth bound to matter; the trunk which inhabits the existential world and bears itself upright like a human being; the branches which inhabit the uranian sphere, air and light, fed by the fire of the sun and cooled by the rays of the moon. The tree is androgynous: self-contained. Its trunk is phallus-shaped; its distribution of branches and leaves are feminine, as are its roots which vitalize its being. [4] Within the tree's recesses lies a body which humankind has transformed into a coffin; the tree plays the sacrificial role of the cross. It also represents evolution and growth.

Simon Agnel looks upon the Tree as a striving force involved in a continuous and assiduous effort to force up his body from inanimate matter. The Tree lives outside and beyond time: *illo tempore*, as attested to by Jesse's Tree, which has been reproduced so frequently in stained glass windows in medieval cathedrals. Jesse was David's father, and it was said that the Messiah would be born of the "rod out of the stem of Jesse" (Isaiah II, 1). The Messiah has not yet come for the Jews; the Christians trace Christ's lineage from the House of David and, therefore, give him roots in the existential domain. In either case, the Tree possesses a mana personality—it contains the "essential sap," that "inner moisture"—which paves the way for man's energetic routes.

Cébès kneels in front of Simon Agnel. "Haven't you learned anything beneath this tree of knowledge," he questions. Adam and Eve had chosen to eat the fruit of the tree of Knowledge and had been cast out of Eden. Had they not fallen into matter, man would not have experienced his earthly sojourn, nor would he have the hope of redemption. As if suddenly struck by a vision, Simon Agnel cries out into the vacant skies: "Cébès, a force has been given me, severe, savage! It's the furor of the male and there is no woman in me." Cébès understands the powerful charge that inhabits Simon's being since he is a mirror image of him. In desperation, the pain stabbing his flesh, he begs Simon to save him, to care for him, to understand the harrowing road he must follow and the ordeal he must undergo. Simon Agnel, strengthened by his own inner pulsations, is ready to face the exposure of lacerating forces, is prepared for his "night sea journey," that descent into blackness and chaos which Osiris, Moses, Christ, Buddha had all experienced during their excoriating initiations. Each must carve his own way in life, sifting through the debris of matter until light emerges. In a moment of despair, Simon Agnel bellows out, as if an open wound had been daubed with acid: "Love me! Understand me! Swear your loyalty to me. . . ." They are fatherless children, lonely, disconsolate, walking blindly into an increasingly blackening night.

Blood will cement their bond; it will also dismember. Simon Agnel slashes his arms and lets the drops of blood flow onto Cébès' head: "so man, although he has no breasts, will know how to give of his milk." The sacrificial symbol of blood, that life-giving force, now binds them forever, appeases their suffering. Like the *logos spermatikos* or "creative, impregnating Word" which Clement of Alexandria identified with the patriarchal society when he equated blood with milk, "The food is the milk of the Father, with which children alone nursed,"[5] so Simon Agnel will both nourish his weaker half with his blood and will concomitantly divest himself of it.

Throughout history blood bonds have denoted intense relationships, both spiritual and physical. When Joseph of Arimathea gathered up Christ's blood in the Holy Grail, it represented eternal life for the Christian. The blood of communion is expressed as follows in Matthew: "For this is my blood of the new testament, which is shed for many for the remission of sins" (26:27–8). Man takes unto himself in the transubstantiation ritual the Godly elements, thus divesting himself of his mortality. In war or in sacrifice, the spilling of blood dazzles Mother Earth, who sucks it up in deep swallows. As the blood travels through the recesses of her realm, it nurtures new growth and fresh sensibilities. In the Gnostic's *Odes of Solomon*, the father, an androgynous figure, gives blood, milk, and semen to those in need.[6]

Simon Agnel's blood causes him both a communion and a dismemberment. For the first time his mirror image —Cébès—will follow him on his journeys, but not as part of him, rather as a separate form: visible, objective, outside of him. Prior to Cébès' appearance on the scene, what he represented within Simon Agnel's personality was so embedded within his subliminal realm that he was unconscious of its very existence. Once it took on life as a projection, Simon Agnel was able to recognize it for what it was, confront it, face it, experience its abrasive and lancinating elements, as well as its gentle and tender side.

Simon Agnel tells Cébès, now covered with blood, to kiss the tree, considered a cross. Similar to the Red Knight of the Holy Grail, Simon Agnel will go out into the world, in the company of his shadow figure, Cébès. Thorns await them as well as sanctification. In a last moment, Simon Agnel lies down on Mother Earth and embraces her deliriously. Strengthened by her limitless force—as Anteros had once been—he longs again for communion with *tellus mater*, his blood surging toward this elemental entity. In his frenzied regression, Simon Agnel finally feels one with earth; the unconscious flows over the rational sphere and is eclipsed by it. Simon Agnel faints. The vast poem, which the trajectory of his life will become, has been inseminated in the earth's bloody bed.

II. *The King's Ritual Slaying*

The action takes place in the king's palace. Columns are outlined on a bleak and desolate stage. A sovereign resides in this enclave. Since time immemorial, palaces have been considered the center of kingdoms, the focus of spiritual values, forces capable of protecting vast treasures within their walls. Metaphysically, the castle represents three spheres: heaven, earth, and hell. In human terms, it symbolizes soul, spirit, and body.

Kings have come to represent ordering, directing and governing principles on earth, all conscious and judging forces. The King *is* wisdom, self-control, the energetic factor. In *Golden Head*, however, an old, negative senex figure walks the stage. Decrepit, weak, reminiscent of the old man of Part I, the ailing Grail King, Amfortas, makes his way before the viewers. Having served his purpose, Claudel's king is no longer a golden principle, a strongly structured being. He is decomposed, barren in his outlook. He bears the patronym of David (in Hebrew David means "beloved"). His namesake had once been a hero—the killer of the giant Goliath—the one secretly anointed king by the prophet Samuel, when Saul was still on the throne. Claudel's king has outlived his creative period; he has slipped into arid times. Abandoned by his army and ministers who fear the attacking hordes, he walks about the stage barefoot, distraught, his clothes in disarray. He groans and laments in throbbing and spasmodic overtones. He worries that his kingdom will be subjugated by the enemy, and he knows he is incapable of defending it. His agitation grows. Even the treasure has been removed, including the diamonds he had so carefully conserved. Luminous beings, diamonds represent light, intuition, adamantine and unconquerable forces. Now, however, they no longer reside within the palace, an indication that what they stood for has also vanished. Overrun with mold and rot, the king and his entourage have, symbolically, served out their earthly function.

The time is midnight: the dividing line within the twenty-four hour cycle, the halfway mark, that instant prior to the zero hour that marks the dawn of a new day. Numbers are archetypal: they arouse energy, rhythms, patterns in space and foment a dynamic process. They are "idea forces," developing virtualities or possibilities in space; they may be considered latent experiences or shapes that lie dormant until consciousness experiences them in the form of images, thoughts, and typical modes of behavior.

The dividing line, as the king is now experiencing it, is no abstract concept. It must be taken seriously: the enemy is at the gates, his kingdom is weak; it wobbles on the brink of destruction. Cébès lies wounded on the floor, dying from some mysterious disease. He cannot sleep and refuses to drink the water offered him, despite his terrible thirst. His pain is perpetual. Simon's departure has caused the inner devastation from which Cébès suffers. The dismemberment is complete. Nevertheless, Cébès longs for the return of his blood brother.

In contrast to the silence of Part I, we now hear noises emanating from everywhere. Clashing of metallic instruments, groans, gasps, create havoc; the atmosphere crackles with intensity. The king is perpetual motion: he wanders about, frantically, from the kitchen to the upper floors, from room to room, hall to hall, as if assessing the damage wrought, searching for some miraculous remedy. Watchmen lie about the stage, half asleep, they are "blind, ignorant, simple." They need to be led, he states, as do the masses; they must serve; they cannot see clearly; light blinds them; power must never reside in the hands of the weak. One at a time the Watchmen awake from their somnolency. They express their annoyance with the king who can no longer protect them. A new leader must be found, they claim, strong, virile, able to enlighten the shaded, support the feeble, and govern the whimpering.

The darkness is opaque. Someone scratches at the door. The Princess enters. She symbolizes royal virtues, as yet undeveloped and unfulfilled; she is the ideal, the essence of beauty, love, and purity. Claudel wrote that the Princess is a composite of "all the ideas of pain and suavity: the soul, the woman, Wisdom, and Piety."[7] In Proverbs, to which Claudel refers frequently, woman is characterized as "I am understanding; I have strength" (8:14) and "I love them that love me" and "those that seek me early shall find me" (8:17). The Princess is a sublimating force: Divine Wisdom, Sophia, alluded to by the kabbalists as Chochma, by early Christians as the Holy Spirit and Logos. Wisdom was also looked upon as Divine Energy, manifested in Jesus and communicated in the Holy Spirit. It was through Sophia, it was said, that God created the universe.

No longer the earth/woman who was buried in Part I, the Princess walks the stage of life, in many ways reminiscent of those exquisitely wrought, Carolingian ivories of the Virgin Mary from the eighth and ninth centuries. Solitary, courageous, the Princess comforts and nurtures by her very presence. She enters the proceedings at Midnight, as though she were the one to order primogenial chaos, giving birth to the Beginning, allowing light to flood blackness, and sublimation to emerge from unregenerate forces.

Cébès cries out his terrible thirst; unquenchable like that of Tantalus, who had been condemned by Zeus to perpetual thirst and hunger although in the presence of water and fruit he could never reach. Water rather than blood was used for communion purposes in the early days of Christianity. St. Cyprian, the third century martyr and Bishop of Carthage, celebrated communion with water: "If man thirst, let him come unto me, and drink. He that believeth on me, as the scripture hath said, out of his belly flow rivers of living water" (John 7:38-9).[8] Water, as does blood, spells eternal life. Cébès' rejection of it indicates that his zest for the existential domain has vanished. He merely awaits Simon's arrival and has no other desire to go on living. He will recede from this world as the earth woman had at the outset of the play. When, therefore, the Princess attempts to comfort him, to assuage his terror, he retorts brutally: "Woman, you will not console me and I shall have nothing to do with you." He refuses to be saved. He anticipates his joy at being the sacrificial victim. He awaits his "older brother," his only *raison d'être*.

The Watchmen articulate their anger as had the Chorus in Greek theatre: singly and collectively; participating in the action, yet remaining detached from it. War, not passivity, is their way to success, according to one of the Watchmen who says: "the sword is held above you and will not cease [its work] until it has devoured you." They believe in the sword: it dismembers, cuts, separating the mass of chaotic instincts. By severing, it gives insight, permitting light to flow through what had once been solid thought, mass feelings. The Cherubim, placed in the east of the Garden of Eden when Adam and Eve were exiled, bore "flaming swords which turned every way, to keep the way of the tree of life" (Gen. 3:24). So Christ of the Apocalypse is described as holding "a sharp two-edged sword" (1:16) in his mouth; and here, too, he struggles to enlighten. All is closed in the palace, sealed, stuffed: "Cemented and shuttered with nails of iron." There is no free access to the outside world. Only an immense force could tear down the doors of this fortified prison, thus allowing fresh food to be offered, and clean air to replace the sunless, decaying, mephitic matter.

Cébès cries out, longingly, for the Sun's return. He reflects upon his past, bathed in elemental forces: mud, water, grass, the brilliant countryside he had once known as a young man, where all was fresh, when life seemed a burgeoning and limitless experience. A palette of powerful colors crackles in verbal array as he articulates his doleful dirge.

The Princess had withdrawn into the palace and now

returns. No longer passive, she has donned a red dress, covered by a golden cap from head to foot. A miter, the liturgical hat worn by archbishops, symbolizing authority, has been placed on her head, and a long thick braid hangs down her back. The red of her vestments is a transposition of the passion of martyred saints, of John the Evangelist setting out on his conversion crusades. Red is a kratophany, a manifestation of force.

With closed eyes, the Princess walks about the stage in slow and pensive steps, as though measuring her every motion and breath. In this posture, she is reminiscent of the fifteenth-century Amiens School paintings of the Virgin (1473). The Princess stops midway between the light and shadow dividing the stage. The transformation ritual is now underway: she has taken the first step out of darkness, from the unformed Princess-state to that of heavenly Queen: from earth to celestial sphere, flesh to spirit. No longer human, she has grown remote, awe-inspiring. She is Wisdom, emanating from divinity; she is the sun's earthly counterpart.

As the Queen of the Night, however, she is not yet ready to fulfill her function. She still remains a vision, an image, a feeling. Her eyes are still closed as she circumnavigates about the stage: sightlessness implies an imperfection in visionary or intuitive powers. These must be perfected and sharpened before she may accede to the next step of spiritual evolution. She suddenly opens her eyes and questions: "And what is this lamp over there?" The Watchman answers: *"Lampas est expectationis"* ("That is the torch of hope."). The Lamp is light—concentrated flame, wisdom which reflects the doctrine, life, continuity, futurity—the presence of God.

Light has penetrated the palace, which is no longer sealed. A dynamic force is at work. The door which had previously divided the unknown from the known, light from darkness, activity from stasis, is now ajar and invites both communion and death. "Death is coming down the path, and the door is still open." It is the narrow door which allows for access to heaven, the scriptures say; this same door leads to the inner man, to revelation. "I am the door; if by me any man enter in he shall be saved and shall go in and out, and find pasture" (John 10:9). Good enters through the door: "Open to me the gates of righteousness: I will go into them, and I will praise the Lord (Psalms 118:19).

Different from Parsifal, who had not sufficiently matured to ask the Grail King the question which would have helped him experience a higher initiatory level, the Princess does question, and several times: "And why did they put the lamp on the ground?" The answer is forthcoming: in order to see. The Princess quests her inner being and in so doing loses her identity and her way. "I no longer know who I am." Development, growth, evolution leads to disorientation particularly when undertaken too rapidly. The Princess demands an answer. She extends her hand toward the fourth Watchman and commands him to stay, to reveal, to unearth meaning in the most unyielding of substances: matter.

The Princess/Queen, reminiscent of Sophia and Mary, both anima figures, incorporates past, present, and future. She reflects the loftiest and purest qualities known to humankind as the soul of the world. She is the domain of ideas (pleroma) or plenitude; she is love etherealized, the living replica of the Ideal. So sublime has the Princess/ Queen become that the Watchmen are ashamed to look at her. "We salute you O beautiful one! We salute you." She is mystery. "All women are but mothers. I am she who raises and nourishes." She observes in silence. No one can hide from her now. Her eyes are powerful, luminescent forces, adamantine orbits. She inhabits the realm of the strong and powerful; a feminine Christ, she is ready to pierce through matter as does the eye of God in darkness. She knows the sin of each individual, the vanity which accompanies thought, the egotism implicit in gesture.[9]

The Princess/Queen is empowered to cure Cébès, but "You must believe me, Cébès, and love me." Cébès rejects her terms. He is not yet ready to experience the feminine principle. "I have taken an oath of allegiance to only one person, and I shall die before yielding it to another." He has no faith in her healing quality, nor does he accept this *sponsa:* her need to elevate the degraded, to bring luster to the tarnished. As such, the Princess/Queen has failed. Standing center stage, she speaks to her father. No longer as the archetypal Princess/Queen, the prime mover, Sophia/Virgin, but as an earthly creature once again, filled with the turmoil and terror of being. She begs to leave. She feels her way to the door. Blindness once again overtakes her.

Alone now, the king must face the terror of defeat. The battle rages outside of the castle. Steel clashes and grinds. Screams, strident and painful, intrude upon the stage happenings. "Chop me up, carve me into pieces, and my dismembered head will jump up and bite," one of the Watchmen threatens. Thunder, lightning; malediction reigns as the atmosphere vomits its rage and ravages the world. Cataclysmic occurrences pervade: devastating, crushing, molten lava breaks down the walls securing the palace.

A Messenger arrives announcing victory. The heat generated by this news encourages the Watchmen to express their feeling tones. The king is jubilant. He sings out his benediction and drinks to joy and festivities. They imbibe the waters of heaven and earth, toast to life's renewal.

The Messenger describes the battle. Simon Agnel's soldiers have won because they buried their fear, their arrogance, and marched in humility toward the enemy; they
waded through mud, fought on horses whose power seemed
unlimited, similar to ·Perseus' horse when rescuing An-
dromeda. As for their leader, a man of unusual beauty, he
massacred, pillaged, spilled the blood of enemies—crying
out in rage—in harmony with the flaring cannons and
piercing color tones.

Simon Agnel enters. He has been proclaimed Golden
Head. "Head" stands for the active and ardent governing
principle; it is the world of spirit and light as opposed to the
darkened realm of the body. A spherical shape, it stands for
the universe, a microcosm: a sun. The gold of his name
symbolizes the highest spiritual values, the purest state of
being, the most precious of metals which never deterior-
ates. It is that igneous characteristic in the sun which is both
royal and divine. Decorations on religious figures in Christian, Buddhist, and Egyptian religions reflect celestial
forces, divinity's light, yang qualities. For the Christian,
Light and Sun are Christ; the spiritual head of the Church,
its strength and life.[10] Artists have drawn Christ with golden
blond hair, a Christianized Apollo, with a halo or zone of
light glowing and resplendent around him.

The king greets the conquering hero. He is triumphant.
He has given his countrymen a will to live. He is that great
solar hero now; that fighter eternal. He has even taken on
the stature of those sixth-century Byzantine equestrian
statues that seem to have shot fullblown from a rough, red
granite rock.

Cébès calls to Golden Head. He tells him that he, Cébès,
will die the following night, before Noon, before the dividing time of that moment when the sun reaches its zenith,
when the intensity of its light bruises and blinds. It is not

death that he fears, Cébès confesses, but the spiritual and
physical torture which this transformation ritual implies.
Similar to François Villon's *Grand Testament* (vers XL),
in which the process of death is described in detail—the
bursting vessels, the flow of bile as it floods the body, the
shriveling skin, wrinkling, blueing, parching, and wasting
away—so Cébès' life is consumed. Cébès rejects the turgid,
stifling atmosphere that permeates the castle. He yearns for
strength, but is engulfed in weakness.

Golden Head has taken on the dimensions of an eagle, a
Superman. He is the insurmountable conqueror whose
solar force fulminates. Yet, in a moment of outstanding
humility, he takes Cébès in his arms, holds him close,
endows him with his flowing feeling, in a communion
death pact—a love duet. Cébès yields to death, no longer
seeking to burden his brother with the weight of feeling.
Golden Head may now forge ahead alone, undaunted,
ready to fulfill his drive for power and to establish his "own
empire."

Golden Head has chosen action. He seeks to become
king. The court with its Adversaries creates tensions. They
could have won the war without him, they claim. Golden
Head speaks out, forcefully, truthfully. No façades, no
masks, no hypocrisy; the lie is banished from his world. The
Adversaries fled when the enemy was at the gates, Golden
Head states. Having pusillanimous natures, they hid and
slept when their land was invaded. It was he, with his
men—the lion in him—who saved them from being devoured. Encircled by a group of Adversaries, they screech
for equality, the rights of the people.

Anger rages within Golden Head. He removes his helmet
and his long blond curls fall loosely to his shoulders. "Look
at this woman!" they scream. They call him the "ferocious
virgin," and Golden Head confesses to being woman: ". . .

and look at the kind of woman I am!" He is "Seduction, Flame, Invincibility." Similar to the Virgin awaiting the Holy Ghost, Golden Head may be likened to the Immaculate Conception; to the androgyne, a self-reproductive creature. He is fire and flame, the Phoenix which dies in the conflagration and is reborn from its own ashes, the eagle, devouring the world about him, insatiable in its appetite, ingesting, digesting, expelling. Reminiscent of the male/female Walkyrie, a martial goddess, an amazon who hunts down rivals and would-be killers, Golden Head is a *complexio oppositorum*: "I am neither the hoe, nor the sack, nor the scale, / I am the fire and the sword!"

The king refuses to give up his throne. He is the head of the kingdom, the *pater familias*, the one to rule the empire created by his fathers. No usurper will intrude. Golden Head, the power-to-be, the virile, new, creative force takes his king prisoner—as in a chess game. Weak, wasting away, and blemished, the butt of insults and ridicule, the pontiff represents a dead past. Unlike Simon Peter, who only cut off the high priest's right ear after Christ's betrayal, Golden Head kills the king; he slashes, symbolically, all that is archaic, unregenerate, and fallow. He stands gigantic over the king's corpse. Golden Head now declares himself ruler, intermediary between heaven and earth, the centralizing and regulating force, a military man who sees to the prosperity of his subjects. It is he who will purify the area, wash away the perverse, scour the mold. The king will be dismembered, he says: "I shall tear him apart and throw the pieces in your faces." Golden Head is not a peacemaker, any more than Christ was: "Think not that I am come to send peace on earth: I came not to send peace, but a sword" (Matt. 34–5).

The sword, an expression of warlike feelings, is a mirror image of the struggle taking place within the unconscious.

Used by Christian knights such as Roland, Olivier, Turpin, Charlemagne, Ganelon and others, swords dazzled with their luminosity. St. Michael, the Archangel, was depicted frequently in Renaissance paintings wearing his handsome coat of mail with his sword sparkling as he thrust it into his enemy, his shield and bejeweled crown always battling Satan and demons (Rev. 12:7–9). Swords are phallic, solar powers, and when emerging from Christ's mouth, procreate fire, speech, standing for the "Spermatic Word."[11]

The ritual slaying of the king has been accomplished. Fertility will return to the land and prosperity to the people. Golden Head is the new king, the Father and Son to his countrymen, a unity (homoousia).[12] He stamps on the ground, laughs, then takes his hands, bloodied from the regicide, and rubs them all over his face, thereby reliving the earlier blood ritual. No longer sharing a prior communion with Cébès, he now generates his own energy, incubates his own life force, fertilizes his own being. He shares the blood with no one; it is self-referential: "the beverage of immortality" covers his being. He has not only consecrated himself with the communion blood, but when he stoops to take the crown from the floor, he also places it on his own head, thereby solidifying his power, both temporal and spiritual.

As a quasi divinity, no one dares to come near him. He is the possessor of an instrument mightier than the sword: the power and fire that reside within his own being dazzle, scintillate, mesmerize, invoke, and provoke. He rules as had the Crusaders of Medieval times: killing for the sake of God, pillaging for the sake of God; converting for the sake of God all those they consider prey to "imbecility," to "inertia," thereby obliterating, in their mind's eye, the corrosive and decayed elements of man and society. Golden Head's every word, gesture, and glance become transforming agents: earth, wind, storm, mountains, pyramids, sulfurous and igneous elements are all personified by him, relate to him, and focus upon him. Through contact with these forces he is endowed with renewed vigor and is ready to pulverize his Adversaries, crushing those standing in his way. He is the world of violence, fire, flood, and whirlwind: that charge capable of "washing away their shame" and raising man from his depths by leading him to victory.

Yet, no evolution has really taken place within Golden Head's psyche. He has merely furthered an ancient custom: that of liquidation rather than differentiation. Had he become detached from the events he was experiencing rather than submerged by them—had he been able to experience harmony within his instinctual domain rather than chaos—his world of affects would not have acted and reacted in muscular contradictions. Wisdom would have prevailed; discernment, evaluation, discrimination would pave the way for deeper knowledge.

Golden Head calls his men to arms: "Advance upon the world," he tells them so they may "know the universal world" and gain possession of it through strength. The court officials refuse to follow. They want the Princess or her brothers to wear the crown. Lineage must continue. In a moment of bravura Golden Head takes his sword and extends it to anyone who seeks it. No one steps forward for in his heart each fears this mighty being who has become a totem: a spirit.

The Princess enters. The new king is not afraid of her. He has saved her land, her kingdom with his sword. She, however, remains unforgiving: he has killed her father. "My father's blood is upon you; it has fallen on you like rain / And yours will gush like an underground spring," she states (p. 164). Golden Head banishes her.

Engulfed by the thought of victory, drunk with its special "perfume," excited by the sound of military music, blatant and forceful, salivating at the clatter of hardware, he looks at the dead Cébès, briefly, and then brandishes his sword as St. Michael, the warrior, had in times past. He departs. Smoke wafts on the stage and large cloudlike formations permeate the atmosphere, warring against the sun's blazing brilliance as it, too, attempts to force its way onto the proscenium. Two forces are at work, antipodal, each seeking to exterminate the other.

III. A Hero Eclipsed—The Agape

The Caucasus is the setting for the third part of *Golden Head*: the gateway to Asia, the divide between East and West. It is here that Prometheus had been enchained to the rock, that his liver had been torn out nightly by an eagle. Jagged cliffs stand out in sharp relief; a vertical trench cuts through the mountains to the West. Blackness, except for the constellation, the Big Bear, which alone is visible, clothes the scene.

It is significant that only the Big Bear of all the constellations is clearly defined. In ancient times, she was represented as a mother figure, a nourishing force, particularly in the role she played in the myth of Atalanta, who was fed by the bear when fleeing from the wild boar.

A creature covered with animal skins crouches on the side. No longer dressed in regal vestments, the once Princess/Queen has regressed to her primitive nature. Hunger, thirst, and cold overwhelm her. She, hunted down and pursued, has fled from man. Reviled and exiled, she has fallen out of grace, deformed by spiritual tyranny and abusive ways. She is not the potentially spiritual force she had once been: she is indistinguishable from beast, unrelated to humankind.

Golden Head and his soldiers have reached "The Door," the last dividing line between Europe and the rest of the world. One of Golden Head's men, Cassius, tells him to look about, and, "Take, for everything is yours." All the earth has to offer could be his: the vast domains which remain as yet unconquered excite his lust for possession. Suddenly, Golden Head sees something hiding in the bushes. Is it an animal? or human? he wonders. He recognizes this entity as the Princess. He pities her and tells his men to give her water; he extends a crust of bread to her, as well as his cloak. The Princess remains mute. She opens her mouth, however, to receive the sacred bread: the consecrated host. She is the sacrificial victim (*sacrificare*, "to make sacred" or to "consecrate").[13] The transubstantiation is to take place: the water (blood) and the bread (the *corpus mysticus*) will be ingested for the agape.[14]

Golden Head marches on with his men. War is imminent. Exulting at the thought of conquest, he is renewed by the thirst for battle; the odor of freshly slaughtered men propels him. He reaches out into the infinite expanse, a demiurge who stills waters, and incubates the divine spirit within and outside of himself.

Meanwhile, a Deserter walks on stage. He recognizes the Princess from the palace. He had despised her then, as he does now. He grabs the bread from her; he sees a tree, pushes her toward it, nails her to it, using stones for a hammer. Suspended midway between earth and heaven, her face expresses the magnificent sorrow of the Avignon Pieta (1460), with its silent, twisting anguish. Suspended motionless, the Princess takes on the value of cosmic emanation in a timeless and spaceless universe. Neither earthly nor celestial, she hovers between two destinies: a binary way of life.

The Deserter observes her, taunts her: "The blackbirds will extirpate your eyes," he exclaims, reminiscent of Villon's *Epitaph*. He eats the bread before her and watches her tears fall to earth. She begs God to take pity on her; yet she never despairs. On the contrary, she is proud of the role she plays—that of the sacrificial force. The Deserter leaves.

The soldiers return, marching with their standard bearers and flags. The sounds of war hold sway. Mass movements, considered as concrete examples of energetic impulses or thoughts rushing into consciousness, arouse excitement. Suddenly, the Messenger rushes on stage. "The King of men is dead," he misinforms. He explains how the accident took place and describes the battle, with the sun beating down on Golden Head, on that fiery face. The sand was dry and parched as he advanced toward the enemy: "Screaming in a terrifying voice and dragging here and there the living prison" which was his body. For the Gnostics, such as the second century Carpocrates, the body was looked upon as a prison, and only after it completed its worldly sojourn could the soul be released and unite with divinity. The existential experience was to be looked upon as an initiation: the soul within the body—in the somatic world of the demiurge—had to fulfill its pain and trial so that it could be worthy of overflowing into divinity.[15]

The King/Golden Head is brought on stage. He is dying. The Centurion approaches him and calls him Agnel Simon, a name he has not heard since he donned the vestments of hero and king. His daring feats as well as his nearly divine image have now diminished in size. He has been branded, stigmatized, and daunted. He, who had wanted to seize the earth, now realizes the impossibility of his goal. By fighting, scorching, branding the world with his essence, he has reached the heights and depths of life: "I have lived," he says, as had other greats: Buddha, Moses,

Christ. Similar to them, he has known life in all of its many phases. His blood has washed the world and his trajectory has come to an end; the skies darken with pain "A Gorgonian lament fills the mountains and valleys!"

Once dual, now cosmic forces have unified. The Big Bear holds the sun in its clutches; the Gorgon has been killed by the fleet-footed Perseus. Cataclysms have disrupted the face of the earth, uprooting stability, unleashing myriad forces, compelling the unshakable stone to shudder.

The King/Golden Head sees the Princess nailed to the tree—that starving animal to whom he had previously given his bread and his cloak—but she has survived her crucifixion. She is spirit who has defeated animal nature. Although severed from the earth, she has not yet reached heaven, but remains midway between the polarities in an *imitatio Christi*. She has experienced the stigmata; she has cohabited with divinity in mystical union.

Claudel's image of the crucifixion is innovative in the fact that a female has been attached to the tree: the embedded nails in her extremities are similar to so many painful thoughts; they are lancinating feelings which fester in her subliminal realm. Comparable to the Maiden in *The Acts of Thomas*, she is now prepared to become "the Mother of Wisdom," the female worshipped in the Eucharistic Prayer.[16] Both Mother and Wife to Christ, who had been forced into the marriage bed of the cross, she will play a parallel role with Golden Head.

King/Golden Head, in a moment of extreme heroism, rises from the ground, and pulls out the nails from the Princess' limbs with his teeth. Bloodied, but still strong enough, the unleashed Princess now carries him to his mortuary bed. She wishes she had been nailed by him to the cross; then she would have experienced true ecstasy. "And I would have closed my eyes to better feel. / And in loving you I would have died in silence." The values of suffering and pain are held most sacred by the Christian; no longer are the virtues of bravery, physical courage, and strength, once exalted by the Romans, uppermost.

King/Golden Head is dead. The Princess leans over him and kisses him on the mouth, thereby cementing their union. The kiss of peace, as in the Agape, has been performed. In early Christian times, it had signified altruistic love, that of God for man. The Princess is the King's bride (*sponsa*), the human soul; she is a replica of Christ's mystic marriage with the Church. The Commander and Officers of Golden Head's army proclaim her Queen. They remove the crown from Golden Head and place it on her. The sublime honor is hers and she accepts it. She is Queen Mother, Bride, and Sister—as well as Virgin (*Parthenos*) —reminiscent of other matriarchal figures: Isis, Demeter, the Virgin Mary. Slowly, she dons the sacred vestments of royalty. The stage is flooded with light as a *hieros gamos* is experienced: the union of Heaven and Earth, spirit and matter. Although her strength is ebbing, the agape and love she has known allow her to experience a *mysterium fascinans*. She dies retaining the powers invested in her, a divinity ordering the cyclical flow of universal forces.

Violence and cruelty mark *Golden Head* as they do the dramas of Racine and Genêt. The crisis of youth, spiritual and physical, is dramatized: a dismemberment takes place. Characters are torn, ripped apart, burned and bruised in an Agavelike blood ritual. Tenderness and nuanced relationships are banished from Claudel's world; yet a longing and need for these qualities exist in the antagonists who are unable to give of themselves to others. Man is unable to love woman. Even at the conclusion of *Golden Head*, it is the woman who performs the agape after the hero's demise.

Titanic and blinding forces rule Golden Head. He experiences his existence in a series of explosive acts. Unthinking—and in this regard the antithesis of Perseus, who was never turned to stone because the Gorgon was seen only through a mirror—Golden Head braves the world blindly and impulsively. Similar to the Babylonian Gilgamesh, Golden Head attempts to dominate and cajole fate, but fails to do so. He is overcome by the disease of conquest and possession, these rankle in his depths. Rather than viewing his urgings objectively and in bold relief, as one does a graven sculpture, he succumbed to their virulence and was ruled by them.

Claudel's characters are numinous forces; similar to magnets and energy charges, they attract and repel. They are transformers, who convert raw and rich instinct into a refined work of art. Etched into the very nerves of the stone that masks a soul in torment, these ancient markings —archetypal figures—are covered by an eroding acid. Despondency and despair are not the way of the Claudelian hero. Rather, he shakes the world, devours and claws at those forces that will not yield their riches; he brands, thereby paving the way for a complex credo and set of relationships to come into being: thus, the play *Golden Head*.

There was no turning back for Golden Head or for Claudel. Life for both was a quest and a conquest, a constantly renewed and renewable experience, food for the poem/play. As Claudel wrote: "Life is always new for us and always interesting, for with each second we have something new to learn and something important to accomplish."[17] Life is a perpetual communion, a blood ritual: it is an Agave which dismembers, and an Agape which brings the multiple into the one known as creation.

A youthful work, *Golden Head* explodes with talent and power, a play that today still moves and arouses audiences, holds them enthralled.

"Blood is the union of water and fire."
PAUL CLAUDEL, *Journal*, I.

3. THE CITY:
FIRE AND BRIMSTONE

The City (1890, 1897) is naive in its ideations and heav-
ingly emotional in its poetics. It is the drama of a seared
soul; a young man who, prior to his conversion, lies gasping
for want of air, starving for need of food, parched in his
desire for water. The work of an adolescent—far more so
than *Golden Head* which is a work of art—*The City* is more
of a thesis play: rigid in its ideations and simplistic in its
answers. Claudel wrote *The City* when "plunged in one of
his depressed states, overwhelmed by the insalubrious
fumes of Sodom and Gomorrah."[1] Overcome by sensations
of anger and repugnance for life around him in the me-
tropolis, with negative reactions concerning his own inner
state, Claudel feared for the future and was obsessed with
guilt concerning his past. To relieve the piercing feelings of
torment, Claudel frequently took long walks in Paris, reacting to this indifferent, unyielding, and unresponding
conglomeration—this immense reservoir of structures and
groupings of human flesh—with anguish.

Claudel's isolation in the midst of many, his spiritual
poverty when faced with plenty, his emotional aridity when

Maria Casarès (Lala), Alain Cuny (Coeuvre), and Georges Wilson (Lambert de Besme) in *The City*.
FRENCH CULTURAL SERVICES

in the company of joyous friends, served to further disorient him and increase his despair. The austere and distant relationships he had known as a youth had left a gaping maw: he felt drained, parched, empty. His mother had never responded to his need for understanding and warmth. His father had never opened his heart to his son, particularly after his parents had separated. As for his sister, Camille, she dominated the family scene—tempestuous, passionate—a whirlwind in her modes of behavior. This talented, extraordinarily captivating creature was intellectually and psychologically responsive to him. He looked toward her with admiration; he adored and worshiped her—perhaps he loved her. Haunted by an unconscious fear of incest, he did not know what to make of his feelings or how to cope with them. Repression was the family way, even though expulsion of impulses in torrential outpourings was habitual with his sister. When at Villeneuve, he looked toward nature in all of its splendor to answer his desolate cry. In the city, however, Claudel felt estranged: no more foliage, lakes, streams, and fields to assuage his terror. The city, in some respects, had become a fortress of negativity for him, a mechanical monster swallowing, destroying anyone in its way. It became a collective entity in which respect for an individual no longer existed; it professed a work ethic from which the joy of labor and fulfillment had been annihilated. Years later Claudel wrote: "no feeling of charity nor of patience and support for one another, but a kind of reciprocal belligerence and continuous tension, secret wars waged by all against all."[2] This was Claudel's vision of the city at this time. After his "conversion," however, hope was restored to him, and a God-filled world allowed dreams of perfection to exist and the utopian myth to take root.

The City is divided into three acts. The first version of the play, written in 1890, featured Paris as the focal point of Claudel's spiritual tirade. The second writing, completed in 1897, after Claudel lived in China, focused on a collective grouping of people, that is, any city. (It is the latter which will be analyzed here.) China had taught Claudel the meaning of exile: this would have a positive effect on his aesthetics as well as on his spiritual evolution. Distance encouraged reflection; it compelled Claudel to indwell and, perhaps in this manner, to achieve more independence in his thoughts and feelings. Important, too, was the fact that upon his return from China he realized that the machine age was anathema to him. He could not relate to impersonal groupings, to commodities alone. What he yearned for were individual relationships in which love and harmony were in the offing.

I. *The Garden*

The City opens on a hill, in a Garden belonging to two brothers, Lambert and Isidore Besme, the first a politician, and the second, an engineer. It is night. Similar to Japanese Noh drama which was to influence Claudel's dramaturgy in later years, no specific locations or time schemes are given, thereby increasing the mythical quality of the drama. Night symbolizes the end of a way of life, the conclusion of a civilization, of structures of thoughts, masses of beings. It also represents the unconscious, the timeless and spaceless dream world that was soon to hold sway: intuit, feel, experience life as it infiltrates the atmosphere.

That the action takes place in an Edenesque Garden, a paradisiac state of cultivated order, underscores the vegetal level of the psychological situation. The Greeks had their Garden of Hesperides in which a condition of immortality could be enjoyed, nature forever being born and reborn; the Persian and Indian Gardens were continuous sources of inspiration for poets, reflecting beauty and love. In Claudel's *The City*, the Garden represents all of these things, as well as worldly success and wealth: the fruits of a long life of toil, of planning by the Besme brothers, who had believed that one day they would enjoy their life's work, relax in serenity and happiness.

Lambert de Besme, an old man, is standing in his Garden, which overlooks the city. As a politician, he has always dominated the populace he sees below. He rejects disorder and has spent his time lulling the masses into a state of subservience, feeding them panaceas, encouraging them to live out their lives in unawareness and oblivion.

Lambert is talking to the Miser, an archetypal figure who stands for Transformation. The Miser is against passivity; he is intransigent in his ideations, uncompromising in his attitudes, violent in his ways. He triggers activity, seeks to alter, to differentiate. A nonconformist, he understands the need for change. A catalyst, he is changed into spirit as he passes unknown and unseen amidst the populace, expressing his rage and furor at the city dwellers, arousing them to rebellion, even murder. He is that *power* that foments dissatisfaction, creates conflict, and brings about knowledge. He is the antithesis of Lambert, who seeks contentment and peace. Man must be freed from subservience to the machine, or to anything else, the Miser contends. Nameless, the Miser, an impersonal entity in the play, is given virtually extraterrestrial powers: he becomes the instrument of awareness in the drama.

Since earliest time the city in general has been viewed as a feminine figure: positive in that it encloses, protects, and comforts in a maternal manner; negative by its very constriction, since it may lead to imprisonment and suffocation. Young men have been killed fighting for the city, each wanting to usurp power for himself, such as the sons of Oedipus, Etiocles and Polynices, or Romulus and Remus, prototypes of countless more. In both the Old and the New Testaments, the city has been labeled lascivious, sensual; for Claudel, it is Babylon, Nineveh, Sodom, and Gomorrah.

The Miser refers to the city as a giant harlot: a proud, cruel and inbred monstrous conglomerate. Its glittering lights radiate and illuminate, but they also blind. Impenetrable as a mask, it also yields excitement; perplexing in its mobile, chaotic turbulence, it "vomits an eddy of black smoke," the Miser suggests; it encloses countless human sheep, who bow and scrape before a master, ruler, or lord. Complex as are the lobes of the brain, and equally incomprehensible, the city is a mystery, inciting fascination and fear.

Lambert informs the Miser of his plan to marry the young Lala, if she will have him. He had adopted her after she had been orphaned and raised her. Her beauty radiates as does her glowing heart; she is tender and exquisite in nature. His entire life, he explains, has been spent politicking, trying to achieve stature and power. He has, reminiscent of Faust's plight, overlooked love, the warmth of human relationships. Now, he longs for communion with a woman who will bring him peace, and seeks to withdraw from life's activities. His bride, he believes, will answer his needs, respond with "invincible tenderness." Lala, the anima figure par excellence (man's unconscious image of womankind), is for Lambert that pristine and pure virginal force, that angelic, virtually divine comforter. She is an all-giver. In her embrace he will find repose and serenity.

The Miser derides Lambert. Is this what the one-time "powerful politician" now wants? Is this the outcome of a lifetime of leadership? Is this the fate of "the pastor of cities?" The Miser states in no uncertain terms: "Peace is not in repose. I do not desire repose," but excitement, growth, decay, life. Looking down upon the city, he comments, "They are swarming all of them, souls and members, blending their breath and their excrement." The city tantalizes, provokes, and animates the Miser.

Suddenly flames invade the center of the city. A large fire is eating away at the stores, theatres, factories with frenetic haste, swallowing everything with which it comes into contact. Even the Palace of Justice could burn at this pace, the Miser muses; the fire is sputtering, crackling, humming in the cellars—those subliminal realms—it is the fate of all of man's creative élan.

The Miser laughs at Lambert. This is no time to think of marriage, he says, not when an entire city is going up in smoke. Values are being lost, rebellion is about to break

out, punishments must be administered. The Miser comments with lustful excitement on the "brilliance of the fire"
as it engulfs everything in a sea of purified flame. The den
of iniquity; lies and deceits will be consumed. The Miser
admits that when people listen to him they are astonished,
surprised, shocked by his forthrightness. Wherever he is, he
speaks truth. Sometimes, when visiting people, feelings of
imprisonment invade him; he is revolted by their perpetual
gossip, their gross jaws moving up and down like endless
mechanical openings bobbing up and down, and he grows
impatient. When he can bear the situation no longer, this
archetypal force sets the place aflame, destroying these
parasitic entities, these clustering nonbeings. Fire, representing energy, life, vitality, destroys when it consumes,
but it also creates through its warmth, nurtures via its light,
encourages relationships as it melts down rigidity of form
and character. The city, the Miser warns, will be destroyed.
A *Götterdammerung* will take place—a twilight of the
Gods—after which nothing will remain.

Lala enters. Onomastically, her name sounds like a
baby's utterance, as well as the musical note "la," the sixth
of the scale, a replication of the sixth day of Creation when
God had completed his work. Lala may also be associated
with the Hebrew name *Laila*, meaning "nocturnal" or
night. The woman who works in the shadows is a mysterious force, since within her lives the germ of future life. Lala
is all of these things: infantile, because she is unspoiled,
new, and virginal; musical, because within her feeling
qualities have developed, giving her tones which mesmerize, titillate, but also pain. When Lambert expresses his
love for her and his wish to experience the fruits of the earth
through her, she accepts his advances innocently. She does
not understand the meaning of love.

As the archetype of purity, beauty, and all-goodness,

Lala also encloses within her being, for Claudel at least, Grace and Wisdom. That she is placed in the Garden encourages an affinity with Solomon's personification of womankind in Proverbs: "I (Wisdom) love them that love me; and those that seek me early shall find me" (8:17). Lala represents the wonderment of discernment, the rapture of understanding, as well as love/perdition.[3] She is the source, both visual and sensual, of inspiration and fantasy. She is love in that she fecundates, cajoles, but also lulls her captive in her warm embrace, enclosing him in her feeling world where he may remain forever, unknowing, stifling, and dying.

Lala lives in a nebulous time scheme. As an archetype, she has no personal character traits, only remote modes of action. She answers a need. She fulfills a function. Never does she assume any life of her own. She exists as a projection for Lambert, a medium figure; later on she answers the needs of other *dramatis personae*. When looking at her, Lambert is enraptured; he is filled with lightness, as new feelings of bewilderment swell within him. She calls him "my adopted father"; he sees her as a "fairy," something removed from this earth, angelic, vaporous, idyllic in her way. So moved is he by her presence that he says, "if you love me, I'll open my heart to you—that of a father." He asks her to be his "consolation" and his warmth.

Lambert's brother, Isidore, enters the Garden. An engineer, he represents the pragmatic world. He has constructed with mathematical order and precision the city below. It is his work; his calculations brought it to fruition. He responds to the world of reason, to the conscious domain; but, emotionally, he is held captive by pessimistic views—death, darkness—a joyless realm.

Coeuvre, the Poet, enters the Garden. Onomastically, Coeuvre's name encloses *oeuvre* which means a work in French, and implies *chef-d'oeuvre*, a masterpiece. He is the creative factor in the play. In lyrical terms, he expresses his vision of the city bathed in night, in fleeting shadows, "dreadful agitation." Contrasting the Garden to the cluttered and cloistered city, he welcomes its darkness and mystery as consoling forces. The blackened world with its invisible aromas, silent sonorities, offers him the peace and solitude he needs, the retreat which will allow his creative élan to unfold, unburden, unbend, and take on life in its own way. The Poet does not attempt to explain nature; he seeks to transmute its beauties into comprehensible form, delighting and delecting.

Isidore de Besme asks the poet "what use are you?" a question posed to artists since the beginning of time. The creative individual is not conventional. When discovering his proclivities, when propelled to carve out a future from his own flesh, he responds to an inner urge. He lives for and on inspiration, intuition, the amorphous and subliminal realm. He cannot answer a utilitarian need, only a spiritual longing. Through his art the Poet creates and recreates the world, as he sees and feels it, using artificial means. The word *art* implies artifice, artificial. He humanizes life, individualizes it, subjectivizes it. "What use is the orchid, in the heart of a virgin forest?" the Poet questions.

Coeuvre speaks of the poetic principle, of inspiration, in metaphors: as filling one's lungs with fresh air, breathing in deeply of the outer realm, of dilating the inner sphere with new factors, energies, potentialities and transmuting these contents into flamboyant images, lilting sonorities, multiple hues and rhythms; then one exhales the completed work into the life flow. It is the poet's function to fill form, ejaculate sensation, explore sound; he must create a living language of the soul.

Isidore de Besme cannot follow Coeuvre's panegyrics, the mysterious harmonies involved in the poet's creative urge. "Where is this exchange, this mysterious respiration about which you are speaking?" The pedestrian, pragmatic thinker cannot possibly hope to understand the poet's way, those tremulous vibrations that inhabit the subliminal spheres. Isidore is a man who relates to the thinking process alone. He cannot function in higher altitudes, in rarefied atmospheres, areas where poetic fancy takes flight, entranced and enriched by its very expansion and inner light. Isidore is important, however, to society, as well as to *The City*. He peers into nature and man, finding vanity and intrigue. Empowered with vision, and the glow of a certain type of life that he had built and constructed, he had once seen into the future. "If only I had not been born," he now says. "Or if I had not received that fatal gift of vision." It is this inner sight—this third eye—which allows him to measure the measureless. Intuition is his, then, but in insufficient amounts. Once his work was completed, once he had seen the city in operation and mechanization brought to its highest peak, he felt a crippling void within him, which nothing could fill, neither the love he had never known nor the poetic principle which he could not fully understand. His world is the half-moon, the negative quantity now. The Poet, on the other hand, endowed with the imagination, excitement, fervor, and furor of life, sees the other side of the picture, or believes he does.

Coeuvre is not devoid of conflict. He is surrounded by doubt, fear, and terror. He experiences himself as his own echo: living in two domains, outer and inner, created and uncreated, abstract and amorphous. Something is missing in this world: Eros. He has never really loved and wonders if he is capable of experiencing such sensations. Only slowly does Isidore begin to understand the Poet's real torments.

As the moon rises in its course, Coeuvre salutes "the Queen of the Night." For him, she is the harbinger of the uncreated, the unconscious within which all treasures are stored. Yet, revealing only one side of her nature to man-kind, forever alternating her form, she radiates light in blackness and makes the invisible visible. An inspiration for Coeuvre, she offers majesty within ephemerality.

For Besme the moon responds to his world of reason, to the conscious domain: she is a "light-bringer," as Lucifer was, imposing upon him the world of conflict and aware-ness, rather than the one of serenity for which he longs. The moon provokes tides, rains, cataclysms of all types, with which the engineer and visionary must deal. This very force, however, assuring that the earth is drenched, nourishes the vital substance with the waters of creativity, similar to those inhabiting the womb: the elixir from which life emerges.

Lala castigates Besme for speaking of death, perpetually. She spells life, futurity; she is maternity. It is she who sees to the constantly renewing factors in the visible world. She is the Earth/Moon: "O Foolish man, why speak of death when you are alive?" She is happiness and represents the forces of nature: a rising moon, not one sinking into obliv-ion. She is wisdom: she seeks to have her beauty accepted, its freshness understood. She neither questions nor probes. Nature is her force: youth her joy; life her Garden.

Lala turns to Coeuvre. It is he whom she wants to marry now. The poet, the wanderer who knows no course in life, no boundaries. It is he who will still sensations, radiate tenderness. Unadaptable, untamable, the poet is the man who "traversed a sea" and who after "vomiting water, ar-rives at the other side."

Besme's threnody follows this hymn to life. Seven times he repeats his dirgelike saying, "Nothing is." The worth-lessness of existence overpowers him; the "horror of the useless" pursues him and drones on in oratorial fashion. Coeuvre turns around and, in contrapuntal tonalities and

rhythmic devices, sings out once again to the forces of
creation: the moon in its course, the warmth of the rising
sun; the waters streaming forth, the moisture under foot;
the vines growing and fermenting in all of their darkened
beauty; the glistening grass, shining, like mirrors in the
softly glowing light, nurturing animal and man; the freshness of the dew instilling feelings of cleanliness and purity
in a soul desirous of maternal tenderness. He tells Besme to
turn toward the sun as it bursts forth through the heavens,
explodes in golden rays, enveloping the cosmos in its joy.
But Besme cannot alter his course.

Lala will marry Coeuvre, and in a moving love duet,
when the poet tells her to remove her veil, he sings out "O
Star of the Night, is it you?" and encloses mystery, beauty,
and anima in his embrace. A replica of the flower, water,
and trees which exude their yellow and bluish hues, Lala
becomes nature, resplendent before him. "Let me inhale
your odor," he says, "the odor of earth." Inspiration, youth,
and sexuality are now wedded to the creative principle.

II. The Grave

Act II opens on a cemetery, which now dominates the
city as the Garden had in the opening act. It is morning. An
undefinable period has elapsed. Lambert has become a
grave digger. He hosts death. Neither future nor past exist
for him. He lives in an atemporal era, detached from all
living beings as well as from inanimate entities. As the
archetype of the old man ready to make peace with life, he is
in the process of digging his own grave, his underground
palace, his bed, where he will return, serene in the earth's
belly.

Lala enters. Lambert does not recognize her. She walks around the gravestones, the odor of death infiltrates the atmosphere with decay, decrepitude. Lala has given Coeuvre a son, we learn, then left them both. Now she lives with the Miser, but he needs only her presence, nothing more. No longer the adolescent whose life revolved around happiness, a future, ebullience, she has known sorrow and rapture. These experiences have served to detach her from the world, free her from constriction. She has lost her identity in the process, however, and has become what each person considers her to be. Never anything but a medium figure, she is divested of all personal life. In this capacity, she helps others to reconstruct their worlds, to be reborn. She entreats Lambert to leave his tombs and stones and to follow her into the light, to eat of the earth, to partake of bread and wine. He asks who will dig the graves if he does not. "I am the laborer of death and not the guest of life."

When Coeuvre arrives, he does not recognize Lala. He has emerged from her embrace divested of everything. No longer young, no longer believing in the flowers and glories of nature, he has searched for a more profound reality. Yet Lala's withdrawal from his life has enabled him to experience the solitude necessary for meditation, to reshuffle ebullient emotions which merely inhaled and exhaled their harmonies. Her departure left him tossing about for long periods of time, wildly, frenetically, experiencing the tumult necessary for *renovatio*. Lala has opened access to another realm. She tells him "I opened the door to leave and filled your room with the light of the moon."

Lala speaks to the Miser. The city, once active and dynamic, has now come to a standstill. Nothing is budging. Stasis. "The City has retired from its work." People are indulging in repose, waiting, expecting. They are bored, inconsolable; emptiness follows them during all the days of their lives. There had been a time when they took pride in their activities, labored on a thing of beauty, felt fulfilled with a job well done. Lala laughs at the Miser, stridently, unfeeling. He does not understand her raucous reaction. She reminds him of those olden days when man consulted oracles and misunderstood their revelations, their incomprehensible prophecies; of those women who danced their Dionysian revelries, bleeding and tearing the guts out of a calf, slaughtering a lion, dismembering a human; of those witches who sat cackling next to a boiling cauldron, preparing their mixed brew of unfathomable moment. Lala, the Eternal Feminine, brings love and hate, serenity and madness.

Besme understands life in his own way: "The earth is impregnated with salt and poison. The more beautiful this world, the more it laughs in the freshness of its leaves"; thus, the greater one feels the sting of mockery, the more poignant is the cut.

The Miser intercedes. "Breathe in for the last time the odor of the City, dilate your nostrils and inhale the odor of this heap of human beings." The city is to be destroyed. Lambert has withdrawn into his grave. As for Besme, although he has never known love, he weeps his untried feelings. "My whole life has been spent attempting to relate causes to causes, but my intellect was never satisfied." Thinking had occupied his existence, until he discovered that he was ignorant of life. Humility has replaced the hubris of his prior attitude. Now he knows that there is "a science beneath science, and we call it Ignorance." He understands the meaning of mystery, the inexplicable. "And what is this hunger which devours the mind"; why this "need to know"? What forces man to discover, to sound out, to seek and to unearth all? It is at this juncture that Besme gives his sapphire ring to Coeuvre: "this limpid atom" which is the outcome of years of study, probing, digging, cutting, lancinating of the earth's surface. This sapphire possesses its own luminosity in its blue flame: spirit, divinity, flamboyant in its radiance—in the six equal cosmic paths of its facets, similar to the *la* note of *lala*— an expression of the six days of Creation. Besme will die, but not in ignorance; he will die with the knowledge that he has experienced illumination.

Cannons are fired, shots heard, and a flag is hoisted. Besme's head is now visible in the distance, mounted on the bayonette of the revolutionaries who have razed the city.

III. *The Charred Remains*

The third act is the weakest of the three; it reveals the charred remains of what had once been a forceful city. A vision comparable to Revelation is offered; it is a city which had once been a den of lust and sensuality, a Babylon with its Hanging Gardens; a harlot/mother as alluded to in the last book in the Bible.

> And upon her forehead was a name written, MYSTERY, BABYLON THE GREAT, THE MOTHER OF HAR-LOTS AND ABOMINATIONS OF THE EARTH (*Revelation 17:5*).

A city worthy of destruction, slaughter, fire, and brim-stone.

The Miser has fulfilled his destiny and despite entreaties from his officers, two of whom are on stage, he seeks to withdraw from the world and live out the balance of the time allotted to him elsewhere.

Coeuvre arrives on the scene. Dressed in bishop's robes

and followed by members of the clergy, we learn that he has converted. Older, his desires, he explains, are no longer exclusively of the earth; they embrace cosmic spheres. He longs for the "harmony of things in their accord and their succession." Coeuvre hears God within him and exists for the present alone, not for a past or a future. The present is the "circumference of a permanent eternity," he states.[4] Happiness, he tells his entourage and his son who is now on stage, is not a luxury, nor does it stem from lust. It resides within the treasure trove, hiding in the recesses of the soul. Punishment is also part of the life process and must not be excluded. Indeed, "it is our hope," he declares. Happiness stems from suffering "as knowledge" exists in darkness; there is "salvation in the suspended sentence."

Lala appears. She is a stranger to all those present. No one has really understood her, she claims, neither husband nor son. Coeuvre's mind "attaches itself to causes which he gathers around him in the profound cavity of his mind, as clouds from which thunder and lightning escape"; whereas she has reached that state in which she feels free enough to "maintain" herself in the "very vibration of light," no longer succumbing to the needs of either mind or body. Whether her hair turns gray or white, her beauty remains in the very life force of the mystery which she is. "I am the tenderness of what is; as well as the regret of what is not."

A new order is to be established. Coeuvre's son, Ivors, having learned the lesson his father instilled in him, will found a new City with Deity as its center; he will recreate Order, his brand of utopia. As is written in the Epistle of Paul to the Galatians, "But Jerusalem which is above is free, which is the mother of us all" (4:26). The celestial Jerusalem now engendered will be the one of the mind, not of the flesh.

Although *The City* is puerile in its ideations and simplistic in its conclusion, Claudel's insights concerning the dangers of an overly mechanical society and man's lack of understanding for humankind in his social relationships are significant. What remains incised in the reader's heart and mind is the poetry that exudes from Claudel's pen, words which fulminate, spilling his rapture. As if Claudel were cloaking his writings with transpersonal vestments, music radiates from the very heart of the sensations described; its resonances implement the hierarchy of kaleidoscopic tones, redefining and reworking the complex and ambivalent feelings with which *The City* is replete.

As attested to by *The City*, Claudel's life course was difficult. Unable to adapt to the mechanical age, to masses of buildings, the grayness of a stultifying environment, the foulness of its stench, he took refuge in sundrenched nature, or its cloudy and stormy moods. In the city, Claudel's solitude mounted. His inability to find a common denominator with others on the deepest levels was accentuated. He did not really relate to women. They were either wives, that is, homebodies raising families, focusing their life's work in maintaining households—cold and reserved as was his mother—or they were *femmes séductrices*, *femmes fatales* who lured him into their clutches, holding him captive for a period. Either sensual and lustful creatures from whom he could never extract enough, or the hyperdulian Marylike types—pure, spiritual offering comfort —untouchable forces emanating from divine spheres, they were composites of opposites. The Woman/City repelled and delighted; she spelled inspiration for Claudel.

4. BREAK OF NOON: A COSMIC AWAKENING

Ten years had elapsed since Claudel wrote *The City;* ten years spent traveling in the Orient and Occident, living his great adulterous passion. *Break of Noon*, one of the great plays of all time, centers around "adultery": a wife, a husband, and two lovers. It dramatizes the struggle between "the religious vocation and the call of the flesh." The flesh dominates. Every word in *Break of Noon* breathes with Dionysian fervor and jubilation. Counterforces follow each euphoric experience, shedding feelings of shame and guilt in their wake. The intensity of these clashing emotions—exquisite sensuality in pursuit of the forbidden fruit on the one hand, and the terror engendered by the belief in the damnation to follow on the other—heightens the excitement and titillates the senses.

Break of Noon is a giant cosmic awakening in which the four Aristotelian elements (sun, moon, water, earth) activate and energize the stage happenings. Each element, in consort with the protagonists, participates in the drama aboard a ship sailing on the Indian Ocean to China. An animistic world is therefore brought to life, which allows

86

the four characters to bathe in primitive powers and to experience viscerally the mysterious and inexorable forces that are to decide their fate.

Break of Noon dramatizes a transformation process: from a leaden, earth-oriented and physiologically chaotic condition to an attempted purification of the soul and the establishment of a harmonious *golden* essence. It is not the "common gold" of existential man who, like Midas, so frequently identifies with gold and becomes possessed by it; rather, it is the "invisible" and "incorporeal" philosopher's gold, a symbol of the highest spiritual values.

Break of Noon is autobiographical. Claudel wrote it at a time when he was undergoing a severe personal crisis, at a turning point in his life—a "break" between his past and his future. It was vital, he confessed, that the torment eating away at his system be expelled. Since the experience from which the play was born was so abrasive and the events so closely blended into the fabric of his emotions, Claudel had *Break of Noon* privately printed. He refused permission to have his drama produced on any stage until 1948, when Jean-Louis Barrault, working in consort with the author, was given this singular honor.

The title, *Break of Noon*, is in keeping with the semiotic approach to language. It implies a cleavage, a schism, a severing of one life and the beginning of another. "Noon" for Claudel, the metaphysician and numerologist, signifies a midway mark in the sun's course through the heavens, when it has reached its zenith and is preparing for its descent. "Noon, the center of our life."[1] Noon is also the hottest moment of the day. For the Medieval mind, noon represents that "immobile" moment when the sun is believed to be at rest, when calm has set in and man is most receptive to divine as well as to demoniacal powers—that fateful instant when the intensity of illumination may blind. For the ancient Egyptian, the Sun was Ra; for the Greek, it was called Apollo; for Claudel it was God (the Three in One). Only the pure of heart could look at this body without flinching. Lot, because of his sinful nature, was unable to gaze at the Noon sun; Abraham, however, whose soul was spotless, could view God face-to-face, when this celestial body reached the peak of its burning force. So Claudel's protagonists would similarly attempt to gain insight into themselves by means of this solar force.

Numbers had particular meaning for Claudel. Noon is number twelve. When referring to the twelve months of the year, the twelve disciples, the twelve signs of the zodiac, it signifies completion. The protagonists are four, and when multiplied by the three acts, or stages in their evolution, equal twelve. The number four, associated with terrestrial existence, the earth element for the alchemist, the square, the four seasons, the cardinal points, also brings to mind the Tetramorphs: the four faces Ezekiel saw in a vision (the faces of man, the lion, the ox, the eagle), the four surrounding the Throne of God in Revelation (4:6—8). Each animal, according to St. Jerome, expresses a religious function: the ox symbolizes passion and sacrifice; the lion, resurrection; the eagle ascension; man incarnation. Each represents one of the four Evangelists: Matthew is man; Mark is the lion; Luke the ox; John the eagle. Throughout *Break of Noon*, Claudel makes reference to these animals and others, and to the Evangelists and their individual personalities with reference to the protagonists.[2]

Onomastically, the characters' names correspond to measurements. The name Ysé (wife, mother, and mistress) comes from the Greek *isos*, meaning equal, as are the two sides of an isosceles triangle. Iconographically, the Y in her name represents one form of the alchemical cross: unity which has become duality. No longer is Ysé the *one* woman who blends harmoniously into her surroundings, but rather one woman as opposed to the three men, her antagonists. The schism between the one versus the three underscores the tension existing in life: spirit and matter, active and passive, imprisonment and freedom. The Y is significant in alchemical symbology in that it stands for a *rebis*, the hermaphrodite with two heads. Ysé is psychologically bisexual: man and woman, the incarnation of certain aspects of the dramatist's psyche. She is very much like Isolde (Tristan's beloved), ever-alluring, yet virile and powerful in her attempt to "subjugate" the men on shipboard. She is Mystery incarnate, suggests Claudel. "She represents the possibility of something unknown. A secret being charged with significance."

The name de Ciz (Ysé's husband) spells division, friction, and tension. Associated with the word *ciseau* (scissors), *ciselure* (carving), *ciseler* (chiseling)—all cutting instruments that alchemists used in the course of their dismemberment operations—his name corresponds iconographically to his personality. De Ciz is weak, irresponsible, drawn here and there, cut off from himself and the world at large. His instability takes him wherever business looks intriguing. Unlike St. Cizy, the eighth century martyr killed by the Saracens, de Ciz will die in a less valiant fashion.

Mesa (the character who most closely resembles Claudel and who became Ysé's lover) comes from the Greek word *mesos* meaning moderation, balance. He is the antithesis of balance; and is given to extremes. Searching for beatitude, longing to give his life to God, but prevented from doing so by his superiors, he has been thrust into a world of temptation, a den of iniquity. Immoderate in his thoughts, feelings, and deeds, perpetually dissatisfied, egotistical, self-centered and inflated with feelings of spiritual superiority, he is chaos striving to become cosmos.

Amalric is Ysé's second lover. His name may be divided

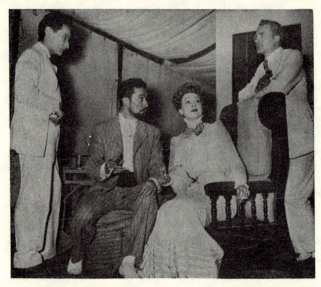

Jean-Louis Barrault, Pierre Brasseur, Edwige Feuillère, and Dacquénime in *Break of Noon*.
FRENCH CULTURAL SERVICES

into three syllabic counts, corresponding to the three stages of life, the triangle, and the Trinity. The other protagonists spell their names with two syllables, representing duality and unresolved conflict. Only Amalric will, therefore, emerge whole from the ordeal. Other factors in his name serve to externalize personality traits. The syllable *mal* (evil) and *mâle* (male) are included in his name. He is very masculine, driven by a love of life, a need for conquest. He seeks to embrace a universe, encompass a world, and like Atlas, nothing is beyond his strength, no burden too heavy to bear. Strong, courageous, expansive, Amalric resembles his namesake Arnauld Amalric, the promoter of the crusade against the Albigensians (12th century), who also fought the Moors in Spain. Amalric is not destroyed by the harrowing events about to occur, nor is he given to bleak-

ness of mood. The energetic principle he represents encourages him to span nations and continents, to plunge
with fervor into universal existence. He is the most authentic of all characters; the one who accepts himself as he is,
seeing through the ambiguities of life most perceptively. He
knows that the so-called equilibrium, which seems to exist
at the outset of the play, is frail and false. "Here we are
engaged together in a game, like four needles; and who
knows what kind of wool destiny will have the four of us
weave together." The image drawn by Claudel may be
likened to Christ's Passion, since four nails were used in
depicting the crucifixion in the early centuries: two piercing the hands and two the feet. Only later were three nails
used: one nail piercing both feet, thereby associating the
entire crucifixion with the Trinity. As for the wool Amalric
refers to in this passage, it corresponds to the lamb, the
sacrificial animal. In view of Amalric's statement each
protagonist will experience an *imitatio Christi* in his own
manner.

I. *Sun/Water Ritual*

As Act I begins, Amalric and Mesa are on deck talking. A
stillness permeates the atmosphere; it is a static nothingness, sameness. Mesa sums up the feeling: "The days are so
much alike they seem composed of a single great black and
white day." The image imposes a cyclical time scheme
upon the proceedings; events take on mythical dimension.
Unlike the Westerner's eschatological time, we are plunged
into the Oriental's mythical view. "I love this great immobile day," Amalric comments, instilling a more powerful sense of repose into the atmosphere by contrasting it
with the mobile waters that are carrying the ship to its
destination.

The sun pours down from an endless sky onto vast emptiness: "water behind us and more water in front of us." A kind of Taoist "glorification of the void" is implied here, a condition which enables man to experience "a state of perfect availability," simplicity and detachment. Soon the idyllic image alters its focus, and from the world at large it centers on a "black" dot, the ship—the microcosm. Heaving, tumultuous, oceanic inner forces now propel four people along their journey; these will be enlarged and dramatized.

The vessel navigating through the burning/icy waters symbolizes the human being in his spiritual quest—a soul in its mysterious wanderings—reminiscent of *The Flying Dutchman* and his search for redemption. In this sense the ship becomes a vehicle for self-discovery. An analogy may be made between Buddha, called the Great Ferryman, who crossed to the other side of the ocean of life to experience nirvana, and this quaternity of passengers, who try to divest themselves of passions and acquire tranquility during their sojourn.

The protagonists feel disoriented and dissatisfied. They exist in an aimless, goalless sphere. They are "a wandering troupe," Mesa says. "I have no place any place," Ysé confesses. Each in his own way is cut off from purpose, from God. They are souls in exile.

Mesa, de Ciz, Ysé, and Amalric undergo a Sun/Water baptism. As Jonah said to God "thou has cast me into the deep, in the midst of the seas; and the floods encompassed me about . . . even to the soul" (2:3), so Claudel's protagonists are now severed from their peripheral existences. During the period of isolation, their energies are to be directed within, thus activating unconscious contents and paving the way for new conscious attitudes.

Mesa, hard, brittle, and one-sided, had to become more malleable, flexible, and bending. Unable to relate to others

Edwige Feuillere and Jean-Louis Barrault in *Break of Noon*.
FRENCH CULTURAL SERVICES

or give of himself, his solitary, taciturn nature needed
recasting. Even Claudel described him as "very hard, dry,"
as "antipathetical," egotistical, and preoccupied with himself and his own salvation. "He had to be transformed," in
any way possible.[3] Mesa's longing for God was his only
preoccupation. It had become obsessive. The Sun/Water
operation—incineration and drowning—would allow vol-
atility and fusibility to be born, and with it a flow of ductile
sensations. To experience the tortures of the damned, as
had the wicked in Job, thus making their iniquities conscious, would also be Mesa's lot: "His roots shall be dried up
beneath, and above shall his branch be cut off" (18:16).

So Mesa would be burned after which he would experience a chaotic, preformed, and regressive condition.

Mesa is the first to mention fire (an aspect of the sun), commenting on the ship's siren. "What a cry in the desert of fire!" The siren, compared to a human cry—shrill, penetrating—tears him asunder, reinforcing his sense of loneliness, isolation, and exile. Life for him is a desert; it is arid—a wasteland: the vast oceans and endless skies replicate the dryness of his life. The fire which had burned within him—the fire for God—has consumed his serenity, desiccated his feelings, depleted his energies. His unacceptability by God served to weigh him down with grief, leaden his outlook. His stance is that of an automaton. He would have to remain in his watery desert—as the Hebrews, escaping from Egypt, stayed in their sandy desert—facing his inner wilderness in order to discover his Promised Land. The ship will lead Mesa into temptation; and the sun's blinding rays will vivify his demons, which will calcinate and bruise him.

Whether fire emerges from the sun or from a man-made flame, it has a dual function. It generates or consumes, fecundates or destroys, ushers in life or death. The struggle between light and darkness, Good or Evil, is the focal point of *Break of Noon*, as well as of Manichaeanism. St. Augustine (and Claudel was an inveterate reader of his works) had been a Manichaean. After his conversion to Christianity by St. Ambrose (387), he wrote vociferously of the evils of his erstwhile religious affiliation. In his *Argument Against the Manichaeans and Marcionites*, St. Augustine stated "EVIL THEREFORE IS NOTHING BUT THE PRIVATION OF GOOD. And thus it can have no existence anywhere except in some good thing." Evil is thus relegated to a defect in good things or to the figure of the Antichrist, as C. G. Jung suggested.[4] For Claudel, however, Evil is a very vital force, active and powerful, which must be fought at every turning point.

Fire/Sun will serve to illuminate the "evil" in Mesa: his impure, arrogant, and egotistical ways. It will bring to the open what lies hidden and repressed within him; revivify what is dead or dormant: love, feeling, emotions for and toward others. According to certain Medieval legends, the alchemist Christ and his Saints succeeded in revivifying corpses by passing them through fire as a metalsmith does when refining his metals—achieving a golden state. Mesa will experience his ordeal by fire, his sacrificial ritual: that inner burning which brings gnosis to the one who seeks it, perception to the one who sheds the outer core and burrows to the heart of humankind. Fire/Sun is heaven sent, Mesa believes. It originates in the celestial spheres, and then descends into terrestrial regions. Its purpose is to remold man. Just as Lucifer (light bringer) fell from heaven into the flames of hell, so Mesa will bring illumination, but he will be consumed in the process, and hopefully, reborn from his own ashes as was the phoenix. "Heaven smiles down to Earth with ineffable love," wrote Claudel.[5]

De Ciz must experience the Fire/Water ordeal because he is weak, disoriented, and irresponsible; he is always yielding to his desire to go elsewhere, to do something new. Referred to as "thin" and "with tender eyes," with "woman's eyes," he represents for Claudel the male failure. Although Ysé does not love her husband, she is nevertheless drawn to him sexually; and when he looks at her in a certain way, she feels "shame." He does not love her and she knows it. "He loves only himself," she remarks. Amalric describes de Ciz as a "parasite," a "glutinous creeping ivy," a "rubber plant." Too fluid and too unstable.

Ysé, blond, beautiful, sensual, and proud, needs to be loved and longs for the affection and security denied her by her husband. Only her senses have been aroused until now, not her soul. Her unfulfilled existence has made her consider herself "a stranger" to the world at large, imprisoned in superficiality. Ysé is not weak; nor is she a shrinking violet. She is strong and elegant, even virile. Amalric describes her as a "warrior," a "conqueror" and not a "coquettish" person. She must "subjugate" others, "tyrannize," or else "give herself" completely. She was made to become a "chieftain's wife," to have "great obligations" to tie her down. Amalric calls her a "high bred mare," and he adds that it would "amuse" him "to mount her back, if he had the time . . . She runs like a nude horse." He also sees her as a "maddened horse, breaking everything, breaking herself." Amalric knows her well. They are alike in many ways. He understands the power of her instincts and the lengths that they would take her if sufficiently stimulated: they would lead her to disrupt her present well-tempered, conventional existence.

Ysé is an "autonomous" person, Claudel wrote, remote, ambiguous, chaotic. As an archetypal figure, her power works in mysterious ways. She is the sun's female counterpart: the one to light the flame of passion; the agent who consumes and is consumed—the one to touch off the catastrophe or transfiguration process. Similar to Amaterasu, the Japanese Sun Goddess, about whom Claudel wrote a poetical essay, Ysé dazzles those in her entourage with her brilliance and beauty. Important too in the association made between Ysé and Amaterasu is the name of the island on which great temples to this Sun Goddess had been built—Isé—located on the Island of Isé, pronounced in French in the same manner as Claudel's protagonist.

Sun and water will work in consort for Ysé. The Indian Sea and her psychological submersion within these primal waters will be the source of her renewal and purification. As a female principle—yin as opposed to yang—water darkens and ices; it spreads lugubrious and unworldly feelings. "There is no solidity around me," Claudel wrote in *Verses in Exile*. "I am situated in chaos, I am lost in the interior of Death." These words are applicable to Ysé.

Amalric is courageous, powerful, a conqueror. He will be put through the Fire/Water ritual as part of a life experience, and will be the only one to pass the crucial test. He enjoys the world, feels comfortable in it, relates to people, is ebullient and naturally joyful. He is handsome, virile, sensual. Women cannot resist him. Authentic in his outlook, he follows his penchants and travels from one end of the globe to another. He is able to face facts, to "see clearly, to see thoroughly / Things as they are." He had met Ysé ten years prior to the events taking place on shipboard, before her marriage, and had wanted to make love to her then. She resisted his powerful advances, because she felt he did not really need her. Her pride and her independence of attitude were instrumental in rejecting his advances. Claudel singles Amalric's hand out for scrutiny: "With this hand here, with this hand you now see, and which is large and an ugly hand. . . . When I choose, my warrior, I shall place this hand on your shoulder." Hands are supportive entities; they symbolize activity in the outside world and serve to orient. For the Romans hands spell a life attitude: *manus* corresponds to authority, the *pater familias*, the emperor. For the Buddhist, hand gestures (*mudras*) take on religious significance; they manifest an inner spiritual situation and the exteriorization of inner energy, when the unmanifest becomes manifest. Hands are instruments, tools, armaments, which convert passive into active. Ysé predicts Amalric's success in life because he is "clever with his hands." Mesa comments on his "pleasant hands," which are well suited to milking a cow: they draw nourishment and are earth-oriented.

Although self-reliant and independent, Amalric is

caught, nevertheless, in the play of light, the sizzling heat on shipboard. At first he is troubled by sensations of blindness, by cutting pain. "I am blinded as if by a gun shot. That isn't a sun! . . . One feels horribly visible, like a flea between two panes of glass." Unlike Samson, who was divested of his masculinity when Delilah lulled him into a state of sleep, then cut his hair, which led to his blinding by the Philistines (Jud. 13:16), Amalric was blinded by Ysé's sensuality, but only for an instant. Despite his implacable desire for her, he has quickly regained his composure and would not humble or weaken before her. A man of the earth, his legs and hands were always balanced, oriented, thus giving him the equilibrium necessary to cope with the events to come.

As a solar hero, Amalric is a source of light, heat, and life. Not a sweet, gentle, understanding illumination, he is more a brash and violent fire. Amalric is invincible: the *Sol Invictus*, the active male, the yang principle. He is the antithesis of the Solar Christ, whose daily rise and fall spelled the cycle of light and darkness, ascension and descension. Amalric will not change dramatically during the course of the play. He will remain righteous, as he faces the sun in eagle fashion, with exultation—at times with a tinge of terror. Nothing can disrupt his realistic life attitude, not even his passion for Ysé, which intensifies, duplicates, replicates, heats like a furnace, stimulating his lust for life still further. The conqueror in him vibrates at the thought of possessing her, the Eternal Feminine.

As the trip pursues its course, the sea turns into a limitless mirror, a reflection of God's universe. Striking, brilliant, and perverse, the water/mirror is shot through with solar rays that magnify, enlarge, delineate in sharp, crystalline tones what had only been subsumed at the outset of the drama. The mirror holds and retains the formerly fleeting, coagulates the flowing, reveals the hidden to the all-seeing and roving eye of the Creator. It contains, absorbs, reproduces, and distorts the protagonists' feelings. As the speculum (Latin for mirror) on a telescope or surgical instrument allows more accurate observation by enlarging the image before it, so the water/mirror examines more minutely the passengers' needs, thus leading to greater speculation about their real motivations.

Each protagonist in turn reacts to the Sun/Water/Mirror complex. De Ciz sees it as clusters of infinitely replicating flashes of lightning. "How small and how consumed one feels in this reverberating oven." His personality assumes form in this one image: lightning consumes and destroys because its energy is so powerful and concentrated that it reduces everything which comes within its reach to cinders. The oven, like the womb, corresponds to the alchemist's athanor, which melts and smelts metals. De Ciz will be annihilated during the course of his inner trajectory—a *regressus ad uterum.*

Mesa looks upon the Sun/Water/Mirror complex as a "hard" substance which possesses a "resplendent backbone": as a "vat of dye," a "deep pane of glass." Each of these images indicates durability and liquidity, which will be transformed through the heating process—the tension aroused by the events to be experienced—into a new creation.

Wind is also a catalyst. It synthesizes the four elements: earth, water, fire, and air. It generates, fecundates, and destroys, as when the wind demolished the Spanish Armada. Wind gives rise to hurricanes, instability, and agitation. It unleashes, symbolically, a Titanic spirit, an elemental force that may, if unhampered, blind with rage, annihilating everything in its wake. Yet, wind (*ruh*, in Hebrew) means breath, the spirit of God as it moved over primordial waters in the beginning of time and Created the World (Gen. 1:2).

Amalric recalls the Sunday when he and Ysé met. There

was "a ferocious wind" blowing; it swept over everything, breaking, bruising "like the cutting mistral." It brought "the moonlight, the darkest night" with it. The wind "slapped him hard," shook him to the very foundations of his being. At the time Ysé was returning from Egypt, and he from distant lands, the remotest areas of the world; their love was born as was Venus from the wind-blown waves. Sunday, the day they met, was tempestuous: *dies dominicus*, the day of the Lord, of rest, the first day of the week, the beginning of their Creation from the Waters. Amalric expressed his baptism into her life in liquid terms: "Having imbibed my first great drink of life." He was not drowned by the experience, but drenched; not destroyed, but troubled; not despondent, but excited.

They met at ten o'clock. For the numerologist, Claudel, numbers are of metaphysical import. Ten is considered the union of One (God) and Zero (eternity). Ten also symbolizes the Ten Commandments, which Mesa will eventually break.

Ysé adores the wind because it forces up the salty spray from the ocean. Salt brings excitement, tingling sensations all over her body. It revitalizes the pagan and "silvery" Ysé; it glazes and makes everything "embarrassingly clear"; it disquiets, since it shears masks, reveals the mystery of being, releases repressed and reviled instincts. Salt for the alchemist blends, mixes: it is a universal go-between. It represents quintessence, a mediating force. Salt is a *complexio oppositorum*: it purifies when used in baptism; spells wisdom and spiritual nourishment in purification rituals; it preserves and renders incorruptible when blended in food. Salt, however, if placed near silver, corrodes, destroys, poisons.

The ship lunges forth to its destiny in a world where Sun/Water/Salt battle it out: purity/impurity; black/white.

The Manichaean forces of Good and Evil—, having acquired universal dimension, vie for supremacy—a struggle
between God and Satan. For Claudel, sin becomes a necessity, as already stated, if man is to earn redemption. Man,
born from darkness and sexuality, experiences an earth or
leaden condition during his lifetime. He must, therefore,
attempt to ascend the ladder from darkness to light, earthly
to spiritualized sequences. He must, also, experience the
world of instinct.

To underscore the elemental forces surging within
man, Claudel's universe becomes populated with images of
cows, horses, dogs, tigers, each representing the animal in
man in a hierarchy of values. The horse, for example, to
whom Ysé was compared, is looked upon as an animal of
darkness, a chthonian spirit representing unbridled instinct, night (the mare as in nightmare), terror. As a
nourishing force, the horse is said to be able to force water
out of springs by stamping his hoofs on the ground. In a
Medieval French epic concerning the four sons of Aimon,
their famous horse Bayard did just that: water emerged
when they needed it, thanks to their "magic" horse.
Psychologically, the horse awakens the unconsious world:
imagination, impetuosity, desire, creative power, youth,
energy, and sensuality. The mare, as Amalric called Ysé,
was "highly bred." As a mare, Ysé incarnates the Earth-
Mother who energizes and revitalizes. Ysé, however, compares herself to "an old white horse who follows the hand
which pulls it." A white horse implies majesty, as when
Christ mounted one (Rev. 19:11). It brings death, however,
when an overly impetuous outlook is allowed to flourish.
"And I looked, and behold a pale horse: and his name that
sat on him was Death, and Hell followed him" (Rev. 6:8).

The cow is also a protagonist in *Break of Noon*. Mesa
compared the cow to water, to a feeding, fecundating,

fertilizing force: a Primal Mother. Such associations are understandable, since water is linked with vital heat. The lover of Baal, the Canaanite fertility God, whose worshipers indulged in human sacrifice and sexual orgies, was a cow. Mesa mentions Baal in opposition to Christ. The cow, however, has spiritual values. Brahma's female aspect was given the name of "Melodious Cow" and "Cow of Abundance," underscoring the positive and nourishing qualities of this animal. Thus Ysé, depending on her relationships, can be positive or negative.

The dog is an active participant in the shipboard drama. Mesa calls himself "a yellow dog," a cur. Associated with death, Anubis, Cerberus, Garm, the dog is a complex of opposites in that it brings protection as the keeper of the flock, and devours when provoked to anger. Mesa is that terrified, yellow cur whose ordeal lies ahead.

Just as animals reflect man's inner climate through analogy and identification, so do colors. Claudel's universe is a giant network of ever-fluctuating and interacting tonalities: a canvas of kinetic hues, a conglomerate of active, aggressive, and brutal chiaroscuros. Light, Claudel wrote, "decomposes obscurity." It produces "the seven notes, in accordance with the intensity of its work."[6] Pigments, then, are related to sound for Claudel, as they were for Pythagoras and his "music of the spheres," or for Aristotle in his *De Coloribus*, when he compared the seven basic colors to musical intervals. Claudel's reservoir of musical analogies, derived from clusters of images, transforms *Break of Noon* into a veritable tone poem, with all the shadings, visual as well as sonorous, thus expanding and deepening its impact.

Color serves to generate excitement. It accentuates gradations of emotions and intensities of feelings. It is nature's metabolism, and aids in analyses of the protagonist's spiritual and physical outlooks. In that color is endowed with emotional equivalents, it is not surprising that

Claudel's colors should be violent, harsh, powerful. Mesa speaks of greens, tobacco-color, fired red "in the teeming clear chaos." He loves fire, white, yellow, strident and striated hues; striking pigments struggle and clash with each other, are forever at war. The greens mentioned by Mesa have particular significance. Outside of the conventional allusions to fertility and productivity, it also refers to the Holy Grail, to that emerald chalice, which legend tells us contained the blood of Christ; to the emerald on Lucifer's forehead, thus equating green with both salvation and perdition, ascension and descension. When Mesa looks down at the water around him he calls it a "wine pocket," associating it with the blood of Christ and the transubstantiation ritual. The brilliant sun in Act I has become a "scarlet sun" at the finale of the act, thus fusing spiritual with carnal essences; a premonition of the blood sacrifice to follow.

Gray is also mentioned in *Break of Noon*. Ysé tells Mesa that she has "gray eyes." She also speaks of "gray fish." Gray is a half-way color, a mediating tonality between black and white. It is the color of cinders, pain, semi-mourning for Hebrews and Christians, and the grayness of spirit, nebulous, enigmatic, and unclear regions. The slang word for tipsy in French, *griser*, comes form the word *gris* (gray), thus reinforcing the connection with the color and an irrational condition: the loss of lucidity, the diminution of gray matter in the brain. Instinctuality, under such circumstances, is allowed to dominate. Before Mesa met Ysé, his world was bleak, clouded. He was unable to see clearly into his own soul; his arrogance, pride, and egotism blinded him. He lived only in a remote and nebulous region: "I have left humanity." Ysé extracted him from these cold, dank, remote, leadened realms and forced him to experience the turmoil and ecstasy which would ultimately, she hoped, bring him (and her) equilibrium.

Black is also included in Claudel's palette. Ysé wears a

Ysé wonders how Amalric recognized her after ten years had elapsed, he says: "The same blackness suddenly appeared in the air"; black is the color of sublime beauty as in The Song of Songs: the Shulamite or the beloved is black. Black is death, Ysé informs Mesa. Love is an "operation to be undergone," in which ether, as a soporific, will be used to bring about a loss of consciousness, a moment of exquisite passivity—a "death." It was during such instances of nonbeing and nonfeeling that Adam and Eve conceived their first born. Mesa lets himself be cradled by Ysé, the Black, the Great Mother, the archetypal figure. She calls herself "A mother of women and men!" Within her being, as in black, there exists a synthesis of all colors: "all beings exist in me!" she declares. "You must yield, You must die."

Ysé, the catalyst, will pave the way for Mesa's death and transfiguration. Why, he questions, has she been placed in his path? Why must she "disturb" his "peace of mind?" Serenity, not battle, is what his soul seeks; repose, not activity; indifference, not attachment. Mesa is aware that he will never be able to give himself completely to Ysé; that he will never be *one* during his earthly sojourn. "There is no way that I can give you my soul, Ysé." Entrenched in the world of the spirit, he does not know how to cope with the emotions which swell within him. A man seeking moderation and measure, Mesa, when aroused by Ysé, reacts as the anchoret when enticed by the courtesan, Thaïs.

There is a side to Mesa which longs for earthly love despite all of his statements concerning his spirituality. "I long for love: O the joy of being fully loved!" When possessed by Ysé, his world begins to fall apart. What had once been a rigid attitude, a certainty—his desire to sacrifice his earthly existence to God—has become porous, weak, malleable. He compares himself to "a broken egg." The analogy is well-founded, since according to Egyptian, Tibetan, Hindu, Chinese, Japanese, and Greek beliefs the world was born from an egg. So in *Break of Noon*, the sea water was transformed into "a reverberating oven" that was then set aflame, thus paving the way for the evolution of the protagonists. Mesa's "hard" exterior had now been shattered, broken into components, allowing nutrients to flow inward and dormant contents to leave the protective, imprisoning sphere.

Ysé poses a terrible conflict for Mesa. She has come between him and God. His feelings of guilt do not allow him to look her in the face. As their journey pursues its course, however, she forces their eyes to meet, pitilessly. Mesa looks away. He refuses to share his pain with her; nor will he open his heart to her. "This, at least, belongs to me," he tells her. The solitude and loneliness were flowing outward, passing over his former unbending and metallic covering. "It is hard to keep one's heart for oneself," he tells Ysé. "It is hard not to be loved. It is hard to be alone. It is hard to wait. And to endure, and to wait, and to always wait." No longer intractable, his ductile sensations flow forth.

II. *Air/Earth Ceremony*

The curtain opens on a cemetery in Hong Kong. It is shaped in the form of an omega. The sun has lost its glow; the heavens have darkened. The April monsoon season is about to erupt. An unformed, leaden, cloudy atmosphere envelops the scene. The blackness of the day and the omega-shaped cemetery are the perfect backdrop for the dismemberment ritual to follow. As the Gospel according to St. John states most clearly:

> Except a corn of wheat fall into the ground and die
> it abideth alone; but if it die it bringeth forth

much fruit. He that loveth his life shall lose it and he
that hateth his life in the world shall keep it unto life
eternal *(John 12:14)*.

All must experience death and decay before it can be reborn, revitalized, and reworked into new surroundings.
The omega also represents a stage of *renovatio*. The
twenty-fourth and final letter of the Greek alphabet, it
corresponds to the beginning and end of a cycle of life. The
arms of the omega also ensnare, envelop, imprison—as
well as protect. The outcome is ominous either way.

Mesa "trembles" in the bleakness and blackness of the
cemetery, which Claudel calls "a rotting place for heretics." Mesa experiences nausea. He looks about and says:
"What a shadow on the earth! My footsteps cry. It seems to
me that I am speaking in a cavern." Shadows, cavernous
regions, reflect his inner climate. The cavern, which has
been equated with a womb, represents the realm of the
unconscious: an area where unknown forms roam about
and archetypal figures rumble. Plato's cave represented an
area of imprisonment, where darkness gave birth to light,
where possibilities could develop into positive characteristics. A condition of yin prevails in these inner regions. Only
under cave conditions can the inner world become known.

De Ciz, the "watered down" husband, whose furtive,
fluid, and unstable nature would have to take on consistency or would break up completely, decides to accept
Mesa's offer to go on a dangerous mission into the heart of
China. He would stand to gain a lot of money, which is
what he wanted. He leaves Hong Kong, despite Ysé's pleas
that he remain or at least to take her with him. She needs
him, she confesses. She fears for her future and for her
children's. She has a premonition of disaster. "I know it,
there are terrible things in store for me. I am afraid of this

land which is foreign to me." Twice she asks him to take her with him. Twice he refuses.

Mesa will now reach the height of his power. His energy will radiate. They meet in front of the cemetery. Neither looks at the other. Suddenly, Ysé raises her head, opens her arms to him. He embraces her sobbing. "It's all over," he cries. The beginning of the end. The gray condition had encouraged light, lucidity, rationality to vanish. Drunk with euphoria, Mesa had yielded to his impulses and experiences the ecstasy which comes with abandon. "O Ysé, don't let me return." In this sequence Claudel has created an aesthetic of unconsciousness: a sense of absence overwhelms the protagonist. What is uttered is no longer as important as what remains unsaid, unmanifest; emotion prevails rather than thought; feeling instead of the verb.

The emotions previously directed toward celestial spheres are channeled by Mesa toward the Eternal Feminine. "I am like a starving being unable to contain his tears at the sight of food!" The once hard, unbending Mesa has grown malleable, tractable. "I shuddered when I recognized you, and my entire soul has yielded!" Mesa looks at Ysé. She is as "beautiful as a young Apollo!—" he says, as resplendent in the darkness of the day as she was in its radiance; as "straight as a column," as "clear as the rising sun"; and her hair is comparable to strands of "gold." Although the instrument of perdition, the vehicle through which Mesa is to sin, Ysé is alone the means of his redemption. To compare her with gold, therefore, the purest of elements, to the "rose," the Medieval symbol of the Virgin Mary, to the "tree," which represents the marriage between Sol and Luna, "dawn," the beginning of life, the "flowering acacia branch" signifying *renovatio*, not only reflects the scope of her powers, but is also an animist's way of virtually deifying her. Ysé becomes a hierophant in this

scene. Of singular interest is the analogy Mesa makes between Ysé and the Bird of Paradise. In the Bardo-Thödol
this bird represents the throne of Buddha; for the Christian
it stands for the Solar-Wheel, its tail is the sky constellated
with stars—an incorruptible soul; its hundred eyes correspond to the "all-seeing" Church.[7] It is an almost premoni-
tory image for the very much flesh and blood Ysé, who will
take on celestial values later on.

The "bridal chamber" is the cemetery. It is here that two
archetypal figures will be joined. Mesa takes possession of
Ysé. The sin has been committed. Two principles are
welded together: sensuality and eroticism take over. Time is
abolished, and the external world repudiated and made
void. Mesa and Ysé bathe in universal forces; their voices,
like musical interludes, rhythmic sequences, acquire amplitude and depth. Onomotopoeias, metaphors, analogies,
repetitions, alliterations take on the value of objects, which
jar, bruise, abrade, and corrode as do chemicals biting their
way through the elements; beauty is injured, patinas destroyed, the whole cut asunder.

Ysé understands the chemistry of their union, the goal of
their lust, and the stakes for which they are playing. "But
what we want is not to create, but to destroy . . . and the
rage . . . and to destroy . . ." says Ysé. "Detestable are these
clothes of flesh. . . . It is not happiness I bring you, but
death, and mine with it." Maceration and laceration occur
as two bodies unite. Mesa's emotions are expressed in
imagery: "the great black flame of the soul which burns,"
referring to his old theme of a "devoured city."

Ysé's rapture ushers in feelings of "shame" which are
experienced like flaring sparks, knives, needles. Torment
envelops her body with additional desire. Her hatred for her
husband mounts. She no longer knows de Ciz, she claims.
Although colors are few in Act II by comparison with Act I,

they are, nevertheless, still potent and flammable, hazed and muted as well. Beneath the blackness of the cemetery atmosphere, the grayness of the colorless realm evoked, unfathomable depths are reached: nonverbal dimensions contained in the fulfilled experience of earthly ecstasy. Mesa has become alienated from God. He has turned toward the world; enveloped in Ysé's all-consuming presence. He lives and breathes only her. The loss of his Paradisial state has advanced his wholeness; it has led him to become a man of the flesh, thus continuing the congenital schism which was his lot.

III. Nox Profunda: The Lunar Phase

The curtains open on a large room in a "colonial" style house surrounded by verandas and enormous banyan trees in a port town in Southern China. Mesa's inability to give himself wholeheartedly to Ysé led her to leave him a year prior to the events now taking place. "I did not possess him, there was something strange about him. Impossible." Nor had she answered his letters. Amalric is now Ysé's lover and is caring for the child born to her and Mesa. Their happiness seems short-lived because of the insurrection taking place in China. Ysé and Amalric are to be killed along with the other Europeans in the town. Rather than accept capture and possible torture, however, Amalric has set up a time bomb slated to blow up the entire building. They prefer to be masters of their destiny rather than passive recipients. Amalric faces his end as he has his life, with equanimity.

Ysé is more complex. Her thoughts focus on her past: her "sins." She lingers on her infidelities toward her husband, her abandonment of her children, and her betrayal of

Mesa. Death will serve a purpose, she feels. It will wash away her torment. She greets it not with fright, but with a kind of relief. Yet, she feels trapped, anguished, and lines of grief and pain mark her face.

Amalric asks Ysé to make some tea. For the Chinese, tea has a very special significance. Its imbibing corresponds to a communion, an offering, an Oriental agape. For the Taoist and Buddhist, the tea drinking ceremony implies the overcoming of antagonism in the earthly spheres and the emergence of a state of serenity, sobriety, and detachment. Not an escape from life, the tea ritual ushers in the creation of a more contemplative existence. The cosmic principle of Sun/Ocean in Act I has now been reduced to a less potent and glowing fire; the expanse of water has also been diminished in size: both are contained in the kettle—the percolating water over the flickering gas flame. Limitations, it is implied in this image, have been imposed upon Ysé and Amalric. The world is no longer young; life is no longer ahead of them. The end is approaching.

As Ysé stands near the stove, she begins to sob. Her tears are a mirror image of the boiling tea on a still smaller scale; each in its own way reflects the circumstances. Only one cup of tea is left, which she gives to Amalric. He can also have the little milk which remains. The child will no longer need it, the intimation being that it will die. By giving the tea to Amalric, Ysé is symbolically nourishing those factors that he represents: courage, straight-forwardness, a realistic attitude. Ysé's course is different. "O hunger and thirst for death," she says.

Ysé walks toward the mirror and peers into it. She smoothes down her white woolen bathrobe, loosens her long blond hair, letting it fall freely about her shoulders. Flowing hair in Medieval paintings symbolized "penitence," a state Ysé will soon be experiencing. Amalric leaves the room.

Ysé hears a noise on the stairs. She shudders. The door opens. A shadow becomes visible; the form is reflected in the mirror. Mesa enters. Ysé remains motionless and speechless. He questions her. Why hadn't she answered his letters? What had he done to deserve such treatment? He cannot live without her, he tells Ysé. Mesa grows irate because Ysé does not respond. He accuses her of having an "iron" heart—a metallic personality—of being unbending, unyielding, inflexible, and brittle. Ysé has branded him, fettered him. Mesa's anger mounts. He informs her of her husband's death, and the fact that they are now free to love each other "without secret and without remorse." He begs her to leave with him. He will save her from death and take her children with them. Mesa informs her that he has a pass for two people which will allow them through Chinese lines. Still Ysé remains silent.

Reacting violently to her ironlike exterior, Mesa's attitude alters in consistency. It ignites and the air abounds in heavy dank fumes and smoke.

> Bitch! tell me what went through your mind the first
>   time you gave yourself, after having decided to do
>   so, to that stray dog,
> With another man's fruit in your body, and when the
>   first signs of my child's life,
> Mingled with the frenzy of a mother tingling with the
>   excitement of a double adultery?
> I gave you my soul and I communicated my life to you,
> You prostituted these; and what thoughts went through
>   your mind during those heavy days when my child
>   was ripening in you,
> And you brought it to this man, and you slept in his
>   arms while my son's limbs were filling you?

Mesa approaches the rigid Ysé. He is carrying a "sepulchral" lamp; the dark flames invade the scene, reflecting their glow in Ysé's eyes and in the full-length mirror on the side of the stage. Mesa blows out the flame. Ysé has never really understood him, he declares vehemently. "Goodbye Ysé, you never really knew me! This great treasure that I carry within me, You could not uproot it."

Amalric enters. He strikes a match which lights up the room. Both men look at each other. The action generated by the sulfur of the match symbolizes the tension between Ysé's lovers: two sulfuric forces brought together. Mesa declares his intention of taking both mother and child with him. Amalric will give up neither. He asks Ysé to choose: to die with him or to live elsewhere with Mesa and the child. Mesa, who cannot stand the tension, draws a weapon from his pocket. Amalric throws himself on him. Ysé watches the struggle in the mirror: an outer manifestation of an inner conflict. Muted moon rays, replacing the burning sun tones, now penetrate the room and encircle the two struggling men.

The fight has ended. Amalric has thrown Mesa to the ground where he lies lifeless: broken in body and soul. His right shoulder has been dislocated; his leg "demolished." The dismemberment ritual has begun, on the physical plane, with the displacement of his limbs, symbolizing a break with the manifest world. Mesa will no longer be able to order or orient himself in the existential sphere —relationships will be severed. Amalric carries him to the couch. He removes the "pass" from Mesa's pocket. Ysé goes to the next room to get the infant. She remains there for a time and then returns alone. The child is dead. Amalric extinguishes the lamp. As they leave Ysé begins laughing hysterically.

In keeping with the classical monologue which French dramatists have been using since the seventeenth century to reveal a protagonist's inner conflict, Claudel wrote "The Song of Mesa," also a monologue, but inspired by the Song of Songs. The Biblical poetic dialogue between two lovers is considered by mystics to be an allegorical representation of God, the bridegroom, and Israel, the bride; or the human soul in union with the Divine beloved. Christian exegetes look upon the blissful encounter in The Song of Songs as an expression of the union of Jesus, the royal bridegroom, with the Church, his bride.

Moon rays now glow in the night atmosphere. An entire universe becomes visible from the room. Stars and planets shine; their light corresponds to illumination fighting darkness in the soul; it is spirit in conflict with matter, fragmentation versus unity. The Star of Solomon, made up of two interlocking triangles, symbolizes the conjunction of multiplicity: fire/earth/water/air.

Mesa's Song begins with a salute to the Heavens above, the Constellations, the Queen of Heaven, that is, the Virgin Mary, reminiscent of the image drawn of her in Revelation, standing on the crescent moon wearing a crown of stars: "And there appeared a great wonder in heaven; a woman clothed with the sun, and the moon under her feet, and upon her head a crown of twelve stars" (12:1).

Mesa's love for the terrestrial woman—Ysé—has now evolved from its existential and impure condition to the collective image, the cosmic figure: the matrix of the Christian world, the Virgin Mary. From the creature of flesh and blood, Mesa now communes with the "Mother of Mothers," the resplendent Moon Virgin. Moon rays flood the stage in a kind of epiphany enveloping the entire atmosphere in the glow of a religious mystery. The tea ceremony enacted earlier was a prelude to the events now taking place: the sublimation, decantation, and distillation of emotions.

The numinosum is experienced. The light filtering in from the heavens above in variegated forms and hues transforms the dismal room into an awesome and majestic cathedral. Mesa's Song, with its mysterious rhythmic and tonal patterns, takes on the power of a chant.

> And from left to right, all over, I see a forest of
> torchlights surrounding me!
> Not illuminated wax, but powerful heavenly bodies,
> similar to those great flamboyant virgins.

The entire universe responds to his offerings, as though the celestial spheres inhabited by the Patriarchs, the Bishops, and the entire Clergy—all constellated in the stars—were reaching out to each other and to the penitent in a sublime cosmic tone poem. Mesa asks for the remission of his sins and prays for his sanctification as the Biblical David had done centuries before: "Have mercy upon me, O God, according to thy loving kindness; according unto the multitude of thy tender mercies blot out my transgressions" (Psalm 51).

Mesa has grown detached from terrestrial longings —from the mortal Ysé. He is ready for the "highest form of drama," Claudel wrote: the sacrifice. Spirit has intervened. His human soul "vibrates," and "contemplates." *Pneuma*, the breath of divinity has taken hold. Mesa's heart and mind, once exiled from Paradise by God, then geared to human needs, had been crushed, broken, pulverized, and mutilated by the forces with which they collided. Only now is his soul allowed to leave what he calls his "detestable carcass."

Ysé returns and walks through the room as if in a "hypnotic trance." She is like an "automaton," a cloud, and crosses in front of the mirror. The whiteness of her gown, the blondness of her hair, accentuated by the reverberations of the moon rays in the mirror, concretize the sanctity of the preceding moments. Ysé goes to the room where the dead infant lies and cries strangely. Mesa calls to her. She returns and again passes in front of the "spotless mirror" in search of something; then pauses "inundated by the moon," as Artemis, Isis, and the Virgin Mary had when experiencing moments of similar sublimity. Ysé's image is caught in the "occult mirror," to use Claudel's words; it is flooded by the Moon's spiritual essence. The soul has been purified. It has suffered enough.

Until now Ysé was a carnal female principle. As she walks toward Mesa and sits at his feet, however, he experiences her presence as a soul force, an anima. Their love has now been sublimated and bathed in pure visual essences. "Full of glory and light, creatures of God," Ysé says, "I see that you did love me, And you have been granted me, and I am with you in ineffable tranquility." Similar to Goethe's Marguerite, whose past came to her in a series of visions prior to her redemption, so Ysé relives her sins. It was earthly love that had compelled her to act in such a despicable manner, which had bound, tortured, and imprisoned her. No longer the sun-drenched Ysé on that August day at Noon, she has become the Ysé of the night hours, of Midnight. "This is the Break of Noon," she intones, "And I am here, ready to be liberated." The cycle has been completed. The number twelve, representing the new Jerusalem in Revelation, has become actualized for her (21:1). *Nox Profunda*. The Great Work has been completed. "All veils have been dissipated and the Flesh now becomes Spirit."

Although both protagonists are doomed to die, it is Ysé who emerges in her golden essence. Sacrifice which leads to redemption, according to Claudel, does not seem to be authentic on Mesa's part. He returned to Ysé to take her and his child away with him. After his struggle with Amalric he was physically unable to leave; the pass had been taken from him, therefore, the choice was no longer his. He could not escape. Ysé, on the other hand, of her own volition chose to return. Her sacrifice was profound and complete; it earned her transfiguration and redeemed her from the weightiness of her leaden and earthly condition.

Break of Noon, Claudel's most dramatic and poignant work, has universal appeal. Audiences identify both emotionally and spiritually with the conflicts experienced. They leave the theatre deeply moved; deeply troubled.

5. THE SATIN SLIPPER: PENITENTIAL? SACRIFICIAL? OR SADO-MASOCHISTIC?

Claudel wrote *The Satin Slipper* (1919–1924) when he was fifty years of age. He had already worked in government service for twenty-five years, had traveled throughout the world, and had experienced the political, economic, and spiritual impact of World War I. *The Satin Slipper* is the most involved, ambiguous, and lengthy play of Claudel's career. It dramatizes the Sacrament of Penance and Sacrifice: a spiritual flagellation and psychological humiliation, a prolonged test of man's will to transcend the flesh, to battle matter and the Devil in order to experience God in His plenitude. It may also be considered a staged sado-masochistic ritual.

The Satin Slipper completes and resolves what had remained unfinished and in a state of suspension at the conclusion of *Break of Noon*. It is Claudel's nebulous answer to the question plaguing him throughout his life: What is the meaning of love? Since the severance of his relations with Rose (1905), the prototype of Ysé, Claudel claimed to have suffered deeply from a gaping wound that could not heal. Only years later, after another encounter with Rose, did he succeed in transforming his tremulous love into a drama revolving around what he considered to be the joy of renunciation.

The Satin Slipper is baroque drama. The word baroque was used by jewelers in the Iberian Peninsula to define a pearl with irregularities. In this context "baroque" indicated, for the Westerner, something which was imperfect. For the Oriental, however, irregularity indicates a sought-for condition: that of incompleteness. The Japanese artist, for example, tries to create imbalance in his art forms. Asymmetry allows viewers to absent themselves from logical thinking, from formalism, or conventional, geometrical, and rational regularity, and to become aware of the fact that nothing is "complete" or "fixed" in the phenomenological world. There is always *more* to be seen, *more* to be experienced. The visible, then, is incomplete and imperfect; it is one aspect of a continuous life process of perpetual becoming.

The pejorative notion that the Westerner had originally associated with the word "baroque" has changed. Claudel looks upon it as the expression of the Counterreformation. Whereas Gothic art, he explains in *The Eye Listens*, was direct, straight in its form, clear, and its trajectory toward the heavenly realms, speedy and unimpeded, Baroque art is sinewy, vaulted, and complicated. The Counterreformation had to fight off enemy attacks; it could no longer translate feelings into simple and unobstructed vertical lines. The movement toward God had to be compressed; other outlets had to be fused for "the reactive energy" to reach its destination. The dome in Baroque art strains, curves, arches, strengthening itself for that giant push toward divinity. Subtle movements, reminiscent of the "gymnastics of prayer," reach their destination in this fashion.[1] At the very outset of *The Satin Slipper*, a prayer is said for the hero, asking that he attain his goal to experience divinity, rather than be bogged down in the matter, entrapped in the flesh. The hero's way may be circuitous, Claudel indicates, so let it be: "and if he does not go toward you by means of his own clarity, let him seek you through obscure ways; if not through direct paths, than by indirect ways. . . ."

Claudel's drama is divided into Four Days; not the Seven of Creation, since man's job is incomparable to that of the omniscient and omnipotent God. Over a hundred characters inhabit the stage. Were the play to be given in its entirety, it would take nine hours. Barrault produced it in 1943, but cut it extensively, dividing it into two performances to be given on consecutive evenings. Even such reduction in size did not simplify Claudel's complex of contradictory and multiple ideas. Activity is forever altering structure and texture in *The Satin Slipper*; tension is rampant, propelled by his driving desire to break out of limited spheres and forms into boundless realms. Some of the characters appear only once, while others are occasional walkons. Still others play significant roles. Some are essences, appearing as a vision or a flesh and blood being acting as a device to contrast or harmonize with the prevailing mood surrounding the protagonists. Passions from the most sublime to the most insidious ferment —spasmodically, spectrally, condensing, crystallizing—as each pursues the object of its search. The two main characters, Prouhèze and Rodrigue, weave their web throughout the globe, crossing continents (Asia, Africa, Europe, the Americas), communicating by means of waterways. *The Satin Slipper* is a giant conglomeration of disparate and fragmented factors—byroads and sideroads—networks of involutions and convolutions; it is an aggregate of genres and feelings—a storehouse of irony, comedy, tragedy, whimsy, parody, burlesque, satire—almost unending riches which a febrile imagination puts to good use.

Geneviève Page and Jean-Louis Barrault in Jean Wiener's adaptation of *The Satin Slipper*, music by Arthur Honegger.
FRENCH CULTURAL SERVICES

The theme of *The Satin Slipper* is love: a love bond as colossal as that of Tristan and Isolde, a love destined and predestined to be unfulfilled. Powerful, consuming, abrasive, Prouhèze's passion for Rodrigue cannot be satisfied because she is married. To commit adultery would be to defile the sacrament—the Catholic Church and God. Her passion, therefore, must be dominated, repressed. At one point in the play, marriage would have been possible, but here, too, Claudel has fate intervene to prevent the completion of earthly love. It was Claudel's belief that to experience an all-embracing or total love on earth is to diminish humankind's love for God. To opt for a finite relationship is to consider salvation, which is infinite, of lesser importance. *The Satin Slipper*, then, is a network of events in which the protagonists are forever being punished, flayed, dismembered; a willed refusal on the author's part to ex-

Jean-Louis Barrault and Geneviève Page in a scene from *The Satin Slipper*, in a production by Jean-Louis Barrault at the Théâtre de France.
FRENCH CULTURAL SERVICES

perience physical fulfillment and pleasure. Earthly love must be sublimated, energy dispelled and channelled in some other direction, drawn away from obsessive love. Love is a catalyst, an energetic force, particularly when it remains unsatisfied and incomplete; it creates tension, and tests character.[2] Claudel gives historical examples of such unrequited emotions which forced men, such as Napoleon, to make war, to build a world or destroy one. Owing to Rodrigue's seething torment, he becomes a mighty conqueror in the Americas, establishing his court in Panama. He even attempts to take Japan. As for Prouhèze, she governs a small Spanish possession, Mogador, in North Africa. Since Prouhèze and Rodrigue are forever repressing their feelings, dominating them, arming themselves with stoic and aescetic disciplines, they never experience the meaning of compassion, tenderness, or gentleness. Feelings are minimized, dismembered, flagellated. They must serve for larger purposes. The protagonists grow bitter during the travail that is their life. Love must be replaced with shame. A product of the will, humiliation, if earned, paves the way for redemption. Never is an action on the part of either Prouhèze or Rodrigue accepted for its own sake, but rather for a cause, a goal, whether it be for divinity or another. *"Punishment Serves the Soul."*

"Order is the pleasure of reason: but disorder is the delight of the imagination," writes Claudel, as he descants upon his view of sixteenth-century Spain, the period in which *The Satin Slipper* takes place. It is an era as ambiguous and unsettled as is the drama's opening scene, which takes place on the Atlantic Ocean, midway between the Old and New worlds. The broken mast of a great ship floats by, as if propelled by some unknown force; it is a single, tiny, insignificant object compared to the unlimited expanse of shimmering constellations. A Jesuit Father is tied to the mast—tall and thin—an El Greco figure; he experiences an *imitatio Christi*. We learn that he has been captured by pirates while on his way from Spain to America; he is Rodrigue's brother, who prays for him, hoping that he will have the strength to struggle against his "animal" nature, his instinctual longings, thus becoming pure enough to approach God. The Jesuit Father thanks God for having "bound him" in this manner, for having oriented him as he had, allowing him to suffer in the most excoriating manner amid the swirling waters of an open sea. Pain has stabilized and fixed his previously mobile and seething soul. Only now, tied to the cross, he really knows torture; only now has be been able to consider himself truly as belonging to his Creator—and only to Him. He calls upon God to aid

Rodrigue and Prouhèze in their obsessive feeling for one another, so that they may be worthy of the rarefied crystalline passion given only to those who have vanquished their need for physical contact.

We are told at the outset of the play that Rodrigue of Manacor is a powerful, ambitious, handsome, virile Spanish nobleman. He seeks to brave the world, cross frontiers, discover life in its multiple mysteries and riches. Reminiscent of many of Claudel's heroes, Rodrigue is also Promethean. He is ready to awaken the urge within him, to discover the energetic principle in a fearless universe. He does not yet know the burden of the flesh, the weight of sexuality, the excoriating pain the man of faith undergoes as he tries to live up to God's commandments—His love. Rodrigue will have to learn the meaning of "desire" and of "passion" so as to be able to struggle against these forces and to dominate them. Conquest of nations is only one part of the terrestrial order; there is a soul with which each individual must contend. In an epigraph to *The Satin Slipper*, quoting St. Augustine, Claudel wrote, *etiam peccata:* sin serves. God avails Himself of sin to save souls. It is through sin that awareness of purpose may be realized, that the will and mind prove their powers over the flesh, and that humankind begins its ascension toward the divine sphere.

Rodrigue first set eyes on Prouhèze when a tempest hurled his ship, which was sailing around the Spanish coast, onto the shores of Morocco—a tiny area dominated by Spain at the time. Rodrigue became ill and was cared for by Prouhèze, the wife of Don Pelage, the ruler of the area. Fate bound them from that moment on, irresistibly, deliriously. Their passion would never abate; it was all-consuming, each ravishing the other. Near or far, Rodrigue's voice always resounds in Prouhèze's ear, just as hers becomes an echo within his.

Prouhèze had married an old Castilian nobleman whom she did not love. Solitary, uncommunicative, deeply religious, Pélage, already advanced in years, had fallen in love with her, then proposed marriage. Before he asked Prouhèze to become his wife, however, he consulted a statue of the Virgin in front of his home. He understood her response as one of encouragement. The marriage, however, brought neither partner happiness or contentment. Prouhèze wanted life, struggle, excitement, and challenge. Pélage sought peace, harmony, a withdrawal from world experience. He looked upon her as an anima figure, as the ideal, as existing for him alone. Pélage represented stasis: "I tried not to cause any movement at all in this area," he said to Rodrigue's mother.

Prouhèze's love for Rodrigue (and his for her) was based on secret affinities, mystical inclinations, superhuman vibrations. It was of such a nature that each was forever inundated by the other's strength, each opened the other's soul, awakened the other to life, communicating spectacular joy as well as piercing sorrow. Rodrigue knows from the outset that Prouhèze awards him inestimable "joy"; she is unique and represents the divine soul, the heart, the Gnostic Sophia. "Joy alone is the mother of sacrifice," he said. His recognition of the role she is to play in his life, his understanding of the magnetic power she wields within him, allowed him to accept—with difficulty at first—the meaning of their protracted separations. There are some men whose path toward God is straight and acquired with relative ease. Such was the man of the Middle Ages, as represented by straight, pointed, smooth, and simple cathedral spires. Rodrigue's way, however, would be arduous and lengthy, tortuous and difficult, a replica of baroque architecture. Rodrigue, when he first meets Prouhèze, is unaware of the network of tortures awaiting him. So filled is he with Prouhèze's presence, so inundated by excitement, that he "forgot to look at her." Prouhèze, from the moment Rodrigue set eyes on her, has taken on the luminosity of an astral vision, the sparkle of a "splendid" star, a radiant point "in the living sands of the night."

The same sensations inhabit Prouhèze. Were she to yield to her passion, shame and dishonor would be brought upon her, her husband, and her house. Pélage, therefore, plays an important role in shaping her destiny; he places his confidence in her. He knows she is boundless in her rectitude; he senses that though her desire for Rodrigue foments, ceaselessly, unabashed, it will never be fulfilled. Her flesh will never know his. Indeed, throughout the drama when Rodrigue and Prouhèze do meet, they barely touch each other. To touch, to experience bodily contact would lead to giving the other what is not the other's to give. Prouhèze's body belongs to her husband; she cannot dispose of it as she sees fit. Throughout *The Satin Slipper*, therefore, the body for Rodrigue and Prouhèze, is defined as a "prison," an "enemy," a constant reminder of man's mortality. Rodrigue's mother talks of it as a "stifling" force. It is the body which paves the way for agony, a garment to be carried throughout life. It is unalterable, weighty clothing or a heavy mass which grows, inflates, then suffers and decomposes. Flesh is what Prouhèze and Rodrigue share with humankind; it is this very element, paradoxically, which separates them. To love totally on earth, then, is to deprive God of his pound of flesh; of his need of man. Total love is to be given, Claudel declared, only to the Creator.

To make certain feelings do not dictate Prouhèze's acts, she takes an oath: she will never commit an act of evil, never dishonor her husband or her house. As a pledge of her word she removes the satin slipper she is wearing and places it in the hands of the statue of the Virgin that stands in front of her house.

> I leave myself in your hands! Virgin mother, I give you my slipper! Virgin mother, keep my unfortunate little foot in your hands! . . .

> But when I shall try to walk the evil path, let it be with a limp: the barrier which you have placed . . . .

> Keep it next to your heart, O terrifying great Mother!

Prouhèze must cope with a double burden: not only must she resist her love for Rodrigue, but she must also stand the presence of her own husband. Aware of her perplexed situation, Pélage suggests she leave Spain and go to Mogador in Morocco, a tiny outpost controlled by the Spaniards. If she cannot forget her love for Rodrigue, she will at least channel her energies elsewhere in important and worldly affairs. Pélage asks her to make Camillo, the present ruler of this area, her lieutenant. He knows that Camillo has always been passionately attracted to Prouhèze; he is also aware of the fact that she is revolted by him. In this manner, Pélage has set another test for Prouhèze, another trap, another ensnarement, to see how powerful a force her will and word are, checking how strong and God-filled her soul has become. Camillo is a difficult, dishonest, disreputable renegade; he is an impetuous and strange Castilian. Prouhèze's function, then, will be both social and political: she must protect herself against Camillo's advances, and Spain (Catholicism) against the inroads made by the Moors (Islam). Camillo, it has been thought, had converted to Islam; it is Prouhèze's obligation to see that he returns to his faith. In addition to all of these difficulties, Prouhèze must deal with a rebellious army. She will find her match, her husband believes, in this desolate area heaped high with sand dunes. It is here that her struggle will truly begin and that her life, through this conflict, will take on meaning and stature. Pélage is convinced of this, and in his heartlessness declares: "Too bad; she found her destiny and her destiny found her." Pélage believes her will to be unwavering. Therefore, he swells with excitement at the thought of her plunge into "a feast of pain" and the "excruciating inflammation" which will "envelop her insides."

Prouhèze accepts Pélage's offer. She will leave for Mogador, alone. "I am a woman. It is I who must safeguard this forsaken area between sea and sand?" The King of Spain, nevertheless, voices his disapproval of such harsh treatment for Prouhèze. The exile is arduous, even the most stalwart of his officers would find it severe. Prouhèze, however, considers it a challenge: she will fight brigands, betrayals, and Islam—as well as Camillo's constant advances.

Prouhèze's ordeal is not over even after she begins her toil at Mogador. The King of Spain intervenes. He asks Rodrigue to penetrate the network of searing emotions by giving him a letter to deliver to Prouhèze. Both monarchs and Pélage suggest that Prouhèze return to Spain, abandoning her work at Mogador. As the King talks of Rodrigue's future encounter with Prouhèze, brought on by the delivery of the letter, he virtually salivates at the thought of the pain their meeting will engender.

> I want him to see the face of the woman he loves again, once again in this lifetime! let him look at it and let him become drunk with it and let him carry it away with him!
>
> Let them look at each other in good faith, face to face! (p. 172).

Let each know of the other's love, openly, and let each decide once and for all upon separation—forever. Only through such an ordeal can the soul know purification and be saved, divested of all that roots it to earth, all that binds it to other humans. Cutting the bonds—the umbilical cord with earth—is the lifetime goal of Claudel's creatures. Sacrifice and temptation, therefore, are encountered every step of the way in sequences, clusters, and conglomerates in *The Satin Slipper*. For Claudel, these ordeals direct energies and lead to God: "Cleanse forever cupidity and lust" from being.

Rodrigue follows Prouhèze to Mogador. His ship nearly overtakes Camillo's, but a cannon shot from Prouhèze's frigate fractures his mast delaying him for three days. He sees part of the prow of his brother's ship, *The Santiago*, float by; the one which had led to his brother's demise. He considers it an omen, forcing him to reassess his life, his calling, his relationship to humankind, and God. He thinks back upon his past, his yearnings, his passion for Prouhèze. He castigates Pélage for having delivered Prouhèze to Camillo. His anger swells: At the sound of her name, suffering reentered his life. He longs for Prouhéze: "I need her body, nothing else but her body," he states. Rodrigue looks out at the sea; the swells are comparable to an infinite number of floating crystals, glass beads, sparkling in unison, in subdued and blinding tones, hurtling against one another—abrasive, scraping, grinding, rubbing—each the instrument of the other's illumination: a giant fomenting baptism. The sounds, reminiscent, paradoxically, of discordant harmonies, appear to him "all round in the night, as the fire of this ship in the depths of darkness which approaches to take us beyond the visible. . . ."[3] As the waters move about, agitating, battling their way to the top, the black masses grow translucent, opaque, ductile, as well as intractable, an outer world hiding, veiling the tremulous creatures inhabiting the mysterious sphere buried deeply within the oceans; masking Rodrigue's own unconscious world of pain and fracture.

During such moments, when the heart cries out for love, the mind grows desperate, pensive, and agony dilates. Parallels between the canvases of the Spanish seventeenth-century artist Zurbaran and his delineations of saints may be made: the flame contained within the depths of their religious experience is reminiscent of Rodrigue's own struggle to contain that searing, generative force. There is, however, that other aspect of his spirit, reminiscent of the baroque seventeenth-century Flemish artist Jordaens, who exploits feelings and senses, which also flare, burgeoning in fullness and joy. Rodrigue macerates his passion, attempting to become the ascetic his brother was, trying to fit the mold he has created for himself, when, in fact, his El Greco nature is filled with a full-blooded Rubens force. How many times must Rodrigue have asked himself the question Claudel always posed, a query which must have eaten away at his vitals, daily, throughout his long life: "God has granted all of his creatures to follow their nature; how could I resist mine?"[4]

Prouhèze sees Rodrigue's ship from a distance. "How small his boat seems! A little white dot." In this metaphor, the insignificance of the human being is set against eternity. The microcosm vanishes in favor of the macrocosm. What is a grain of sand? with respect to the universe? Therefore, Claudel's protagonist's love, on a personal and earthly plane, is just as unimportant compared to eternity and the beatitude that God's domain offers.

Rodrigue arrives in Mogador. Camillo goes to meet him. The stage is divided by a dark curtain. Prouhèze, who has refused to see Rodrigue, stands behind it. The entire scene rests, virtually, on a play of shadows: dark and vaulted in the dismal world inhabited by Prouhèze in contrast with the burning sands outside. Rodrigue sees only Prouhèze's shadow which remains motionless, sad, as it leans pathetically against the wall, acquiring its strength and sustenance from this immutable stone. Rodrigue knows she is there; he senses her presence "at the sound his soul makes when speaking to him." Twice Rodrigue calls her name, longs to speak with her, to experience her physical presence. Twice she refrains from answering. He will not call her name a third time, although Camillo encourages him to do so, even prods him along. Rodrigue knows that she might be unable to resist a third call, that she might yield in desperation, losing control of her febrile emotions. Rodrigue helps Prouhèze contain herself, live up to her oath, fulfill her calling. He does not pronounce her name, therefore, but in controlling himself further lacerates his heart, increasing his wound, allowing it to bleed freely. Then, Camillo, with almost uncontained glee, shows Prouhèze's note to Rodrigue, a note which states "I am remaining. Leave." Thus, he serves both Prouhèze's and Rodrigue's cause. He becomes the instrument of their torture. His sadism parallels their masochism, playing into his need for self-destruction.

Stilled with sorrow, Rodrigue feels drained of life. Motionless, solitary, Rodrigue—and his shadow, which Claudel now personifies on stage in an extraordinary scene —suffer from a deadly disease: "My soul has been struck." A Double Shadow now comes into view: that of a man and woman, "formless" in their blackness; each an aspect of the other: "my light belongs only to its obscurity." Each is imprinted onto eternity: "For what has existed but once becomes forever part of the indestructible archives." Silently, the Double Shadow moves about, accompanied by dirges, lamentations, and yearnings for unity with God and his creatures.

The moon rises in the following scene, the Double Shadow having disappeared. Mystery and majesty penetrate the atmosphere, as the rays float and glide about, the only other form on stage is a palm tree which grows ever more indistinct. Luminosities, energized by the moon, cascade in radiant circles, stretching, expanding, lulling the pain experienced by the protagonists into the sleep of oblivion. The pains "of woman buried in light" are utterances which link the protagonists to each other, inextricably: "Never will I be able to be without him and never will he cease to be without me." Paradise, consisting of mutual "torture," opens up for Rodrigue as he sails out into the vast expanse of blackness.

Ten years elapse as the Third Day begins. Pélage has died. Prouhèze has married Camillo and has had a daughter by him, named Mary of the Seven-Swords. Rodrigue, having sailed and unified the Americas, has been made Viceroy. He now lives in a world of luxury, ruling with virtually unlimited powers in a lush and plush semitropical Panamanian land. He learns that a letter has been sent him and that it took ten years to arrive. It had lost its way and wandered throughout the world. The letter was from Prouhèze; it asked that he come to her because she could no longer bear the solitude and pain of loneliness. Claudel borrowed this lost letter device for his play from seventeenth-century baroque novels; in this manner he was able to realize his tortuous and really outlandish plot. Upon receipt of the missive Rodrigue, despite repeated warnings from his advisors and lieutenants, has his fleet equipped and sails to Mogador.

At this vital and dangerous moment in Prouhèze's life, her Guardian Angel comes to her aid. It always intervened in moments of stress, endowing Prouhèze with fortitude. Grief stricken, she speaks to this outerworldly force, confessing that she hears Rodrigue's voice calling to her, persistently, with urgency. She thirsts for his being, his presence, and lives only through him.

She also knows, however, that the precious gem she had lost from her rosary some time back, has just been recovered; that it is "unique" and now that she has replaced it within the complex of other stones, the puzzle of her existence becomes comprehensible and her life complete. Strangely enough, it was Camillo who retrieved the lost gem. Symbolically, it was he who helped her attain clarity and purpose; it was he who aided her in the pursuit of her own ascension. Prouhèze longs for nothing but death now. In this bleak atmosphere of a declining existence, she sees a shadow, "a man walking in the night." Time and space have vanished. Separations, barriers, no longer prevent communication. She pierces the waters, clouds, sun, all opacities; her vision sees through worldly distance. She rushes about in her home "like an imprisoned animal chased after by a gadfly" and sees Rodrigue in all of his grandeur, his sensuality and physical prowess "who once again takes up his furious course, his bitter faction." Prouhèze, who is now wedded to Africa, identifies with Hagar in the desert; while Rodrigue clings to those poisonous spheres in South America. Finally Prouhèze begins to understand the meaning of sin, the fact that evil does serve a purpose in life, that it must be resisted forcefully, mightily, thereby revealing the purity of one's metal, the singular clarity and strength of one's backbone. "The desire of an illusion? for a shadow, for an ever fleeting shadow." Prouhèze exists only through Rodrigue, the Angel tells her. It is through her and by her that Rodrigue will be saved. She is that force placed in his path to tempt him, to test his valor. The love she arouses within him amplifies infinitely, when directed toward God. Prouhèze has no life of her own. She exists to and for Rodrigue. She is his necessity. That she has nearly fulfilled her mission in life encourages her to long for death. "Let me become a star," she tells the Guardian Angel. She learns from this celestial force that

THE SATIN SLIPPER / 133

her earthly trajectory is nearly over; soon she will take her rightful place in the cosmic hierarchy—as Rodrigue's constellation, his inspiration. Purgatory will cleanse her prior to the assumption of this role. But this outcome is not for now. Travail still awaits her.

Don Camillo castigates Prouhèze. He accuses her, not of overt adultery, but of indulging in a spiritually illicit relationship—"Rodrigue at night, every night, neither the walls nor the sea suffice to prevent" their fusion—the unity of souls from taking place. Prouhèze cannot deny the validity of his statement. Yet, "haven't I renounced him in this world?" she questions. Certainly, but only to possess him more completely in the next. For Prouhèze, Rodrigue "is forever that cross to which I am attached." She has accepted her lot, she tells Camillo, but will never give up loving Rodrigue. Camillo realizes that Prouhèze's soul has already taken that giant leap toward God, that sacrifice has enabled her to detach herself from all that binds her to this earth. To give up what she most loves in life is the sign of true sacrifice. Prouhèze is motionless, her face now takes on the strangely radiant glow of holiness: "From where else would this light now emerging from your face come?" Camillo asks.

Camillo, nevertheless, is not completely satisfied. Prouhèze must undergo one more test in order that her initiation into a more spiritual sphere may be complete. He arranges for a meeting between Prouhèze and Rodrigue. The intensity of the encounter, the control over their passions, creates a situation as inflammatory and as abrasive as Ixion's fiery torture at the wheel. There is no other way, Prouhèze says at this juncture, but death which will deliver her of her earthly carapace. No longer forced to remain far apart, to avoid each other, or to refrain from expressing their love openly, Prouhèze is finally on the way to conquering her yearnings. For Claudel, the eye and ear are organs of intelligence, they are "the delegates" of the other senses, such as touch, which is the most important for Claudel. Touch is the strongest of the senses; it leads most forcibly to fulfillment. Therefore, Prouhèze will have to overcome her visceral attraction so that she may enter into the higher destiny reserved for her. Were Prouhèze and Rodrigue to touch each other, they would have become vulnerable to their passion, accessible to mortal desire. The body is a "tabernacle," its mysteries must be preserved; its inner treasures and configurations left in the shadows. To allow the sense modality to escape, to open the door to the soul, except to welcome divinity, is to encourage chaos and contradiction. Containment is both Prouhèze's and Rodrigue's way. She will remain incarcerated in the burning desert sands; he will sail the high seas, unstable, unwilling to set anchor for more than a few hours, days, or months, longing to experience that one force which would lead to earthly happiness and to infinite damnation.

It is under a tent on the torrid sands of Mogador, near the Ocean, that Rodrigue talks to Prouhèze for the last time. She gives him her child, Mary of the Seven-Swords, despite the cries of the little girl. The scene is poignant and profound; their separation is irrevocable. Rodrigue leaves. Prouhèze returns to Mogador, where she and Camillo will die in the fortress they will have dynamited so as to prevent it being taken by the Moors. Rodrigue, Claudel intimates, will not be as fortunate: he will have to go on living and suffering.

Ten more years elapse. The outset of the Fourth Day, entitled "Windward of the Balearic Isles," includes a cast of thirty-three and action that is complicated to the extreme. Humor and irony mark its movement, while death hovers over it like a litany, stamping its essence with life. When Rodrigue returns to Panama he is disgraced by the King of

Spain for having abandoned his post so suddenly. His replacement now receives all the honors, even enjoying the fruits of Rodrigue's conquests. To underscore Rodrigue's disgrace, he is named governor of the Philippines and surrounding islands. Rather than contenting himself with his lot and living as best he can, his incredible drive encourages him to attempt to conquer Japan. In the battle, however, he loses a leg, is taken prisoner, and is held for two years in Nagoya castle. It is here that he studies Oriental ways, their wisdom, restraint, and art. He comes to understand why the Japanese have enclosed themselves on their island, why they have refused access to foreigners. Once released from prison, Rodrigue returns to Spain, but does not settle down. He keeps sailing from one seat to another, one port to the next, wandering ceaselessly throughout the globe. On shipboard he hires a Japanese artist to paint saints' portraits according to specifications. Times have changed. Vasco da Gama, Magellan, Columbus have altered the globe's configurations. As for Rodrigue, he experiences humiliations anew at the hands of an actress, the King's chamberlain, and a valet. He bears all the reprimands and insults aimed his way.

During these trying years Prouhèze's daughter, Mary of the Seven-Swords, now Rodrigue's child, has grown into a beautiful young girl, courageous, open, and forthright. She met Juan of Austria, fell in love with him, as Prouhèze had with Rodrigue, at first sight. Mary of the Seven-Swords, however, realizes that her father is powerless to help himself or her. Rodrigue's altercations with the King of Spain over political matters resulted in another imprisonment for Rodrigue; this time he was put in chains, considered a traitor, insulted by his own soldiers. After his release, Rodrigue and Mary of the Seven-Swords realize that they must separate; that each must live out his destiny in life in his own manner. She decides to swim to Juan of Austria's frigate, which is anchored in the harbor, at quite a distance from shore. "My dear papa, the king gave you England. You no longer need me. I am leaving to join Juan of Austria. Goodbye." The note also says that when she arrives she will have the trumpet sounded. In that way he will know that she is safe.

Rodrigue, meanwhile, has begun to understand the meaning of divinity, its impact on one's life, both mortal and immortal. Rodrigue looks about at His Creation: at nights in their infinite replications, and at days, in their endless births.

> I have never seen anything as magnificent! It seems as if the sky were appearing to me for the first time. Yes, it is a beautiful night for me—this one—marking my celebration, finally, my engagement with liberty!

The universe seems to have taken on a life of its own for Rodrigue; it has grown in dimension, expanded in form, and exploded into light. Crystals, like white diamonds, flash through the sky, shimmering, sparkling, sounding their ordered and disordered ways, slipping and sliding out of each other's orbit, confronting each other in energetic sequences. Rodrigue stares; the cosmos dilates before him, articulates its emotions, exhaling its needs in spherical and concentric pulsations. Rodrigue knows jubilation.

He is proud of Mary of the Seven-Swords. She has demonstrated courage.

> Brave Seven-Swords! No, no, neither you nor your father is among those the sea swallows up! He who has an arm and who breathes in fully God's air, there is no danger that he should be overwhelmed; he overcomes it, joyously, this great magnificent wave which bears no evil intent!

Mary of the Seven-Swords is free. No obstacles exist between her and her beloved save the water which she dominates.

Rodrigue, however, has not completed his ordeal; he is still mocked and taunted by his soldiers, and now that he has lost his daughter, the jeering and derision is even more harrowing. They read the letter she has left for him, encouraging him to feel further alienated from her, from society. It is no matter. No one can touch Rodrigue now. He is engulfed with feelings of Prouhèze. The constellations speak her name. Prouhèze inhabits him, completely, *absolutely*.

A Fisherman has just picked up the body of a dead girl, we learn. Is it Rodrigue's daughter? No, it is the friend who swam along with her. She could not make it. A nun now enters into the proceedings. She is bargaining with some soldiers, trying to buy and sell objects so as to be able to build a convent for Mother Theresa. Old iron, junk of all types, anything will do, nothing is too decrepit that it cannot be *salvaged* and lead to *salvation*. Rodrigue suddenly realizes that if he helps this nun, he may be allowed to complete his ordeal and to fulfill his humiliating earthly role. The trial would thus be ended. By giving himself to the nun's endeavor he would have experienced the deepest of humiliations, the most wretched of conditions. The nun refuses to buy him. She will pay nothing for this one-legged old, good-for-nothing man. Brother Leon intercedes, however, and finally she agrees to take him. Suddenly, a trumpet is sounded, "triumphant." Mary of the Seven-Swords has arrived safely. "My child has been saved," Rodrigue announces. Brother Leon concludes: "Deliverance for captive souls!"

The Satin Slipper is an example of "total theatre." The action is being unraveled on all parts of the globe as well as among the elements. It is a living incarnation of the battle being waged within the author's psyche—personal and bloody. Prouhèze and Rodrigue are submerged in their passion for one another and intent upon dominating it. Their tension is continuous. Never do they experience the repose necessary to look at themselves directly, to understand the possessive, egotistical, and arrogant views of their intolerable goal. As Perseus needed a mirror into which he could peer while capturing the Medusa, so Claudel's beings look outward for help; angels, servants, captains, kings, husbands, anyone to prevent them from being submerged by their passion and losing sight of the real (or imaginary) goal of welding with divinity. Claudel wrote that the key to self-understanding lies in others: "it is our contact with the next person which enlightens our understanding of ourselves" and also helps us make ourselves understood.[5]

Since neither Rodrigue nor Prouhèze is able to peer within their disparate psyches, their actions remain abrasive, constricting, grief-filled. Never will they know harmony or integration. Throughout they must flex their will, which takes on the contours of a muscle, bending, straining every so often in order to dominate the situation. Rodrigue and Prouhèze are undifferentiated and archaic beings. Their emotions are drained or sucked out spasmodically in protracted expulsions. Never are they decanted in understanding sequences. Prouhèze and Rodrigue are the proud possessors of anthropoid psyches; they are like stiff marionettes who fight, struggle, battle against each other's feelings, either destroying or being destroyed in the process.

Prouhèze and Rodrigue possess wills of iron resembling huge steel jaws leading to a profound dungeon; there instincts are entrapped and enslaved within a dismal, dank, fungus-breeding unconscious. It is in this self-imposed prison that what could have been put to good use and fecundated the earth remained tightly sealed, emerging only as destructive force, gasping for fresh air, yearning for peace of soul. It is through this kind of incarceration that the protagonists carry out the Sacrament of Penance: the penalty each pays for being alive; the punishment each must endure to avoid joy, to know torture and humiliation in order to be worthy of Claudel's God. As the Christians organized processions in the thirteenth century in Italy and elsewhere, during which time they ritualized their need for penance in a "collective *imitatio Christi*,"[6] so Claudel introduces his readers to a similar attitude. Punishment serves the soul, Claudel suggests, by revealing man's petti-ness, his shame. Dismemberment diffuses ignominious traits; it also gives meaning to life. Pain compels man to become aware of his function in the world, his relationship to others, his destiny. Such masochistic and sadistic over-tones are replete in *The Satin Slipper*, each with powerfully sexual innuendoes: when Prouhèze rejects Rodrigue, the object of her lust, it increases his allure and dilates the excitement. The pathological connotations in *The Satin Slipper* are weighty; underlying them all is Claudel's corro-sive and pervasive sense of guilt.

The Satin Slipper poses all types of theological problems. Claudel seems to believe that love plays little or no role in the sacrament of marriage; indeed, it is best that it does not, since if love were to be experienced between husband and wife, insufficient amounts would be given to God. Earthly love must, therefore, be cut out of one's being, as the eagle tore at Prometheus' liver nightly. The will must domi-nate; conquest over oneself must prevail. Claudel, wrote Maurice Blanchot, seems to have had "an almost sick fear of being vanquished."[7] He considered losers objects of shame. To succeed is Claudel's law; to possess oneself is his way. Indeed, Claudel could function only within a world of self-imposed limitations, dogmas, certainties. If these were once removed, if the floodgates were opened, Claudel would find himself in a gravityless expanse; he would be diffused in space, shattered by the vastness and powerlessness of his own elemental world.

Claudel's theological notions serve to separate man from

God rather than unite him with divinity. For some believ-
ers, such views are contradictory and perplexing; for others,
they are manifestations of a pathological condition. To
know fulfillment in an earthly love experience, for many,
allows the mortal to feel closer to God. The opposite is true
for Claudel. Since God is excluded during an all too close
relationship, a separation, therefore, exists, between the
mortal and immortal sphere—man and God—the microcosm and the macrocosm. If this is true, the earth is no
longer connected with the cosmos, the minute with eternity, space with spacelessness. God, then, is neither omniscient nor omnipotent!

Claudel's theological ideas are apparently an outgrowth
of his inability to reconcile his sexual drive with his spiritual
values: for him, each opposed the other, creating chaos
within him, burdening him with the need for repression
throughout his life. *Etiam peccata*, Claudel wrote, using
St. Augustine's words, helped him disculpate himself from
what he considered to be his own misdeeds in life, his own
lust, his need for lucre, his arrogance. Evil is justifiable, he
felt, but only after it has been accomplished in the world of
contingencies, and then paid for through penitence,
flagellation, or any other religious device which may earn
redemption. Self-dissatisfaction, self-vindictiveness, self-
chastisement is the only manner in which Claudel's
protagonists—Prouhèze and Rodrigue—could accept
themselves.

The Satin Slipper, an unwieldy and complex drama, is
marred by too many tangential sequences, and many,
many philosophical and dramatic asides. Claudel's religious ideas also pose a problem for the viewers. Some are
irritated by his concept of evil, others consider the play a
sado-masochistic orgy. Yet, as produced by Barrault, and
when viewed symbolically as a dramatization of a vital

theological problem, it neatly sets forth Claudel's view-point. Certainly not his finest play, *The Satin Slipper*, approached as a meditative work, is rich in thought-provoking material and powerful imagistic poetry.

6. THE TIDINGS BROUGHT TO MARY: "O EARTH, MY NURSING MOTHER"

The Tidings Brought to Mary (L'Annonce faite à Marie, 1911), produced by Lugné-Poë at the Théatre de l'Oeuvre, is one of Claudel's most popular and most accessible works. Its themes, always vital to the author, revolve around evil, guilt, sacrifice, and grace.[1]

The Tidings Brought to Mary is a modernized Medieval mystery play. The word mystery, from the Greek *mustés,* the initiated one, implies an initiation into another level of life. Arduous tests are required of the *mustés,* which frequently demand great discipline and strength of character. Such a *way,* therefore, is not open to all, because mystery requires faith and emotional subjectivity, not rational detachment.

The Tidings Brought to Mary is situated in fifteenth-century France, a period when the performance of religious mysteries on stage had become a popular form of entertainment. Born in the tenth century, an outgrowth of religious services (the Nativity, celebrating Christ's birth, and Easter, celebrating His Resurrection), liturgical drama is said to have begun when two priests read aloud from the

142

scriptures, one in response to the other. In front of the altar, other priests would enact the events described, always in the simplest manner. By the twelfth century, dialogues were lengthened, characters delineated, costumes and decors were added, and the entire production was performed on the parvis of the Cathedral. Different incidents revolving around the life of Christ were now included; stories of saints' lives were rendered dramatically as were examples of miracles, particularly those involving the Virgin Mary. The Church used the theatre to proselytize, to educate the masses in matters of religion, to elevate their mores, and to unify their spiritual needs.

That Claudel chose the Medieval mystery form for his four-act drama, *The Tidings Brought to Mary*, not only answered a personal need: to teach, to reveal his religious attitude to the world at large (as the play's title indicates in French, *l'annonce*, to announce, to proclaim), but also as a means of expelling his own psychological problems which centered around guilt, penitence, and redemption. To return to the Medieval period, as Claudel had accomplished in *The Tidings Brought to Mary*, allowed him, as it does most anyone recounting a myth, to undergo an *illo tempore*, a return to a collective past, when one experiences oneself not as an individual, but as part of a whole, not as a temporal being, but an atemporal one. The miracle, as dramatized in *The Tidings Brought to Mary*, allowed the religious encounter, a numinosum, to make itself felt, to take root, after which the participants felt cleansed, strengthened and renewed.

Fifteenth-century France was not a period of serenity. The Hundred Years' War (1337–1453) had come to an end, and with it plagues, starvation and plundering were the rule of the day; indeed, armed bands of thieves ran wild through the countryside, devastating entire areas; morality was at an all-time low. It was a period during which the dissolution of the Catholic Church as the single dominant religion in Europe took place, and the seeds of Protestantism and Humanism began to bear fruit in the Renaissance. Voices, such as those of the Czech and English reformers, Jan Hus (1369–1415) and John Wycliffe (1324–1384), spoke out courageously against abuse within the Church, and in favor of reform; the French Lefèvre d'Etaples (1450–1537) was the first to translate the Bible into French, and at the risk of his life, since the Catholic Church forbade such work. Only priests were considered fit to explain such knowledge to the masses. It was a period which paved the way for John Calvin's *Christian Institution* (1536) and Martin Luther's *Ninety-Five Theses* (1517), which were to make deep inroads in England, Scotland, Switzerland, Germany, and Holland. Claudel believed that an analogy could be drawn between the splintering of the once all-powerful Catholicism, which brought decline and decay in its wake, and the even more fragmented religious and philosophical attitudes of the contemporary world, which he believed would be a prelude to its disintegration.

The Tidings Brought to Mary begins with a Prologue which opens on a vast countryside at Combernon, a region Claudel knew well, since he had spent his childhood in such surroundings at Villeneuve. As a youth he had listened to the tales told by farmers about sainthood and the pious who had once lived in the area, as well as stories about feuding families, conflicts, and jealousies. Curious always, Claudel listened carefully. Later, some of these tales were interwoven in his liturgical drama, *The Tidings Brought to Mary*.

The action opens in front of a large barn. Pierre de Craon, mason, builder of churches, devotes his life to spiritual concerns. He describes his labors as being enacted "beneath the ground," occupying himself with laying foundations, or with heavenly matters, when building steeples. Strong, virile, muscular, handsome, Pierre de Craon busies himself by helping to spread the word of God. Alluded to later in the play as Master of the Compas, we come to learn that he is a member of the guild and secret society known as the Masons. The Masons enjoyed special privileges in Medieval times: in this way they were encouraged to fulfill their tasks, which consisted in constructing the great Cathedrals of Europe. The Masons were mystically oriented as well as earth-centered. They participated in the Royal Art or Supreme Work, as they called it: the transmuting of the flesh and blood of man (the individual whose preoccupations deal solely with matter) into a purer, higher, and more spiritually oriented being. Builders and architects, the Masons, ever since antiquity, were considered to have been endowed with special knowledge, to have been initiated into an esoteric (the Greek word *eisôtheô* meaning I make enter) domain. Not only builders of monuments, they were constructors of souls—of inner worlds: "To make enter is to open a door, to offer man the possibility of penetrating from the outer to the inner world."[2]

Pierre de Craon was such an individual. His initiation into the Masonic order had not yet been completed. He was in the process of experiencing it as the play opens. Although seemingly robust, physically, he gives the impression, in some way, of being spiritually crippled. His "Ideal Temple," that of the heart and soul, which would have revealed divinity to him as well as sacrality, was not yet sufficiently sturdy. The inner world, which the Mason considered the *real* one, had not yet pervaded his system. Pierre de Craon still belonged to the outer realm; living for the façades, the mask. The project occupying him presently is the building of the Cathedral devoted to St. Justitia at Rheims. Only the foundations have been started; the body of the building has not yet been touched. He was, therefore, far from reaching the spires which, for the Mason, indicated spiritual ascension.

As a mason, Pierre de Craon, whose task in life is to erect religious edifices, works in stone: durable, hard, permanent matter. Owing to its seemingly lasting and immobile qualities, stone has taken on sacred value in certain cultures: the Ka'aba for the Muslims, the Beth-el for the Hebrews, the Omphalos for the Greeks.[3] Stone fascinates and mesmerizes Pierre de Craon in a similar way. Hewn from the earth, extracted from the deepest of realms, it symbolizes an archaic dimension, a primitive force, powerful and indestructible, as do the *menhirs*, those megalithic funerary monuments that dot the Breton countryside, exciting and inspiring awe.

Pierre de Craon, mason and architect, fashions edifices based on spatial and mathematical correspondences: patterns existing in abstract planes, structures within which color, form—and a soul—dwell. It is he who must find the center of the circle (*mandala*) from which the cathedral will emerge: the point of Creation, which the mystic calls the Beginning/God. To be a Mason not only requires intelligence as well as physical strength, but a very special spiritual attitude, which Pierre de Craon must acquire if he is to complete his initiation into the Masonic Order.

Pierre de Craon had been asked to stop at Combernon to make a passageway in the convent of Monsanvierge on the hill behind the town, so that the Queen Mother could withdraw into this world of sanctity. Monsanvierge was a religious order which removed nuns from all contact with society. Their food, grapes for their wine, wheat for their

bread, was given them through a small slit in their otherwise impenetrable walls. Without doors or windows, those
who entered Monsanvierge never left its sanctum: no in-
gress or exit. When, therefore, Pierre de Craon was asked to
cut a small entrance into the thick stone walls, thus allowing another penitent to enter this world of solitude, he
had to complete his task by sealing it up again after her
entrance.

Pierre de Craon was leaving Combernon as the Prologue
begins. It is predawn, darkness, not blackness that bathes
the atmosphere. He is anxious to continue his real work
—the building of St. Justitia at Rheims—a task to which he
was willing to devote his entire life. During his stay at
Combernon, however, he had strayed from the straight and
narrow path when he noticed his host's daughter, Violaine,
beautiful, young, pure in all ways. He had desired her
carnally: her body, her softness, and all the vigor of
burgeoning womanhood. He had attempted to take her by
force and, in this moment of passion, had used his knife to
make a slight cut on her arm. Violaine, he later said, "had
been the first woman he had touched. The devil had suddenly seized him, taken advantage of the occasion." A year
passed after this incident, during which Pierre de Craon
had experienced the meaning of anguish. Torment had not
left him: it was on that very day he had been struck down
with leprosy.

Sickness in the Middle Ages, leprosy in particular, was
considered God-sent. A punishment, frequently resulting
from some ignominious act, was meted out as retribution
for a sin committed. Since sickness was sent from above, it
was replete with dignity: within lesions and pustules existed
a curative agent that, on a scientific level today, would
correspond to the concept of vaccine. To be plagued with
illness, therefore, was to have been singled out by God

either for punishment or for a very special—and mysterious
—purpose in the existential sphere. Pierre de Craon
realized, when he saw the first spots of leprosy on his body,
that for him, disease fulfilled a dual purpose: chastisement
as well as the more positive God-oriented goal of accom-
plishing something worthwhile in life. He also understood at
this time that he had attempted to take something which
belonged to another; that he had acted thoughtlessly and
without piety. From the moment awareness came upon
him (both physical and spiritual), he remained far from
Violaine and her family. Living in near isolation to keep
from infecting others with his dread disease, he had time to
indwell and to understand that spiritual sickness is as excoriating as physical illness and that evil, in whatever form
it chooses to take, extends its influence and power throughout nature, cruelly, powerfully, and ruthlessly.

As Pierre de Craon is about to leave Combernon, Violaine suddenly darts out from the darkness and stops him by
standing in front of him. The Matins sound from the
Angelus of the convent nearby, and both she and Pierre de
Craon recite their prayers together. Unaware of the real
implications of his act of a year ago, and with all of her
splendid naïveté, Violaine pardons Pierre de Craon. Then
she questions him about the identity of St. Justitia, in
whose honor he was building the Cathedral at Rheims.
Who was this saint? A child of eight, he answers, who was
martyred at the time of Diocletian. The guilds at Rheims
and the nearby towns, as well as the city's wealthy class,
have all contributed to its building. Violaine questions
herself. What could she give? She decides that the ring her
fiancé Jacques Hury had found in the earth when plowing,
would be just right. This ring has very special significance
in the play: it dated from pagan times and its gold content
would be used by Violaine to further the Christian religion

by paying, in part, for the construction of the Cathedral of St. Justitia. As a round object, it links past with present. In that it is made of purest gold, it symbolizes the highest moral values. That Violaine's fiancé had given it to her as a token of his love and that she took it upon herself to use it for another purpose (to further her divine mission in life), suggests her growing detachment from the temporal realm. Violaine was entering into another phase of existence. No longer would she just be the pretty little virgin farm girl growing up amidst plants and trees, whose life cycle would be spent in blossoming, marrying, and then raising a family, all with joy and love. No, her path would be different: arduous even excoriating. She, too, was chosen by God to fulfill a mission.

Violaine, a child of nature, lives in harmony with the earth. As such she understood Pierre de Craon's immense and intense pain. Each time he looks at her—an object of exquisite beauty—he realizes she had been promised to another. His jealousy, nevertheless, knows no bounds. Furthermore, his leprosy forbids him from coming near her: "My presence alone is disastrous." Violaine has never heard of leprosy, and when Pierre de Craon tries to explain it to her by reminding her of the old woman who used to live in the rocks of Géyn, veiled from head to foot, holding a rattle in her hand to warn people of her approach, she remains unperturbed. He tells Violaine that he has not withdrawn from the world as other lepers do, because his bishop has dispensed him from this exile: he wants him to continue building monuments to God.

Pierre de Craon's sickness, because it is both physical and spiritual, is deep. It buries itself within his very fibers; its inner march is precipitous as it inflicts its poisons deeply into his flesh, blood, bones, and muscles. He knows that soon he will be faced with opprobrium, then self-hate,

Loleh Bellon and Danièle Delorme in *The Tidings Brought to Mary* at Théâtre de l'Oeuvre.
FRENCH CULTURAL SERVICES

self-disgust, finally guilt. Pierre de Craon "savors" death; he understands the meaning of "the horrible alchemy of the tomb!" In a moment of distress he blames Violaine for his illness: "It is you who have given me this sickness, your beauty caused it; before I saw you, I was pure and happy." Even her gentle smile, formed by her curved and tender lips, is a poisonous, destructive, venomous force, like the snake in the Garden of Eden.

The pain Pierre de Craon feels, Violaine explains, is not her doing. His flesh is sick, tainted. Now, fully aware of the meaning of her statement and agreeing with it, Pierre de

Craon bursts out: "O little soul, was it possible for me to look at you without loving you." Violaine's perfection is such that she too must become one of God's "untouchables"; she too will have to withdraw from the world and consecrate her existence with divinity. She must become the Lamb of God and take unto herself the Evils and sins of the world in an *imitatio Christi*. As yet, Violaine is unaware of her mission. Her childish gaiety bubbles over; her heart overflows with kindness and tenderness for the less fortunate.

Onomastically, the prefix to Violaine's name, *viol* (from the Latin verb *violo*), which means to treat with violence, to violate or rape, describes Pierre de Craon's attempted act. Her name may be further associated with the flower violet (from the Latin *viola*), the five-petaled flower identified by St. Bernard with "humility" and the Virgin Mary; so it would also serve to describe Violaine.[4] Antipodal to the joys associated with hyperdulian Mary is the purple coloration representing her sorrow and its ramifications in Catholic liturgy. It is the color of Advent and Lent, when penitents experience Christ's death and resurrection. In this connection, the Medieval painting of the *Pietà of Avignon* comes to mind: the markings of deep suffering penetrate the Virgin's face as she receives Christ after the descent from the cross.

Violaine's perfection, both spiritual and physical, was not to be wasted in human involvements. It had to be consecrated to higher matters—God's works—as attested by the fact that she walks toward Pierre de Craon barefoot, not wearing the usual wooden clogs. The removal of shoes before entering a sacred area is a prescription in certain religions: Hindu, Buddhist, and Taoist. In the Bible when Moses was in the presence of the Lord, he heard a voice tell him: "Come not nigh higher, put off the shoes from thy feet: for the place whereon thou standest is holy ground"

(Exodus 5:3).[5] To remove one's shoes is to prepare for entrée into an atemporal sphere.

Violaine describes her love for Jacques Hury as "a great mystery," making the joy she feels that much greater and infinitely more beautiful. She is happiness personified on stage. Yet, despite her feelings of plenitude, an element of terror pervades the atmosphere: something ominous is present, which tingles and irritates at the same time. Panic seizes her heart. Fearing her good fortune, she says:

> Forgive me because I am too happy! because the one I
> love
> Loves me, and I am certain of him, and I know he
> loves me, and everything is equal with us!
> And because God made me in order to be happy and
> not for evil intent or for any pain at all.

Violaine, an anima figure, is man's unconscious image of womankind. She is described by Pierre de Craon as, "O eternal image of Beauty," the earthly replica of perfection. Violaine resents the word "image." She chides him for this appellation as she does for his feelings of jealousy. Jacques Hury is her fiancé. They love each other. Pierre de Craon has chosen another path, and he must make himself "worthy" of "the flame consuming him." He is different, set apart, chosen by God to fulfill a certain destiny on earth: "devoured" as he is, it is for the "glory of the Church!" that he lives.

Pierre de Craon understands Violaine's attitudes. He accepts his lot. His bride, he tells her before leaving, "will be the Church." He will mount it, feel it beneath him, stone by stone, and will erect the edifice, indestructible, to the Almighty: "my work in which God dwells" is his life.

Dawn breaks. Pierre de Craon says goodbye to Violaine forever. As he shakes her hand, she bends over and kisses him on the face, just as St. Francis had done when kissing the leprous. Unbeknown to Pierre de Craon and Violaine, her sister, Mara, had been hiding for the past few seconds behind the barn and had seen the kiss. The protagonists go their own way. Each will experience God's mysterious workings. Claudel can now start the action, since Evil has been accomplished: the crisis has come to pass; the discordant note has been sounded; pain and suffering will ensue.

I. *Pater familias*

Act I opens in the kitchen of the Vercors family at Combernon and centers on a large hearth, a long table "as in a Breughel painting," writes Claudel, and some rustic chairs. The entire family is gathered in this room: Elisabeth, referred to in the play as The Mother, is a collective image; Anne Vercors (a masculine name as well as a feminine one during the Medieval and Renaissance periods), the father, is personalized; two sisters, Violaine and Mara, and Jacques Hury, the former's fiancé, are talking.

Everything in this act is sensorial. One can feel the open hearth, the smell of the newly baked bread and freshly picked vegetables, the odors so characteristic of a farmer's home. Virtually immobile, the family expresses emotions not through a plethora of gestures but, on the contrary, via control: each bodily movement is expended with an economy of activity. Attitudes are simplified with a concomitant density of feeling, allowing words to take on body, melody, rhythmic qualities, resonating in infinite reverberations, amplifications, each denoting myriad modalities of thought.

Anne Vercors, sixty years old, his blond hair intermingled with white, is a partriarchal figure. He lives inwardly, rarely expressing his feelings in clear-cut gestures, but only in rigid, straight-line poses reminiscent of the Medieval wooden carvings of saints and holy men that adorned cathedrals and sanctuaries throughout Europe. Without curves, divested of hidden recesses, or arches, Anne Vercors takes on the power of a principled being; he is incorruptible, straightforward, obdurate. As though constructed from some massive oak tree, his decisions are sharp, trenchant and irrevocable. Within him resides the physical and emotional strength of a man who has lived in close communion with the earth as well as with the heavenly sphere, raising his family according to traditional dogma. There is no wavering of faith in Anne Vercors, no hesitation, no questioning. He is of one piece: the *pater familias* representing authority. As law giver in his own home, his decisions based on what he considers to be high moral principles are final. No arguing, no pleading. His heart is of stone, strong and durable, and just as unfeeling. Unlike Pierre de Craon, who only works with stone, Anne Vercors has completed his life's work: his initiation. He is stone. His will carries out the dictates of his mind. He represents order, consciousness, control, as opposed to spontaneity or instinct. The promoter of institutions, the carrier of the law, Anne Vercors is an archetypal figure who stands for tradition in *The Tidings Brought to Mary*. His ancestors worked the land of Combernon, which has yielded the fruit he now enjoys; they did away with "paganism" so that Christianity could reign; they built the convent of Monsanvierge, which houses the nuns who have severed themselves from the temporal realm. Strong, unyielding, callous for some, Anne Vercors has an announcement he wants to make to his family. He has made a decision: he will leave that very day on a Crusade.

Anne Vercors' journey away from his land, home, and family is tantamount to an exile—a death. It is the end of one phase of his life and the beginning of another. No longer immersed in temporal matters, as father of a household, husband, and farmer, he is preparing for a spiritual existence based on asceticism, pain, his own *imitatio Christi*. He is thankful for the bounty God has proffered upon his farm. He blesses the happiness he has known on this earth. Now, however, these things are not sufficient for his spiritual well being. He is almost immobile on stage; each word he utters takes on the tonality of a powerful electric charge—a yearning and incantatory quality for the world of eternity. He has but one purpose in life now: he seeks to wrest the Holy Sepulchre from the land of the Muslims as others had tried ever since Pope Urban II had preached the First Crusade (1095). Unaware of the destructive side of the Crusades—the mass killings, pillaging, razing of cities and towns for the sole purpose of lucre and personal gain—Anne Vercors' desires are idealistic and pure.

Before departing, however, Anne Vercors wants to settle earthly matters. His favorite daughter, Violaine, his first born, will marry Jacques Hury, who will inherit the land and work it to the best of his abilities. The other sister, Mara, "the black one," an appellation stemming from the blackness of her hair, and which serves to describe her character, will also be given a percentage of the farm. In French, the word *mara* means a kind of rodent: such an identification is also indicative of her nature, which is aggressive, biting, incisive, and bruising. Further analogies may also be made: the word *marais*, so closely linked to her name, means swamp or marsh, and *marâtre* is the unnatural and frequently evil stepmother in many fairy tales. Mara is all these things as well as being "hard as iron." When she wants something, nothing changes her mind: she is obdurate, obstinate, possessive, and jealous. It is she who will spread the miasmic atmosphere into the proceedings and will function as a shadow figure throughout, extending the negative factors which trigger the action.

Both Violaine and Mara are anima figures. The anima is defined as an autonomous complex that represents man's unconscious attitude toward woman. They are, therefore, highly revelatory of an author's inner state, since it is he who projects them onto the figures in his creation. Two sisters brought into such opposition are not uncommon in fairy tales (*Cinderella*) or in myths (*Psyche*), each standing for some aspect of man's soul, each archetypal, thereby possessing nonhuman characteristics.

Violaine is the "angel," a manifestation of divinity; purity resides in her soul. She is the Immaculate One. Although spirituality and a religious orientation mark her ectypal trajectory, she is in contact with the earthly sphere. As such she understands, intuitively, though not consciously, what God's design for her is, causing her to give Pierre de Craon her ring and the kiss.

Mara, the Evil one, is also an aspect of the female archetype, a shadow figure representing that part of a personality which the ego cannot accept and which it casts off as destructive, thereby projecting it onto a collective being. Mara knows that everyone prefers Violaine. She feels unloved, lonely, unwanted. The greater her feelings of rejection, the more she clings to her mode of behavior: she torments others. She tries to destroy happiness that she sees burgeoning around her; she is possessive, jealous, frequently unpleasant, and given to tantrums. She is an "obstructor," a fault finder. She will pave the way for the catastrophe which will resound throughout the drama.

Mara is strong. Similar to her father, she is open, forthright, but also preys on the weak. When she hears that Violaine is to become engaged to Jacques Hury, she takes The Mother aside. She wants her to talk to her father.

Violaine is not to marry Jacques Hury. Mara loves him and wants him for herself. The Mother must change the father's decision. Mara threatens suicide if she does not get her way. She has decided to hang herself, she says, as the cat had done some months before in the woodshed. The Mother insists that Mara is not to worry; she will inherit her share of the farm, but that Jacques loves Violaine and they have been promised to each other. The Mother is powerless to alter the father's decision, which is final and irrevocable; Mara will have to accept the situation.

The Mother, nevertheless, attempts to soften Anne Vercors' attitude. She also does not want him to leave. Furthermore, she questions, where is he going? To a neighboring castle or town? to a city? No, he tells her, he is going to Jerusalem: there is "too much pain in France," he says. His happiness is so great, he tells his wife, that he feels guilty. He has reaped the bounties from his land and, when he sees the starving, the sick, the refugees from a world of torment, he feels that he must serve a *great* cause. He expresses his fears about a changing world—he sees a society about to crumble, dismembered by the war, but also prodded by a new force awakening in Western Europe—a new protesting religion. The old world and its ways are disintegrating. Anne Vercors cannot remain on his farm. He must leave. His wife takes his departure personally. Reminiscent of the thirteenth-century statue of her namesake, St. Elizabeth, sculpted on the Cathedral of Rheims, with its deep furrows, and markings expressing the depth of her pain, so The Mother wonders whether her husband has grown angry with her over something about which she is unaware. Has he grown tired of her after thirty years of marriage: "Now you are abandoning me in my old age." No, he assures her in his cold and dispassionate manner, never allowing his feelings to flow outward, but always containing them within; it is to serve a higher principle. He will depart that

very night, he tells her, his countenance reminiscent of that
of a martyr: unflagging, unbending, unmoving.

Anne Vercors, Jacques Hury, and Violaine are now on
stage. Jacques Hury is given to his beloved Violaine. "Love
her," Anne Vercors tells his future son-in-law, for she is "as
clear as gold." Jacques and Violaine exchange their love
bonds. He will not be present at their wedding, the father
tells them, but in his mind's eye, they are already married.
He breaks bread with them for the last time, though he will
not remain for supper, but puts the crust in his satchel, says
goodbye to The Mother, who tells him, prophetically, that
she will never see him again. To Mara, he says "be good";
he embraces Violaine powerfully, and then leaves.

II. *The Orchard*

Two weeks have passed as Act II opens. A noon-hour July
sun shines on an orchard, which is filled with rows and rows
of neatly planted trees all heavy with fruit. Above the
orchard in the distance, one can see the tiled roofs of
Combernon; on the other side of the hill, the "formidable"
arch of the windowless and doorless Monsanvierge convent.
It is here that the women remain imprisoned in the peniten-
tial order that sacrifices to God: a prefiguration of the action
to take place.

The sun shines harshly. It has reached its full power.
Like an illuminated manuscript, each corner of the stage is
endowed with a specific hue; each flower, tree, leaf is
inscribed with its own luminosity, rhythm, and design,
reminiscent of the fifteenth-century *Book of Hours of the
Duc de Berry*. Musical qualities also seem to cascade from
the stage: tonalities replicate emotions, heightening
worldly love and passion, feelings are allowed to wander

forth in all of their idyllic beauty and harmony. It is in this serene setting that Violaine and Jacques will express their eternal love for one another; here Violaine will reveal her secret, the mystery of the unexpressed and uncreated.

The trees are in bloom and the warmth of their spirit blends with the moist earth in a prenuptial bond: Mother Earth takes into herself the Heavenly Father, July/Sun. Claudel had always felt a kind of veneration for nature's ability to express emotions, to personify feelings, and to renew itself perpetually. Claudel identified with the sexuality and power of elemental life. To be sure, nature is perennial; its colorful vestments radiate joy under a summer's luminosities and reveal sorrow during the winter months when the fruits are withdrawn, the leaves fall, and the land remains desolate and bare, like so many ghostly apparitions.

Joy abounds, at least on the outside, as Violaine and Jacques meet at the fount. Reminiscent of Jacob's encounter with his beloved Rachel, fountains have always played important roles in myths (*Arthur*) and in fairy tales (*Pelléas and Mélisande*). They not only represent the source of eternal life, in that water rises from the depths—its springs forever nourishing, purifying, regenerating, but also psychologically, this upward flow indicates subliminal contents ascending to the light of consciousness with such motility new attitudes, ideas, and emotions burgeon. In Celtic lands, fountains had curative powers; in the Druidic period in Gaul, they were endowed with prophetic faculties to such an extent that Odin sacrificed an eye to drink from the waters of Mimir, thus gaining inner sight and knowledge. The Virgin Mary in Medieval times was called "the fountain of living waters." Allusions to fountains abound in The Song of Songs (4:12) as well as in the Psalms, as attested by the following, "For with thee is the fountain of life: in thy light shall we see light" (36:9). The fountain in *The Tidings Brought to Mary* will prepare the audiences for a turning point in the play.

Violaine arrives. The sun shines brilliantly on her linen robe, over which she is wearing a dalmatic of gold cloth, decorated with large blue and red flowers. About her head a diadem made of enamel and plated gold gives a halo effect; it endows her with special purpose—as though she were the carrier of light—radiance incarnate. Jacques cannot take his eyes off her; nor does he know words to express his love, his admiration, and surprise. Violaine has chosen for her engagement the dress worn by the sisters of Monsanvierge ("except for the maniple"); they wear this dress twice, when wedding God and on their deathbed. As Violaine walks toward Jacques, nature seems to explode in symphonic overtones, glowing, suddenly rhapsodizing, bathing in the golden hues of saintliness—a theophany.

Although Violaine responds deeply to Jacques' tenderness, there is something new, strange, and mysterious stirring within her that draws her away from the brilliant light displayed by nature's abundance; it is a force which beckons her elsewhere, compels her to seek another direction, to enter into a tremulous world that will be hers alone.

A certain disquietude marks her features. Why is she so concerned, Jacques wonders. "Ah, how large is the world and how alone we are!" Violaine murmurs. She feels her solitude. Her father has abandoned her, neither mother nor sister really love her, she tells Jacques. He makes a gesture to take her into his arms. She tells him not to touch her. "Am I a leper?" he answers in jest. In a rhapsodic tirade unparalleled for its lyrical flow, its flamboyant imagery, Violaine confesses her love to Jacques. As the sun beats down on Violaine, it forces out her secret, her mystery; it urges her to unveil what lies dormant within her darkened realm. "Know the fire which is devouring me now! Know it now, this flesh which you have loved!" She asks him for a small knife, then she makes a cut in her linen dress, right under her left breast, and opens the garment to reveal the first spot of leprosy.

Jacques stares aghast. "What is this silvery flower which blazons your flesh?" She is stained; she has caught the dread disease, she tells her fiancé. Jacques' fury knows no bounds. He accuses her of possessing a leprous soul as well: "infamous," "reprobate," "daughter of the devil," "damned" being. Mara had told him that she saw Violaine kissing Pierre de Craon, implying further intimacies between them, but he simply could not believe it. Now he knows the truth and is lacerated by it. He orders her to withdraw from his presence, to leave.

It had been Mara who had implanted the seed of doubt in Jacques' mind. As Satan, the "Obstructor," and Lucifer, the "Light-Bringer," feed uncertainty and suspicion, irritants which pave the way for discord rather than harmony, hate instead of love, so Mara encourages Anteros rather than Eros to germinate.

In a paroxysm of rage, Jacques demands that Violaine deny the accusation, confess her innocence. "I cannot become black in but one instant, Jacques, but in some months, in some months, / You will no longer recognize me." Violaine refuses to defend herself. She says only that Mara never lies; that the silvery flower beneath her breast is proof of the truth. She will leave for the area reserved for lepers, the forested region called Géyn.

What had begun in the clear crisp tonalities so comparable to a Jean Fouquet (1420–1480) miniature, with its exquisite tonal colorations and exact detail, now terminates in cool tones, muted and matte nuances, even darker hues, revealing the inner workings of subliminal depths; these colorations will take on the importance of signs and symbols, tests in the rite de passage which is to come.

III. *The Miracle*

Act III takes place in a large forest in the Chevoche area. Snow covers the ground. It is Christmas Eve. Workers and country people are preparing for the festive occasion: a double one. Not only are they celebrating the Nativity, but the King of France, Charles VII, is also to pass by here on his way to his coronation at Rheims Cathedral.[6]

The peasants talk in joyful anticipation about the nearly completed church at St. Justitia at Rheims. Only the spires and the stained glass windows remain to be finished.[7] The stained glass windows of the Medieval period, such as those in Chartres, Paris, Rheims, and other great religious centers, were famous for their boldness of design, richness of color, and most particularly, for the extraordinary blues interwoven in their complex mosaic patterns. Pierre de Craon has spent all winter in the Chevoche forest heating its very special sand in his ovens, hoping to create just the right "mother color" for his stained glass windows. As St. Paul said: "To breathe on this heavy matter and render it transparent," in so doing transforming "our bodies of mud into bodies of glory," was Pierre de Craon's task. Heating the sand, coloring, then blending it until just the right tonal qualities come forth requires patience, endurance, and spiritual as well as physical stamina. Such work is another test implicit in the Masonic ritual.

As Pierre de Craon works his sand, colors and fires it in the manufacture of his breathtaking colorations, as he heats, burns, and blends matter, so his spirit, through projection, is also transforming, becoming cleansed of impurities and achieving a transparent state. We learn in this regard that he has been cured of his leprosy. He has mastered his Great Work, and has evolved in the Masonic order.

The forested area in which Act III takes place is propitious for the transformation ritual which will be enacted on stage. It is here, in this thickly wooded area, that Violaine has spent the past eight years in isolation, penance, and prayer. The cult of the Great Mother goddesses were celebrated in these darkened regions, as attested by Dodona and Delphi, to mention but a few. Here vegetable life remains free from control, divested of constriction, and burgeons unhampered. In this shadowy world, protected by trees, *tellus mater* reproduces and nourishes.

Individuals enter forested areas, psychologically speaking, when they need to find themselves, to revive what is dead or dormant within their unconscious. Retreats allow individuals to live out their subliminal fantasies, permitting what they consider insalubrious within their psyches to emerge, to take on reality and to expel negative contents in order to understand and eventually reintegrate them within the psyche. To withdraw into the forest (or into isolation) encourages interchange—the revival of lost connections—between one part of the psyche and another which has been cut off and functions in a destructive manner.

Deep introversion, as the forest symbol implies, paves the way for links to be reestablished between individuals and their archaic or vegetative life: a *regressus ad uterum*. Such renewal with Mother Earth encourages the heretofore bruised elements to be healed. Violaine's retreat into this darkened realm, which society demanded of her since she was a menace to it, is a reflection of an inner psychological process. It enables a coalescing of her personality to emerge, a spiritualization of what had been overly earth-oriented: her love for Jacques, her love of life.

Mara enters the wooded area. She is dressed in black and is carrying a small bundle in her arms. She asks the peasants for Violaine, the Leper, the one who has been living in the Chevoche forest for eight years. They point the way, deep into the forest. She is a menace to the community, they say;

a charge to others. Now and then they throw her a stale crust of bread, refuse, anything they do not need. A pariah, this leper has been rejected by man and beast.

A woman emerges from the forest, veiled, small. She is carrying a little bell. One of the peasants casts a piece of bread her way. She stoops to retrieve it. The black form withdraws. Mara follows it much to the surprise of the peasants. A clearing in the forest becomes visible. The moon is shining brilliantly on the area, shedding its soft tones in halo effect. A strange and formidable sight is delineated: stones appear as if forcing their way out of the ground, "monstrous" in shape, "fantastic" in form, reminiscent in contour of fossilized animals, unfathomable monuments, idols of some sort. The Leper takes Mara into her cave. It is small, she says. Violaine is blind and does not know it is her sister who has come to visit her. She asks the stranger to sit down right at the mouth of the grotto, there's more room there.

Caverns and grottoes fostered incubation mysteries in ancient days (at Eleusis and Delphi, for example) and have been the site of such religious practices ever since: at Lourdes, Compostela. These areas are propitious for the enactment of transformation rituals—*rites de passage*—when humans seek to divest themselves of their earthborn state and experience a spiritual one. Saints, martyrs, ascetics have made grottoes and caverns their homes, from St. Anthony to St. Francis of Assisi. Remember, too, that Dionysos, Osiris, Christ all withdrew into caves, darkened areas where death/rebirth rituals were experienced.

It is within the grotto that Violaine had chosen to live out her life, cut off from foreign influences that might deflect her from her quest. Life in her sphere exists in its most elementary form: active in an inorganic state. Severed from the profane world, she lives exclusively within her inner domain, as though she were experiencing her own

center—mandala—that circular form which brings harmony to the disoriented, balance to what might topple. The
disease, having eaten away her eyes, has enabled her to
discover luminosity within, as did the blind Tiresias in the
Oedipus legend or Tobit, whose sight had been taken away
from him during his sleep. The inner eye glows for Violaine, more brilliantly now that the outer eye has shut out
extraneous vision: wisdom, insight, penetrate the thickest
of matter. Because the grotto and cavern are identified with
the unconscious, it becomes a storehouse of energy, thus an
area propitious to kratophanies.[8] It is in one's depths that
energy lives inchoate. To discover the source is to help
fortify the crippled, heal the ill.

That the moon shines brilliantly on the mouth of the
grotto, illuminating the stones within its radius, the trees,
and all of vegetative life, sets the tone for the transformation
ritual. The moon, a matriarchal symbol, guides the mysterious performance which is about to be enacted in darkness and virtual silence. The priestess, Violaine, will order
the transfiguration to begin. Mara is her assistant.

Mara identifies herself, then tells Violaine that their
mother has died. It happened several months after
Violaine's departure. All is well at home outside of that.
Life continues, the farm is producing, new barns are being
built, the stock is healthy. Mara is married to Jacques now.
Violaine asks her if she is happy in her marriage. Yes, she
answers. "He loves me as I love him." Angrily, however,
Mara castigates her sister for having chosen the easy way
out. To be a leper demands nothing of an individual, since
sainthood is so easily acquired in this manner. When Mara
tells her sister that God has punished Violaine and has
made her leprous, she responds: "No more than I de-
served." Why did she kiss Pierre de Craon "so tenderly"?
She saw everything, Mara informs her. There was nothing
else to see, Violaine declares. Jacques thinks she is guilty of

far worse, Mara informs her sister. Why didn't she tell him the truth before she left? Mara questions.

Mara speaks at length about her life with Jacques and their beautiful baby girl. She looks just like Jacques, she tells Violaine, except for her eyes, which are Mara's. Although her joy knows no bounds, Violaine's is even greater. As an elect of God, she has been empowered to suffer: "Here is my body which travails for Christianity, which is dissolving. / Powerful is suffering when it is as voluntary as sin!"

For Violaine the power of suffering has taken on creative value. It has changed her, allowing her to experience herself more deeply, to feel every fiber within her as well as within nature and divinity. After living in exile she began to understand the intensity of physical and spiritual pain: the disease of which she is a victim, eating away at her garments, through her flesh, and the very fabric of her being. Spiritual pain, as well as physical torment, allows the Self to come into being, Divinity to be understood. It cuts off the ego, that clear and conscious part of the psyche; it paves the way for detachment. Indeed, C. G. Jung has suggested that the "fundamental notion in Christianity," the goal of both the martyrs and Christ, was to do away with the ego, that ego-centered or conscious part of the personality. To seek pain, as the martyrs did or to need it as Violaine does, is to believe that by so doing an individual experiences an understanding of Self (the total psyche or God within), and is, thereby, on the road to the "Kingdom of Heaven." Only after being detached from the ego, or individuality, does a larger frame of reference come into being. Aristotle's notion of *entelechia* or the developing of one's potential replicates this psychological process. Within Violaine's sightless reality—in her grotto-darkness—feed the seeds which will burgeon in her new attitude. For this reason Violaine encourages her agony and feels it creatively.[9]

Mara now hands Violaine the bundle she was carrying with her. It is the dead child. Violaine takes her. She feels her cold body, her stiff limbs. Violaine holds her close, covering the baby with her cloak. Return the baby to her alive, Mara orders. Violaine protests. It is not in her power to resuscitate the dead. Mara begs, pleads. Violaine must restore life to her baby. Jacques does not know the child has died. It happened so fast, in two hours. Jacques was not home at the time, and if he finds out, he might never love her again. Mara cannot give him any more children. "Give me my child," she tells Violaine, "alive." She lashes out at her sister. Saints perform miracles, so she can. "I swear and protest before God that I am not a saint," Violaine maintains. As in a litany, Mara demands her baby back, alive, again and again she restates her command. Violaine remonstrates:

> Why don't you leave me in peace? why do you come and torment me this way in my tomb?

> Am I worth something? Is God available to me? Am I like God?

Again Mara repeats: she wants her child back, alive, alive, alive, alive.

The *tremendum* is about to be enacted. Although audible only to Violaine, since her hearing has grown so acute, church bells resound throughout the countryside, stirring its silence, energizing its immobile forms, lightening the gray-white skies. It is midnight: Christmas Eve. "O Mara, a small child is born for us!" Trumpets are heard in the distance. The King, Charles VII, is on his way to Rheims. Joan of Arc accompanies him to his coronation. Violaine is enraptured by the *numinosum*. "Let us pray with the entire universe!" she says. Mara jars the atmosphere of beatitude: Return my child to me, alive, she hammers out.

A crescendo of passion is felt as the entire universe seems to burst into life. Snow is no longer falling. The stars shine brilliantly in the heavens. Violaine asks Mara to read from her prayer book: the Christmas prayer, Isaiah's prophecy. Voices of angels become audible; a choir is heard chanting in Latin. Violaine raises her finger. Silence. Mara listens anxiously. The moment has arrived: a miracle, a mystery is being enacted. Again Mara reads the prayer. Again the angels chant. Again there is silence.

Mara feels unworthy. She must not read the Scriptures. For the first time she has begun to look within, to face her shadow, to understand her real intent. Violaine asks her to continue reading, nevertheless. Singing is heard anew, then another silence, again the ritual is repeated. The stage glistens in all of its pristine beauty. Suddenly, Violaine cries out unintelligibly, as if choking or awakening from an ecstatic experience. "What is it?" Mara questions. Silence invades the atmosphere.

The first rays of dawn burst through. Mara looks at Violaine. Something beneath Violaine's cloak seems to be stirring. Mara looks more closely. A little foot is moving about. She kneels before her sister. Violaine caresses Mara's face and tells her to take her baby. She does. "It's alive," Mara says. The baby is crying. She is opening her eyes. Mara is filled with wonderment. And the child's eyes are blue, the color that Violaine's once had been. A drop of milk is visible on the baby's lips.

Violaine is the instrument of Grace for Claudel. As Aeschylus had written in *The Choephori*, which Claudel had translated, the world is nourished from the earth; Mother Earth gives of herself—soil and water—so that man may implant the seed and turn plant into food. Whether as

Great Goddess of Vegetation, as Hesiod's Gaia, or the Christian's Virgin Mary, nature is eternally fruitful and abundant; its presence, therefore, is sacred. So here, too, life is born—in darkness, under the trees, in the grotto, under the cloak—the very heart of the *rite transformatoire* is the mystery experienced.[10]

Violaine is the modern counterpart of those ancient priestesses of antiquity. It is she who injected life into the dead child, whose name, fittingly, was Aubaine (the noun in French meaning God-sent). It is Violaine who gave this newborn her blue eyes. That this virgin birth occurred on Christmas Eve, that Violaine's milk had nourished the child, allowed her to play the role of fertilizing mother.[11] It also indicated the emergence of a different element within the personality—the spiritually oriented side would now come to the fore. The fusing of the split anima figures (Violaine and Mara) in Aubaine indicated that saintliness had embraced its shadow: Violaine, the blond, pure, idyllic spiritual half had taken into herself "the black" Mara, symbolizing the negative and destructive side of the personality. Aubaine is an expression of the unifying principle: she was reborn with Violaine's blue eyes, the fruit of a dual force which would, at the conclusion, work in harmony—Jacques and the two sisters who are one, psychologically speaking. Violaine, an incarnation of the divine Sophia of the Gnostics, was a mortal manifestation of supernal Wisdom, which directs its energies to elevating mankind through sacrifice and good deeds. Violaine, the hypostasis Sophia (or Virgin Mary), has experienced grace. It is she who is the *Agnus Dei*, the highest manifestation of the female principle. Violaine's *fiat* has analogies with that of divinity; it allowed her to endow Aubaine with life—and experience that moment of *ekstasis*, that single instant when mortals live outside of their own mortality.

IV. *The Coniunctio*

It is night as Act IV opens. Pierre de Craon found Violaine's nearly lifeless body in the sand pit where he had set up his ovens. He has carried her to Jacques Hury's home and has placed her body on the kitchen table. Then he leaves.

Violaine awakens from her stupor. Only Jacques is with her. She asks him if his "wound has not yet healed." She could not spare him, she confesses. He had to suffer, because he was the object of her love; he had to know anguish. She asks Jacques to come closer. She has something else to tell him: she had never ever done anything more than kiss Pierre de Craon. In so doing, she had wanted to fill him with her joy and rapture, her zest for life. He was too sad, she said. But Jacques does not believe her. He refuses even to acknowledge her existence. Only when she places her hand on his head as a sign of complete truth and unity does he begin to believe. He sobs. "If you had believed in me / Who knows if you would not have healed me?" she tells him. Again, as on that day near the fountain, they express their love for one another. Instead of the pure joy of adolescence, their feelings have been transmuted into more ethereal climes, like dirges, they express the pain of a life gone by and their rapture in sacrifice.

Life is ebbing. Violaine must now disclose everything. Mara had not told him of her visit to the forest, of the resurrection of Aubaine, of the child's blue eyes. Violaine does. Anger swells within Jacques. Why hadn't Mara spoken? In rhapsodic terms, he virtually sings his love for Violaine. "O my fiancée, through these branches in flower, salvation!" His joy is immense. "How beautiful it is / To live! and how immense is God's glory." But then, "it is also good to die," Violaine says, and she does. Silence pervades.

The sisters of Monsanvierge were all dead now. The convent was no longer in use. Violaine's departure from this earth had ended a cycle in religious history. Pierre de Craon enters and carries her dead body into the shed her father had built for the poor. She had not wanted Jacques to touch her.

The stage is empty. Anne Vercors enters in pilgrim's dress. He looks about. Nothing seems to have changed. Yet, the house seems empty, desolate. Outside the trees are burgeoning, the branches are heavy with fruit. Nature is arrayed for a feast; wearing her most exquisite vestments, she is grandiose in her welcome.

Time passes. Jacques Hury has told everything to Anne Vercors. A nun passes, searching for a flower to place on Violaine's tomb. There are no flowers in this season, only fruit. Jacques, however, points to a clump of leaves. Only violets remain. The Virgin's flower, then, will be placed above Violaine's tomb. Mara had given Violaine her own wedding dress for her descent into death.

Anne Vercors laments Violaine's demise. On the other side of the stage Mara makes her appearance with Aubaine. The three men look at her. She knows she is still unloved, yet she is the only sister remaining; they will have to accept her for what she is. Mara confesses her guilt now; she opens herself up to the world, to nature, and to God.

It is true, I killed her.
It is I who took her by the hand the other night, when I
    tried to find her
When Jacques was not there,
And who let her fall in the sand quarry and who threw the

> Filled cart on top of her. Everything was ready, there
> was only one king pin to pull out.
> I did it.

It was Mara who spoke to her mother and told her she wanted to marry Jacques, who threatened her with suicide if she did not yield to her wishes. The more Jacques' eyes were welded to Violaine, the more Mara sought to destroy her competitor, to eradicate her presence, tear her out of her mind, dismember her.

Then Mara questions. Was the love Jacques Hury had for Violaine any better? or Pierre de Craon's any purer? How did they react to her leprosy? Jacques threw her out of the house. Pierre de Craon did not aid her in any way. Who is the purer of the two? Who is the spotless one? without sin? "He that is without sin among you," Christ said, "let him first cast a stone at her" (John 8:7).

It is Mara's simple and earthy faith that has saved her, Claudel suggested.[12] Was it her fault that she loved Jacques? She was not able to control her feelings. She felt unloved: she was neither beautiful, as was her sister, nor tender, or altruistic. She acted out of despair, and her motivations stemmed from no other reason. Her love was not born of joy as was Violaine's, but of tragedy. "I committed a great crime, I killed my sister; but I did not sin against you. And I say to you that you cannot reproach me for anything," she tells Jacques. She wants to be accepted by him. She was in Claudel's view *privatio boni*, deprived of goodness. She was Evil, and Evil is a vital and powerful force in life according to the Gnostics. Man must be forever vigilant, struggle to bind and imprison, at least temporarily, this force that can never be destroyed.

After Mara's confession she feels liberated, as though she herself had died and had been reborn; the poisons of jealousy, anger, dissatisfaction had been exorcised from her system and she had gained sanctification. Cleansed of her

Evil, Violaine had told her on that fateful day that she was the only one who had really believed in her, the only one to possess true faith.

The Tidings Brought to Mary, or Violaine's passion, a modern reenactment of a Medieval mystery drama, is an objectification of Claudel's own inner torment. An exile, as was Pierre de Craon, he too tried to build his edifice, a spiritual condition which would have enabled him to transcend the flesh. His powerful desires, however, forever struck him with a leprous condition, which he felt he could heal through sacrifice, torment, and pain. Pierre de Craon, the *pontifex* in the play, was the spreader of leprosy— Evil—and in so doing made God's will known. Violaine's kiss, which enabled her to contract the sickness, was the torture needed to lead to her sanctification. Mara, too, injected the negative note, the lesion which would pave the way for rebirth and the *unio mystica*. Only in times of crisis can the polarities of life be experienced and acts lived out ferociously, brutally, in all of their savage grandeur. The knowledge thus gleaned, according to Claudel, allows the sacrifice to be complete and permits the penitent to *know* the *extreme* and *exquisite* joy in suffering.

The Tidings Brought to Mary, Claudel's most popular play, has been successfully produced the world over. Accessible to viewers of all ages, it possesses a fairy tale quality that activates imaginations and excites feelings.

7. THE TRILOGY:
THE COUFONTAINE CYCLE

Claudel's trilogy, alluded to as the Coûfontaine cycle, consists of three plays: *The Hostage* (*L'Otage*, 1909), *Stale Bread* (*Le Pain dur*, 1914), and *The Humiliated Father* (*Le Père humilié*, 1916). They are the work of a mature artist; the dialogue is marked with restraint; the ideations are explicit, and the conflicts objective. More a philosophical tract than a drama, a debate, a meeting of the minds, the trilogy, nevertheless, brings political and religious antagonisms implicit in a changing society to the stage. No longer are we witness to the hymns or panegyrics to nature, those powerful outbursts directed toward sun and moon that were replete in *Golden Head*; nor does the Coûfontaine cycle evince the lust and sensuality inherent in this youthful work, or even its poetry which exploded, bruised, and inflamed both reader and protagonist alike.

Claudel's trilogy deals with the world of compromise, concession, and arbitration. By the time *The Hostage* was published, Claudel was forty-one years old. He had already held important diplomatic posts (vice-consul, consul, and so forth) in both the Occident and Orient. He knew the

174

behind-the-scenes machinations that took place when laws were promulgated and pacts written. As a diplomat Claudel was part of an international organization in which facades, hypocrisy, accommodation, and deception were built into its very structure. Politics was a game: the winner was the clever individual or nation, the manipulating and conniving force. Far from the naïve lad who had entered foreign service in 1890, Claudel knew now the very profound meaning of "diplomacy," and its name was not integrity. Governments and countries, whether secular or religious, were founded and dismantled by planners, schemers, and opportunists as well as by visionaries.

Historical and philosophical concepts of Vico, de Maistre, and Spengler are interwoven into the fabric of Claudel's trilogy. History is viewed as cyclical, composed of periods of growth and deterioration: renewal is brought about by thinkers and visionaries in abstract form; once these concepts are put into practice, however, they fall victim to the realities of life and, in so doing, decompose progressively. Throughout history it has been shown that intellectuals and idealists were the creators of revolutions: the catalysts that fostered change. The span, however, between the inception of the theory in the book and its concrete manifestation in the working government, was immense. The ideal exists in the world of the absolute; it cannot come into being in the existential sphere—for then it becomes real.

The Coûfontaine cycle, which deals with the period beginning in 1813 and concluding in 1871, juxtaposes the Ancien Régime, with its absolute monarchy, its union of Church and state, and the post-Revolutionary period in France, the Napoleonic era, the Restoration, and the creation of modern Italy. A contrasting of opposites is Claudel's dramatic method: past as opposed to present, the ideal to the real, illusion to reality, good to evil, Godlessness to a God-filled world.

Important, too, is the fact that Claudel had already experienced his great love (1901)—which was to become in time the prototype for other famous adventures in his writings. Having reached inhuman dimensions in his fantasy world, his love could never be replicated in the existential sphere. Love relationships never really ripen in the Coûfontaine cycle. Love does come into being, only to be extinguished suddenly and brutally under the guise of sin or evil. Feelings are forever thwarted and twisted; yearnings are punished. Wedlock is presented as a scourge, marked with pain, and despair, and martyrdom. Discord between man and woman is the rule of the day.

The Hostage

Eighteen Hundred Thirteen. The curtains part on a library in what had been, prior to the French Revolution, a Cistercian monastery. The walls of the library are whitewashed; the decor is stark, even severe, and includes only the necessities of life. A large wooden cross with a bronze crucifix "ferocious and mutilated looking" is visible. The coat of arms of the noble Coûfontaine family is also displayed: two clasped hands and a silver sword impaled between Sun and Moon; its motto is "Coûfontaine adsum" ("I am present"). It is night. A tempest is raging outside.

Sygne de Coûfontaine, the present owner of the Cistercian abbey, informs her cousin, Georges, Viscount de Coûfontaine, who has just arrived after a twenty-year absence, that she has spent all of her waking moments since the Revolution restoring the land holdings once owned by her family. Her accounts are in order; everything is "clear and pure."

In these two adjectives, "clear and pure," Claudel sums up his heroine's personality. She is clear, spotless, stainless, tidy, neat, sharp, clean, with definite ideas. Sygne is uni-dimensional, rational, cerebral, and as such, almost inhuman. There is no conflict within her being, no question of comportment or what her function should be in life. Similar to the Stoics whose activities were dictated by reason, Sygne's unbending will and irreproachable ways are functions or appendages of her intellect. Feeling has been relegated to the background; it is virtually nonexistent. She could be considered a modern Seneca: a Stoic who, when he felt his usefulness to Nero to be at an end, calmly sat down at his table and let the blood flow from his veins until he died.

Sygne's methodical working principle, which guided her activities throughout the chaotic eras of the Revolution and the Empire period following it, allowed her to amass a substantial amount of land and money. Her symbolic role in *The Hostage* is to restore, to preserve, and continue the traditions of her ancestors. Method, therefore, persever-ence, mark her every step. A pragmatist, she also knows that acts alone are not sufficient to gain her point; she must maintain a façade, do away with her individual needs and personal happiness for the good of the collective. Honor and courage have replaced feeling.

Onomastically, Sygne's name is indicative of the role she plays in Claudel's historical and philosophical drama. Sygne, a homonym for sign, signal, emblem, indicates the outer core of something which remains undefined, invisi-ble, impalpable. She is the sign of the as yet unmanifest, unlived, amorphous entity; she bears within her the mark-ings of a larger truth, the mystery of future happenings. It is through her that future generations will be born and archaic notions refashioned; she will be the sacrificial vessel. Sygne also represents past periods, such as the Ancien Régime with its divine monarchy and feudal outlook. She believes in the grandeur and greatness of those past times, which she has now made up her mind to serve. Owing to her extreme religiosity, she is comparable to Constantine the Great (272–337), the Roman Emperor who defeated Maxentius in the battle of the Milvian Bridge (312), and who, it is said, saw a cross in the sky bearing the words *in hoc signo vinces* ("by this sign you will conquer"). So Sygne will also live for the cross, a symbol engraved in the very fibers of her being.

Sygne is first seen seated at her table, going over her accounts. The room is lit by a single candle. Not only the preserver of the lands of her ancestors and of the Church, she also guarded the home fires. In this regard she may be associated with the goddess Hestia (or Vesta, "the hearth"). For the Greeks and Romans, Hestia was an abstract principle, an Idea. Since she was in charge of perpetuating the hearth, sculptors and poets featured her in immobile and unchanging stances. Virgins (Vestals) were called upon to serve her, and it is they who kept the flame burning around her altars. Sygne, in her own way, attends to the homefires. It is she who sees to it that they are fed. Pure and virginal in heart and body, she keeps her ideology unchanged. As such, she becomes the living embodiment of an abstract principle. Remote, distant, devoted to a cause, she is unflinching and unflagging in her ways.

Georges de Coûfontaine is as single-minded as Sygne, but a bit more human. He believes in the heroic values dear to the Medieval knight and the Renaissance warrior and has put these into practice. Since he left France at the outbreak of the Revolution, he has served and fought for his monarch, the future Louis XVIII. Georges is a fascinating figure, because he went to England for his king, sacrificing his happiness, inheritance, wealth, home, and even honor for this man in whom he had virtually no faith, since the monarch was neither a visionary nor a man possessed of integrity or valor. Yet, Georges defended him in all matters, serving him with the same devotion that a feudal lord would have paid to his suzerain. It was in England, also, that Georges lost his wife, along with his children, in an influenza epidemic. Only after her death did he discover that she had been the Dauphin's mistress. Nor does Georges believe in the return of the Ancien Régime. The Revolution and Empire had altered the needs of the people, had changed their ways: the past could never become present. As for his parents and Sygne's, they had died on the guillotine during the Reign of Terror (1793–94).

Why then should Georges defend a future monarch in whom he has so little faith? Why should he try to restore a government he knows will never achieve the same dignity, honor, and power it once possessed? Georges is bitter and angry. He despises the present political situation, and has no love for life. He believes in neither God nor the Church. He considers himself, paradoxically, "a knight of the past," a kind of left-over feudal knight whose heroism is constantly being called into play, although the ideal for which he fights is hollow and meaningless. As long as he lives, he seeks to remain a model figure, maintain an image symptomatic of ancient gallic tradition. Georges rejects the new world, the new way—any change. He is more than willing to give his life to a structure which he longs to see reborn, although he knows it cannot be. Imaginative, adventuresome, active, Georges has created a cause for himself: a fantasy for which he will work. Unlike Sygne, who remains at home, fixed, Georges goes out *into* the world where nations are being created and dismantled, frontiers altered,

Claude Evrard (Father Badilon) and Sylvie Genty (Sygne) in a scene from *The Hostage*, produced by Guy Retore at Théâtre de L'Est Parisien.
FRENCH CULTURAL SERVICES

governments structured and toppled. Georges is flamboyant, impulsive, and cannot function coherently in
the world of reality; he only comes alive in the domain of
illusion—the ideal and unreal.

Georges tells Sygne in hushed tones that he has just
kidnapped the pope, who had been made a virtual prisoner
by Napoleon, and that he has brought him to the
Coûfontaine Abbey for safekeeping until he can get him to
England. Once away from the Continent, the pope and
future king can work together to restore a world that was
torn asunder during the Revolutionary and Napoleonic
eras. The captivity of the pope (Claudel's invention) is
untenable for the devout Catholic. As the "father" of
humankind and God's representative on earth, to closet
him would be to commit a sin. Georges knows that nations
need strong figures to guide people and to keep the masses
in check and, although he is fully aware of the political
manipulations carried on by the Holy See and clergy, he
still defends their cause as he does that of the monarchy. It

is not a question of faith, but of expediency. Action must be taken now, he contends, because Napoleon, his great enemy, is fighting a losing campaign in Russia, while in France the Legitimists are gaining power daily.

When a point of view, whether historical or religious, is unalterable, it ceases to grow; it reaches a plateau. It is then that aridity sets in, that regression and disintegration follow. Claudel had always been fascinated by the notion of change which, as enunciated by Heraclitus, was implicit in nature's course. Only in the divine domain were Claudel's concepts immutable and fixed. On earth, however, everything was subject to transformation. In *The Hostage*, Claudel deals with a fallen monarchy, a regime which had outgrown its usefulness and had reached a point in its development beyond which it could no longer function. A society (or regime) lasts as long as it answers a need. Once stasis takes place, it cannot adapt to new life forces, which are constantly burgeoning in a world governed by flux. The regime, no longer offering healthy and vigorous elements, is then uprooted and toppled; a new one is created having more energetic force.

Claudel's cyclical concept of history was perhaps in part inspired by the works of Giovanni Battista Vico (1668–1744), one of the earliest philosophers to suggest (*The New Science*, 1744) that culture goes through stages of development: the ages of gods, heroes, and men, each associated with certain types of customs, laws, and religions; governments and institutions reach a zenith after which they cease to grow and become plagued with chaos. Decomposition follows and then rebirth. While Descartes, Newton, and La Mettrie believed that nature would one day be understandable to man, Vico contended that only civilization could be apprehended by mortals, since they were its creators; God, who was infinite, brought nature and man into being, and His notions transcend man's understanding. The French

Revolution was comparable to Vico's state of chaos; the Napoleonic era, to that of decomposition.

Despite the fact that Sygne has been living in a cloistered and closed world, she is well acquainted with political, economic, and religious conditions in France. She knows that the Revolution brought about a forced "capitulation" of noble families to their servants, that society has become fluid, and the once powerful aristocracy has been compelled to alter its life style. She senses, also, that there was something degenerate in the Ancien Régime, but does not yet know quite what those factors were. She is also aware of the fact that something has to happen, that new blood must flow into the veins of ancient traditions, so that a revitalization process can come into being.

Sygne is also preoccupied with the question of evil. She has seen it rampant all about her, most specifically, in the decline of the power of the clergy and the Vatican, and in the Revolution itself. What gave her strength all these years, and a goal in life, was the solid belief that "God alone is real," that evil has been placed on earth to test humankind's strength. God, for Sygne, exists behind everything that happens in life, all that exists. His way, insofar as she is concerned, must not be questioned, only accepted. Evil must therefore also be understood in this fashion. "How can he who does not accept evil accept good?" she questions.

The reality of Evil as opposed to Good in the workaday world is a Gnostic notion. The Gnostics, who attempted to accommodate Christian ideas to those of Pythagoras, Plato, and Zoroaster, contended that since the beginning of the created world, two forces were at work and vied for supremacy: Light (Good) and Dark (Evil). For the orthodox Christian, such as Saint Augustine, once a Gnostic himself, such duality was anathema. Saint Augustine stated that Evil does not exist in a God-created world. How could God—all Good—all perfect, create Evil? Evil, then, must be looked upon as a *privatio boni*, without any real substance. Claudel, interestingly enough, seems to have shared the Gnostic credo, although it is considered a heresy by the Catholic church. Evil is an important factor, Claudel contended, in the evolutionary process. Only through the interplay of Good and Evil, that is, polarities, can an individual test his will, feelings, morality and, therefore, be certain of his service and devotion to God. Evil for Claudel becomes a means of redemption.

For Sygne, Evil is a reality. It is also an active force in her life, as is Good. The interplay of this binary force enables her to maintain what she believes to be dignity and honor. It will also inject her with an adamantine essence, feelings of pride and power reminiscent to some extent of those characteristics exhibited by Joan of Arc. Both women lived out their lives in a world of men; both took on many masculine attributes as they carried out what they considered to be their obligations to country and God.

In contrast to Sygne's restrained, poised, reasonable, and masculine attitudes are Georges' flamboyant, impulsive, and foolhardy ways. He does not think before he acts. He feels. He tells her of his love for her, which seems incredible since he had not seen her in twenty years. She, too, had always loved him, but her feelings were always controlled. Only once does Sygne burst into tears and reveal emotion: when Georges asks for her hand in marriage and gives her his glove, a feudal oath which means that such a pact is irrevocable. At this moment, she takes on human dimension, steps down from her abstract pedestal and sheds her vestal virginlike accouterments. She begins to understand the depth of Georges' despair, caused by his wife's infidelity and the demise of his entire family. Minutes later,

Henri Rollan (de Coûfontaine) and Yonnel (the pope) in a scene from *The Hostage*.
FRENCH CULTURAL SERVICES

however, Sygne assumes what has become her normal stance: hard and cold, her tears having dried up and her face wearing the composed expression for which she was noted. When *The Hostage* was first produced (1914), Claudel insisted that Sygne's voice should be monochord, that her acting should be stylized, her words declaimed in rhythmic patterns, and her expression divested of all feelings; that her walk and actions should be devoid of all "residual gestures," that they should be architectural, an expression of "a synthetic art."[1]

Georges, hyperemotional, says with pride that he has done "an incredible thing," that he has brought the pope to Coûfontaine Abbey. He is acting in the finest traditions of

French nobility, he contends. His act, politically speaking, however, is rash and valueless. In no way would the pope be able to help the Church if he went against Napoleon's wishes. On the contrary, the man of God would have more to gain in being friendly with his enemy. Pragmatism, diplomacy, ruse, were some of the Church's most powerful weapons. Georges' act could not be called altruistic, since he felt nothing for either the pope or the Church. It was, rather, a self-centered deed, performed in an endeavor to enhance his own image—his bravura. He could not foresee events. He was no diplomat, nor did he understand the workings of society or the principles involved.

Georges has feeling, however, and sympathizes with Sygne's lost youth, her parents' demise, and the constant work involved in "putting together the disparate plots of land," which he compares to "old, torn lace that one pieces together thread by thread." His use of a feminine image to describe Sygne's work is also revelatory of his personality: fiery and unthinking, but drenched with feeling. It is he who acts; it is he who is the catalyst in this drama, setting events in motion. His unthinking ways provoke the situation that the play solves at its conclusion. An irritant, Georges withdraws from the action after Act I, and lets the masculine forces take over. Unconsciously, he understands that he has nothing more to give to Sygne or to his cause; the vital "sap" that resided for so many centuries in his family tree has dried out with him; his flesh is "Stripped bare, abridged, inflexible, unfruitful."

The pope enters through a hidden door in the library. Georges kneels before him, as had his ancestors, and serves him his meal. He is proud of having been the one to have kidnapped the pope, he informs him. The pope does not understand, however, why he has been brought to the Coûfontaine Abbey.

A senex figure, the pope is neither positive nor negative.

He is reminiscent of a weak branch, blown here and there; he is a cause over which factions fight, but who is no longer vital. The pope, nevertheless, understands the political situation very well: if he is to retain his power, he must embrace the strongest earthly ruling force which, at this time, is Napoleon. He has to accommodate his ways to those of the emperor or be destroyed by him. The pope, therefore, is averse to Georges' plan. He refuses to go to England and remain in exile with the future king of France. He does not want to live among "heretics." He also feels that the king is expendable, but that the pope is not. He reemphasizes the notion that God's domain on earth and in heaven is eternal, while political climates are only temporal.

The "villain" of Claudel's drama—Turelure—makes his appearance in Act II. The arriviste, the self-proclaimed revolutionary, who fought hard on the peoples' side against the monarchy, betrayed his early ideals to join Napoleon. He is now Prefect of the Marne and Baron of the Empire. Turelure is synonomous with Evil.

The appellation chosen by Claudel for his character is significant. Turelure is the name of a village in the Tardenois, Claudel's region, implying that he has come across this type of individual in his own background. Indeed, he states that there is a bit of Turelure in himself. Onomastically, the word *ture* in the Walloon dialect means an old, brutal, and avaricious man; a *lure* in High Middle Ages is a scoundrel; a *lureau* is a ramp; and Turelure is said to have had "a hooked nose."[2] *Turelure* is also an old French refrain: *plus ça change, plus c'est la même turelure!"* implying that such a person is found in all societies and eras. The verb *tirer* may be associated with *ture*, meaning to pull, to draw, to drag; and Turelure did drag himself up from his class, that of servitude, through ruse, artifice, avarice, and a will to power, first during the Revolutionary period, and then under Napoleon.

Turelure was the son of Sygne's servant and wet nurse, Suzanne. It was she who had brought up Sygne in the finest of ancient traditions, helping her save the cross (the one now hanging on the Coûfontaine Abbey wall) from destruction during the Revolution. Suzanne had raised Sygne to uphold the values of her forefathers, the traditions of her class, to behave with dignity and courage, to be submissive and patient. Turelure's father was Quiriace, "a sorcerer and poacher," a man who lived beyond and outside of the law; he was a recluse, a solitary being, a stranger to society and, although he had been baptized, he was not a churchgoer. Suzanne realized that her son had inherited many of his father's characteristics and, therefore, sent him to the Cistercian monastery to be educated. When the French Revolution broke out, however, the monks were either killed or exiled, and the monastery was decimated, and she lost control over the lad.

In many ways Claudel has endowed Turelure with attributes of Joseph Fouché (1764–1864), a minister active during the Convention and Empire, and Prince Talleyrand-Périgord (1754–1838), who assumed an important position in the Ancien Régime, was a member of the Constituent Assembly during the Revolution, minister of foreign relations under the Directory, the Consulate, the Empire, and rallied to the forces of the Restoration.

Turelure also is adept at accommodating his feelings with the regime in power. He knows how to please government officials, how to speak and act the right way—to be hypocritical—when need be. An upstart, Turelure is endowed with many characteristics of this type of person. He is arrogant, aggressive—as is the status seeker—clever,

Hélène Sauvaneix and Alexandre Rignault in *The Hostage.*
FRENCH CULTURAL SERVICES

reserved, composed, and intelligent. He has fought hard to
rise in the social scale and has succeeded. It is for this very
reason that Sygne and Georges both despise him. He lacks
integrity, they feel; his heinous crimes consist of helping
create the Revolution, thereby destroying their family and
way of life. Claudel endowed Turelure with a limp, both
an attribute of the Devil at times and a characteristic of
Talleyrand.

Turelure enters Sygne's whitewashed Abbey, spotless,

immaculate, in which an atmosphere of past grandeur reigns. He talks to her of his youth, his ideals as a revolutionary, his desire to eradicate men of wealth, to divest the clergy of its land, its gold, its lucre, and transform these corrupting and self-righteous instruments into forces that could help the downtrodden. He denies Sygne's accusation that he had certain members of the clergy executed for perverse reasons. "I had them killed for love of country out of the purest enthusiasm of my heart." The Church and its clergy held the poor in bondage; they represented the forces of regression, closeted free thought. The demise of the men of the cloth, he maintained, brought them glory, since they sacrificed their lives for what they considered to be a greater cause: they became martyrs.

Sygne is revulsed by Turelure's rationalization of the bloody events interwoven into the ideals of the revolution. His calculating manner is anathema to her. Sygne and Turelure are antithetical personalities: Sygne is ice and Turelure is fire. Should they merge, she would vanish in the end, melt and then evaporate, while Turelure would pursue his course, guided by the burning force of self-interest. Sygne castigates Turelure in every way possible, and in so doing, sets another dynamic into action: the greater her invectives, the more powerful is Turelure's attraction to her. Indeed, he virtually salivates when looking at her, when pronouncing her name. Turelure grows breathless as he argues his cause. The hunt is on: the prey, although remote, ruthless and retiring, may be caught. A crescendo in the rhythmic interchange now comes to pass. The psychological rape is to take place: the conqueror is enraptured. The "race" that vilified him when he was a child, rejected him as a youth, condemned his boorish ways, mocked his poor clothes, stands powerful in Sygne; but now the tables are turned. She is the remnant of an unproductive and lifeless society. He is authority.

Turelure is Evil insofar as Sygne is concerned. He is an obstacle, a deterrent to her way of life; a destructive force. Yet, he represents a new element in society, the worker, the aggressor, the builder of civilizations. The Ancien Régime had grown degenerate and corrupt. Deeply committed to her ancestors and her religion, Sygne stands for the past. Turelure is the present: a reality with which Sygne must contend. It was Turelure and his cohorts who had, symbolically, leveled King and God, nobles and monks, had bathed France in blood, cleansing it of its unproductive and regressive ways. A Revolution does not happen, Turelure contends, it is planned, brought about, instigated, and fired. Equality, Fraternity, and Harmony were not for the mere asking. There was a reason for such traumatic occurrences.

Turelure altered his concepts in the same way that societies go through transformative stages from primitive idealism to an older and more objective conservatism. When young, he participated in the struggle to relieve man from bondage; he fought hard in the Revolution until he matured and realized that the ideal and the existential sphere were two different ways: one abstract, the other concrete. He understood that if he were to succeed in the workaday world—and he was tired of poverty—he would have to find some way of accommodating his views to the powers at hand.

Turelure, then, is no more Evil than Sygne, Georges or the pope. Each in his own way distills events to suit his or her credo. Claudel, in keeping with Gnostic dicta, understood that man needed Evil in order to foster Good. The Devil is an irritant, an instigator to action; it is the Devil who brings doubt into situations, who activates man's desire to transcend the world of opposites, thereby to create. Blake wrote: "Good is the passive that obeys Reason; Evil is the active springing from Energy. Good is Heaven. Evil is Hell."[3] For Milton, Evil took the form of Satan and became a *principium individuationis*.[4] Psychologically, Evil may be viewed as an expression of the shadow: it embodies those characteristics the conscious mind considers negative and will not accept. These qualities, rejected by the individual and the collective, may be associated for the Christian with instinct and the Devil. It is understandable, then, why the Christian is forever attempting to stamp out the Devil or that aspect within himself which he despises; he undertakes to eradicate the shadow via ascetic practices when, in fact, he should more readily accomplish his goal were he to accept instinct as a fact of life and integrate it into his psyche. Whenever instinct—or the Devil—is subjugated rather than experienced in its own right, destruction is more frequently the outcome.

When Turelure suggests he ally himself with Sygne, that they marry, one may look upon this fusion as an attempt, psychologically at least, of integrating the polarities within the psyche, healing a profound split, experiencing a shift of intransigent attitudes within the human personality and the culture from which it emerges. The more Turelure makes his wishes known to Sygne, the more her hatred for him grows. When he comments on her beauty, the "sparkle" in her angry eyes, "this tight-lipped mouth which smiles, like someone who arms himself in silence," he fulminates. No longer the little boy forced to live in the poor quarters, relegated to darkness in an aristocratic society, he dominates the situation. Her coldness and reticence impress him now; she is a force with which he must contend: that obstacle which he must overcome in order to gain ever greater heights. Sygne's pride remains high-pitched; never does she cower as she humbles his past, his awkward ways, his lowly speech and manner. Turelure responds: he knows that money and power are forceful instruments no matter what the society. "I'll buy you and you will be mine . . . I'll take the land and the woman and the name . . . I'll take the body and the soul." Sygne writhes in anger, but rather than exteriorize her emotions, she directs them inward. Controlled, collected, she conserves her emotions, represses them. As for Turelure, he plays his trump to gain her consent: if she does not marry him, he will reveal the whereabouts of the pope, which could cost the Pontiff his life.

Sygne is alone now. Father Badilon enters. He will convince Sygne to marry Turelure, thereby sacrificing her life to the Church, becoming a modern vestal virgin. It is in the best interests of Christ and His pope, Badilon maintains, to preserve God's earthly domain, to prevent harm from coming to it. Sygne's personal feelings, he suggests, are temporal, ephemeral, merely reflecting passing joys, earthly impulses. Humanity at large will gain eternal life because of her sacrifice, although she may die in the process. Badilon also convinces Sygne that the marriage oath taken with Georges was abrogated, since they were cousins and consanguineous marriages were not harbingers of growth or health. Georges, he tells Sygne, would certainly not be angered if Sygne were to marry someone else; he would surely understand. Nor should she feel the slightest guilt at going back on her word; she will be serving a higher cause.

Sygne must marry Turelure, Father Badilon maintains, even though he helped destroy the monasteries of France and was instrumental in seeing to the demise of her parents. Father Badilon is, in effect, teaching Sygne the ways of the world. She must divest herself of her individuality and assume the role of a "sign"; she must play out the role for which she was destined. To be a victim, to become a sacrificial instrument, to be degraded, scourged, and shamed is to ascend the hierarchy of being. When Christ was crucified on the cross, the Roman virtues of nobility, courage, and physical prowess were no longer admirable attributes but were replaced by weakness and suffering as the most important goals. The greater the pain, the higher its value, implying that the human element is superseded by the divine or inhuman. Psychologically, the ego, or the personal factor in man, is diminished in size, in favor of the collective psyche, the Self.

Sygne is not yet prepared to sacrifice herself in marriage to Turelure. Father Badilon's rhetoric is as opportunistic as Turelure's in this regard: one sides with the Church, the other with the state. Materialism and pragmatism are inherent in both views. As for Sygne, she withdraws into herself in contained rage: she must call "this animal" her husband? she questions. Her body, her pride, her soul rebel against such an outrage. "Were God in the flesh to require it of me," she cries out, she would refuse, categorically. "Must I save the pope at the expense of my soul?" Badilon answers in the affirmative. Sygne rejects his command; she refuses to yield to the Devil, no matter what the cause. In the end, however, after struggling with Badilon's unctuous ways, his soft, nuanced, and suave manner, she is convinced of the validity of his views. It is for God's sake that she will give herself to Turelure. If she does not, she will be betraying Christ and His Church. She must be sacrificed as Christ had sacrificed himself for humankind. To this extreme view, Sygne counters: "I am not a God but a woman." She does not want to play such an immense role, to live out the image of a nineteenth-century Virgin, an ideal, the bride of the Devil, a vessel through whom future generations will be born, a tree which nurtures a seed.

Slowly, however, she comes around to Father Badilon's way of thinking. She must perform the sacrifice. She will yield the fruit needed to save the Pontiff and his office, to see to the continuation of France's very life blood. As Mary took pride in the fruit of her womb, so Sygne will enjoy the role destiny has had her fulfill. Indeed, Sygne nearly revels in the thought: "He will be the flesh of my flesh and the soul of my soul and what Jesus Christ is for the Church, Toussaint Turelure will be for me, indissoluble."

In Act III Sygne is already married to Turelure. A child has been born of their union and, as the curtain parts, the child is about to be baptized. Neither Sygne nor her husband attends the ceremony. The political climate has changed in France. Napoleon's armies have been routed in Russia, the Emperor has been defeated at Waterloo, the monarchy of Louis XVIII has been proclaimed. Turelure plays an important role in the new government as he had in previous ones.

Sygne's hatred for Turelure has not abated. Her attitude is interesting in that her anger rests almost exclusively on class distinction. An aristocrat, she looks upon his common origins with feelings of disgust. Yet, such a view is antithetical to Christ's teachings. But, then, so was the entire monarchical structure. As for her marriage to Turelure, it is devoid of feeling and based on pride. She wanted to equate herself with the great martyrs of the past. Never did she feel compassion for Turelure. In accordance with Father Badilon's view, she felt she had undergone an "immolation" with a death sentence having been imposed upon her. Father Badilon's conscience was assuaged since he believed he was serving a higher purpose; to become a nineteenth-century Joan of Arc furthered Sygne's own aristocratic bent, elevating her still more from the commoner.

Georges has returned unexpectedly. He is outraged and castigates Sygne for having broken the oath they had taken; he rebukes her ways, accuses her of cruelty, of being unfeeling. Sygne grows increasingly distraught and frenzied. Georges has no understanding of her sacrifice, she maintains, or of the fact that she had to yield to Turelure's embrace in order to save the pope. Sygne justifies her act and claims that her "soul" has not been touched. Flesh and spirit for her are two distinct entities, worlds apart. So dismembered and divided is she, that they function in a separate sphere. Her body has been used as a funnel, a matrix, to bring forth the seed which would usher in a new age: a blending of the aristocrat with the commoner. The child born to her and Turelure was conceived outside of her feeling world. She was the *hostage*, the *host* ("the sacrificial victim"), the bread or wafer in the Eucharist. She has given her body in sacrifice and incorporates the idea of sacrifice (a gift offered to God). She is the meal ("consecrated") which, when partaken in Holy Communion, makes God present to the believer during the transubstantiation. The highest point of the Mass in Roman Catholic liturgy occurs when the bread and wine become the body and blood of Christ; then Christ/God enters the human sphere, after which he returns to the realm of the absolute.[5] So Sygne finally experiences her martyrdom as an *imitatio Christi*. There is one difference: she has not given her soul to Turelure and, therefore, the blood remains hers, hers alone. Only her body has been sacrificed; her martyrdom, therefore, is only partial. She was the host upon which the animal or plant fed, giving it existence, making her body its home.

Sygne is proud of her sacrifice: the shame is hers.

> It is mine indeed!
> It is my wealth and it will not be ravished, shame more
>   faithful than praise!
> It will accompany me until my tomb and further, it is
>   sealed on me as a stone, it is incorporated
> To my bones which will be judged!

It was acquired with difficulty. Every step of the way was

fraught with pain; her task was arduous and her joy in the giving of her body made it all the greater. Sygne nearly revels in Georges' accusations, in his humiliating remarks. Nothing has been spared her in the domain of human suffering, and she has grown even stronger, she feels, through the ordeal. Pain and sorrow have not only allowed her to survive, but have also wiped away her feelings of lowliness and disgust, transforming them into sensations of joy. She has given God, His Church, nearly everything she has. Only death awaits her now.

Similar to the medieval *Christian Penitentials*[6] manuals in which sins had been codified and the appropriate pen- ance for each provided, so Sygne's martyr fantasy has also worked in her favor. Humiliation and shame, she feels, have brought her salvation. Echoing the masochist who fuses pain and pleasure, Sygne's martyr complex, which has now reached obsessive proportions, may be looked upon as pathological.[7] Sygne has literalized her suffering, articulating it in abstract concepts. What had been implicit from the very beginning of Christianity (martyrs torn by lions, St. Catherine dismembered on the wheel, St. Sebastian's body pierced by arrows), has now become part of her being, but only superficially—as an intellectual concept. She feels that her sacrifice has taken on the value of sanctity. Such a view is reminiscent of the statement made by Bernard de Clairvaux (1115), who was the second founder of the Cistercian order. Advocating poverty and asceticism, he stated that "humiliation is the way to humil- ity." In Sygne's case, however, pride forced her into the path she chose. For the twelfth-century saint, humiliation led to the dismemberment of hubris, while Sygne's martyr- dom aroused self-pity but not self-compassion. Her view of sacrifice was thrust upon her from the outside; it did not evolve from an inner necessity.

Georges leaves. He cannot kill Sygne. Turelure enters.

Georges then appears at the window and shots ring out. Sygne throws herself in front of her husband. She is hit by a bullet. Turelure grabs his own revolver and shoots Georges, who dies immediately. Life is slowly seeping from Sygne as Father Badilon enters. He reiterates his admiration for her sacrifice: she has served her purpose and may now retreat into death. Ambiguity is implicit in her act. Was it suicide? or did she want to save her husband?

In the last scene, Louis XVIII enters, followed by Ture-lure, whom he considers "the most useful of my subjects." Turelure has accommodated to the new regime; he is ready to negotiate with the government in power, as he had with those of the past. When the king sees the two dead bodies, Turelure explains their presence: it was caused by a terrible mistake; they were actually serving the monarchy when they were shot. Their service must be acknowledged, Louis XVIII states, it deserves admiration.

Dignitaries of all kinds arrive: military, political, and clerical. They all vow allegiance to the new king and pros-trate themselves before him. Although he is far from being "above" the mortal sphere and is in effect a mediocre being, he is now the head of a new nation. The end justifies the means. The pillars of the incoming social structure favor the man at the helm.

Stale Bread

" . . . to negate what one cannot annex," André Gide wrote about Claudel, is a statement applicable to *Stale Bread*.[8] The climate in this drama is negative, destructive, hard, and cruel. Love is absent, as is God. Dissonance and assonance prevail. The characters are shadow images; each proceeds through ruse, jealousy, hatred. They are uninter-ested in understanding each other, or in assimilating the divergent views each represents. Annihilation is their way, dismemberment their goal. As Claudel wrote: "One of the great reasons for art is that it purges the soul."[9] Indeed, *Stale Bread* is just that for the dramatist and his protagonists.

The title, *Stale Bread*, is indicative of the intractable nature of the protagonists. Exiled from his or her existential sphere, each is a pariah, each is cut off from his inner world. Although bread is basic to man's nourishment, Moses said that "man doth not live by bread only, but by every word that proceedeth out of the mouth of the Lord doth man live" (Deut. 8:3). Claudel's creatures are obsessed with the material world: building businesses, attending to commerce, amassing money and power. They do not partake of the bread of life, that is in the Christian eucharist: "I am the living bread which came down from heaven: if any man eat of this bread, he shall live forever and the bread that I will give is my flesh, which I will give for the life of the world" (John 6:51). Their communal meal is unicentered; the hardened crusts are partaken individually, imprisoned in the centroverted world of desire, unyielding, ungiving, unloving.

The action in *Stale Bread* takes place under the reign of Louis-Philippe (1830–1848), a period which saw an incredible growth in industry, trade, and shipping. After Napoleon's defeat at Waterloo, reaction set in against liberal attitudes. Louis-Philippe became king in 1830, not of France, but of the French. He appeared to live simply, as a real bourgeois. His ideas, however, which he carefully kept to himself, were quite different: he was conservative, authoritarian, and felt superior to the rich bourgeois and moneyed aristocracy.[10]

For Claudel the nineteenth century, although a period of development and evolution, was a Godless age that saw the weakening of the Church, the growth of the bourgeois.

class, and an increase in the power of the masses. It was an evil time. Yet, one might point to the fact that when the world was preoccupied with God during the Middle Ages, the Renaissance, and the Ancien Régime, when Church and state were allied in divine rule, a strife-ridden world also existed; worse, since starvation was rampant, dogmatism was impressed upon the people, and free thought was crushed rather than annexed. Although Claudel opted for what he considered to be the grandeur and spirituality of the past centuries, and the world divested of God was his *bête noire*, he, nevertheless, lived in it in grand style.

Act I of *Stale Bread* opens on the same Cistercian monastery viewed in *The Hostage*. Instead of the well-ordered library we first saw, "disorder and dust" have been introduced into the proceedings. Other changes are also manifest: the crucifix, which had hung on the wall in *The Hostage*, has been replaced with a portrait of Louis-Philippe in his National Guard uniform. The crucifix lies on the floor near a pile of books.

Turelure has become President of the Council of Ministers in Louis-Philippe's government. His voice is heard loudly and audibly from another room: he is proclaiming his political and economic ideas. Louis-Philippe, he explains, has made the constitutional monarchy work: one which is "traditional by principle, but modern by institution." He has developed France's natural resources, industry, and agriculture. France shows progress in economics and reform. As for the Coûfontaine Abbey, Turelure intends to transform it into a paper factory. Soon the hum of machines will be heard throughout the area rather than the chanting of prayers, which had sounded in pre-Revolutionary days. Another way of serving God is open to humankind at this juncture—work—which will afford man better living conditions and an easier way of life.

Pierre Renoir and Jean Servais in *Stale Bread* at the Théâtre de l'Atelier.
FRENCH CULTURAL SERVICES

Turelure is no longer the arriviste of *The Hostage* days. He has become anchored in his ideas and stale in his ways: avaricious, despotic, egotistical, emotionally unfulfilled. He believes that by building a fortune, amassing lucre, gold and other precious elements, he will feel secure; he will gain the admiration and respect of his entourage. Claudel was not the first to capitalize on the theme of money or miserliness with regard to theatre. Plautus' *Aulularia* (194 B.C.), Jonson's *Volpone* (1606), Molière's *The Miser* (1668), all revolved around similar notions. These works, however, provoke laughter, are peppered with deep-seated anger and irony, triggering twinges of malaise in many.

Turelure is a miser. He reflects for Claudel the cultural values of the Louis-Philippe period. He is the prototype of the bourgeois who has spent his life amassing wealth and cannot stop. Turelure, as already mentioned, is a reflection in part of the author, himself, who said he was both Turelure and Coûfontaine, the product of plebian and aristocratic antecedents.[11]

The two women, around whom the action revolves, are

Lumîr and Sichel. Each is a product of her environment, each severed from the mainstream of life, each obsessed with personal preoccupations.

Lumîr is blond and Polish. Onomastically, her name may be associated with the Latin *lumen*, meaning light, clarity, and illumination. She represents the idealist preoccupied with gold, the spiritually oriented, obsessed with matter. She tells Sichel that she wants Turelure to return the 10,000 francs she had lent his son, Louis. Lumîr's only thought throughout the play is the return of this money. She had lent it to Louis after he purchased a farm in Algeria. Had she not given him the money, he would have lost his land and his newly planted crop. Now she needs the funds to buy back the Sobieski sword, at present in the Dresden museum. Jean Sobieski (1629–1696) was one of Poland's most renowned warriors. It was he who repulsed the Turks, Tartars, and Cossacks from his land, stopping 300,000 of them at the walls of Vienna. He symbolizes for Lumîr a unified Poland, which had been dismantled after Napoleon's defeat and divided between Prussia, Russia, and Austria.

That Lumîr wears men's clothing and struggles to buy back the sword of a national hero indicates her powerful, aggressive, and intransigent nature. The sword she seeks to retrieve is also indicative of her personality: a cutting instrument, usually associated with specific heroes such as Roland (Durandal), King Arthur (Excalibur), and more. It is also a phallic symbol, and it is no wonder that Lumîr seeks it. Swords represent light as well, because their blades sparkle and shine; as such they were featured in the paintings and replicas of Crusaders who struck down the infidel, mercilessly, ruthlessly—for the love of God. The sword is considered the earth's counterpart of the sun; it is flame and fire. It is also speech: divisive as is a cutting remark, it severs as do sharp statements. Unfeeling, except when it comes to pursuing her ideal (the reunification of Poland), Lumîr stands for the fighter/woman, the amazon type: a female solar force who would resort to any method to achieve her end, even if it meant killing the obstructor. Although a female, physically, Lumîr is endowed with the spirit of a male. She is androgynous, ambivalent in her attitudes, ambiguous in her ways: a typical Claudel woman.

Sichel has dark hair. She is a Jew who seeks to become assimilated. Her greatest wish is to reject her past and her people. Throughout the play Sichel speaks of the difficulties Jews have encountered and still experience in France. Her statements are historically correct. It must be recalled that not until Sept. 27, 1791, were Jews emancipated in France and granted the rights of citizenship. Not everyone endorsed this new law, particularly, the clergy, many of whom spoke of the rights with "horror." The nineteenth century as a whole, however, was one of relative calm for the Jews of France. The belief in the perfectibility of man was popularized; reform and laws designed for the well-being of all would serve, people believed, to bring happiness to the world. This would make it possible for each individual to live fruitfully and positively. From 1816 on, the Jew became part of French society; he worked freely, worshipped without fear, and became one with the French nation—but only on the outside. The writer and politician Benjamin Constant noted that the Jew might now "figure honorably in the administration, no longer withdraw from an army career, cultivate and teach the sciences."[12]

Sichel's father, Ali ("sublime" in Arabic; a name Turelure insisted he use because of its Oriental flavor) Habenichts (German "to have nothing") was in Claudel's play the stereotypic moneylender: the Jew who has been brought to life in plays and essays, in poetry and prose galore throughout the Middle Ages and Renaissance. (It is interesting to note that the Jew, always featured as the userer, was in effect the least important group practicing this trade; the most powerful and most successful moneylenders were the Italians, who charged the highest rate of interest since they ran the greatest risk: Catholic law forbade money lending for interest.) Ali Habenichts was of German extraction, and during the course of the play, Claudel makes certain he speaks some words from his mother tongue, thereby underscoring national as well as religious differences, making him a true alien.

Turelure had taken Sichel as his mistress; he had also forced her to change her name. He did not want to call her by her given name, Rachel. Unconsciously, he must have rejected the biblical association: Rachel was Jacob's wife, the mother of Joseph and of Benjamin. Turelure could, perhaps, not stand the thought of her bearing children by a Christian; thus endowing France with a new "race."

Turelure called her Sichel, from the German word *sickle* or scythe. Thus she is associated with a cutting instrument as well as the crescent, the moon, fertility, and the feminine principle. The sickle is an attribute of Saturn, the god of time, who is also identified with the Greek Cronus, the youngest son of Uranus and Gaea, mother earth. It was Cronus who cut off his father's genitals, thereby making himself king of the world. The sickle also has cutting power in decision making; it stands for differentiation, which must take place in the individuation process, allowing personal and collective evolution to be forthcoming. The sickle is also identified with Ceres, the goddess of the harvest: thus birth, growth, death, and rebirth. The stem which links and binds the roots to the flower must be cut, as the umbilical cord must be severed if the child is to be nourished: "Except a corn of wheat fall into the ground and die, it abideth alone: but if it die, it bringeth forth much fruit" (John 12:24). Mutilation, in all of the foregoing examples, precedes rebirth. Whereas Lumîr stands for light, the sword, and masculine solar force, which fights in the open and will have no place in the creation of a new France, Sichel, a darker figure, works within the land, in secret, and will pave the way for the death of the senex figure. In so doing, she becomes a contributing factor in bringing about innovation.

Turelure also forbade Sichel from pursuing her career as a pianist. Prior to her relationship with him, she had won an international reputation as a virtuoso. When she yielded to his wishes, Sichel divested herself, symbolically, of her feeling function: the tenderness and gentleness implicit in her musical personality. Feeling allows an individual to set up subjective criteria for judging: once repressed or removed, that person is no longer able to understand or even adopt a scale of values. Sichel lost her sense of orientation as well as her identity when she allowed herself to be severed from the world of music, the realm she knew so well and experienced so deeply. Her soul will hear no more music, nor will it create any; no patterns or vocal tones will express the harmony or discord within her. She will not be able to experience the plenitude of nature about her, the correspondences between her individual being and the pleromatic sphere. Cut off from music, she will divest herself still further of her individuality by rejecting her past, her world—in an attempt to achieve a position in society—to profit and use the newly won rights of the French Jew.

Sichel is complex. Unlike Lumîr, whose goal in life was to see to the restoration of her homeland, Sichel considers herself an exile. She has no home, no land, no realm in which she can live freely and love completely. "But we Jews, there isn't a bit of land, not even as large as a gold coin / Upon which we can put our feet and say: this is ours, this is ours, this is home, it was made for us. / God alone is ours." Although equal before the law in France, Sichel indicates that her people have never been accepted into society; their road is still arduous, with few jobs open to them. Only through assimilation, Sichel believed, could she rid herself of the humiliation society has imposed upon her. What Sichel did not realize, however, was that by divesting herself of what she considered to be her shameful origins, she was also cutting herself off from her inner being, her identity, her traditions, ancestors, their laws and God.

Sichel, and Claudel saw this only too clearly, is the prototype of the assimilated Jews who embrace any and all religions in order to hide their origins, thinking this will alleviate feelings of degradation, and abate the turmoil felt as a result of centuries of persecution. In so doing, however, Sichel loses that factor within her which makes her unique: her soul.

The burden of being a Jew was too great for Sichel. She saw only its negative side and overlooked the joys experienced in its beliefs and traditions. She opted for the collective values rather than retaining her individual cultural views. Therefore, she allowed herself to become Turelure's mistress, to attend to his accounts, to give up her piano. She tells Lumîr, "He has reduced me to the state of slavery like the ancient Israelites." She blames Turelure for her own shortcomings. Sichel did not have to become involved with Turelure. She had an exciting and comfortable life before she met him. At first, she had illusions: she thought Turelure would marry her. She realized, later, that the thought occurred to her alone.

Lumîr is centroverted: only one thought preoccupies her, the return of 10,000 francs she had lent Louis. Sichel warns her of Turelure's avarice. He will never return the money, she tells Lumîr, even though that very morning he had received 20,000 francs from Ali Habenichts for the purchase of the Coûfontaine ancestral estate: L'Arbre Dormant. The money is to be plowed back into a business, the building of a factory and other projects.

Lumîr tries to explain herself to Sichel. She had lent Louis the money because he needed it to harvest his crop in Algeria. Lumîr's brother had been Louis' companion in arms; they had later become associated in a 300-hectare agricultural project in Algiers. Now that her brother is dead, however, her cause—the unification of Poland—has taken on the dimensions of a sacred act. Nothing else matters. As Lumîr recounts her past with nostalgia—the fact that her father had fought hard for Poland, that he was a hero, that she had been brought up in a world of men—her eyes blaze. Her personality becomes adamantine, hard and brittle like the diamond, sparkling with luminosity as her name implies. Nothing will stop her from obtaining her goal: money. She would fight if necessary. Lumîr's eyes open onto her soul: energy, excitement erupts as a dream is to be fulfilled. Sichel comments on the nature of her eyes: "they stare; they are serene like those of a child . . . / But when they take on the blackness of rage and become like a fury and one can see the soul burning within. . . ."

Lumîr pursues her cause. She tells Turelure, when alone with him, that she wants her money. She argues that he should not discourage his son from his business endeavors; Turelure should inspire him to realize them. What Lumîr does not know, or will not accept, is the fact that Turelure despises his son. From the moment he was born, Louis reminded his father of Sygne, the woman he could never tame, dominate, or possess spiritually. Turelure also hated Louis because he stood for youth, futurity, and courage. Now that Turelure was old, he was afraid of being supplanted by this vigorous lad whose life was unfolding before him. Poland does not interest him; he is no longer one with revolutions. Although his ideals have vanished now that he is part of the social structure, he, nevertheless, can understand Lumîr's utopian notions. Once a revolutionary, he had experienced the need to overthrow the status quo, to live an illusion. Even now, he confesses, on certain occasions, when he hears the drum rolling at the Tuileries and sees Louis-Philippe walk from his court, he feels that intense excitement. Government today, he tells Lumîr, is a melting pot of different classes, ideologies, and ways of life.

Turelure's reminiscences, his nostalgic forays into his past, are of no interest to Lumîr. Her youth and beauty, however, attract him, and he asks her to marry him. If she rejects his offer, Lumîr knows that she should expect nothing. Proud and stately, she answers peremptorily: "I would rather die a thousand deaths than belong to you." Again the conversation revolves around money, a theme Claudel seeks to discredit, since he considers it the preoccupation of a Godless regime. To focus on money, he suggests, is to divest the world of spirituality, to regress. Yet, gold, whether used to adorn statues of saints and divinities or in the international exchange, symbolizes activity, dynamism, and growth. Gold is all-purposed: it fires and inspires; it represses and suppresses. Both positive and negative, gold is the most perfect and brilliant of metals, symbolically, igneous, solar, and royal. Gold brings enlightenment as well as perversion.

Lumîr was thus far unsuccessful in attaining her goal. Turelure would use the 20,000 francs to build his paper factory, to borrow and lend money, to increase his capital. One stumbling block existed in Turelure's world—the fear of death: "I am afraid of death," he tells Sichel. Fear is his Achilles heel. The doctor has stated that his heart is weak and that the slightest shock could kill him.

The same decor is used for Act II. The shutters are closed; despite the fact that it is daytime, candles are burning. The drama is now to be played inwardly; no outer force will intrude into this cloistered atmosphere. Turelure, Louis, Ali, Sichel, and Lumîr have just partaken in the communal meal; the breaking of the bread is a replication of the sacred ceremony.

Turelure speaks of his projects: among other activities, the foundations are being dug for the building of a paper factory. Louis talks openly of his atheism. To be part of the Zeitgeist, he suggests, is important; and while his father is discarding the books which had once been part of the abbey's library, he should also get rid of the crucifix on the floor: "It's not something one wants to have at home." Sichel is the only one who feels that the Abbey should not be torn down: it stands for a time that was and should be conserved. Louis feels no attachment to the past, still less for France, and he despises the Abbey. He prefers Algeria: the harvest, the grapes, the fertile lands, and the marvelously exciting sun.

Rejected by both of his parents, Louis has known only a loveless world; he is the product of an atmosphere of distilled hatred and anger. His father, shortly after his mother's demise, manipulated her will to divest the son of his inheritance. Louis, therefore, has no illusions either about his family or the nation he has left. His exile from his country and his religion is understandable. As for Lumîr, she too presented a problem. Louis had wanted to marry her, and now learns that Turelure is trying to steal her from him. Louis, Lumîr, and her brother had lived happily in Algeria at the outset of their agricultural enterprise. So closely knit in their suffering, in their struggles and hopes, they had virtually formed a family. In those days Lumîr had played the role of a mother figure for him: she had nursed him when he suffered from those terrible fevers, comforted him when he was overcome with despair and solitude, served as his companion and confidant. Now, however, the situation has changed. She was divesting herself of him and following her own ideals, her own illusory way of life.

Lumîr had changed. Louis was right. Since her brother had died and she had departed from Algeria, she identified more and more with a patriarchal view of life: she thought of her father's heroism, decisiveness, and fortitude. Brought up in her father's world, then in her brother's, she functioned best in the company of men. She thus expects the men who surround her now to be as brave, heroic, and honorable as those she had known. When, therefore, she sees Louis again, pusillanimous, weakly structured, virtually passive before his father, she cries out: "Rise, *hombre!* rise, I tell you!" Be aggressive; be that powerful figure that will protect her, that young man she had once known starting out on his Algerian venture: "Captain Louis-Napoleon Turelure-Coûfontaine!" His answer is *"Adsum"* ("I am present"), a statement inscribed on the Coûfontaine coat of arms and repeated several times in *The Hostage*. Nothing more emerges from Louis' lips. "You are a coward and I spit in your face," Lumîr shouts.

Weak and flabby, Louis can neither believe in her cause nor help her. He does not understand the febrile light coursing through her veins, that electric current which makes of her that fiery instrument, that power which seeks to unite what is disparate. Louis is lifeless, isolated. When Lumîr again demands her 10,000 francs and no reaction on Louis' part is forthcoming, she resorts to extreme measures. She tells him she has two pistols, one loaded with blanks, the other with real bullets. She has learned from Sichel that a shock would be sufficient to kill Turelure. The crime would not be his; he would feel no guilt. The time is ripe, she tells Louis; Sichel and her father are in the other wing of the house. They will hear nothing.

Turelure enters. Louis remains alone with his father. He defends his Algerian project before the old man and refuses to be labeled "a pleasure-loving man." On the contrary, Louis considers himself a hard worker, a conqueror. He went to Algeria at the start of the colonizing period, planted his crop, and would reap the benefits. Practically an orphan, he was not helped by his mother or father. "I am neither Turelure nor Coûfontaine"; he is himself, self-made. He threatens his father. He needs the money: 10,000 francs to save his investment from being seized (then all of his work would be for naught), and 10,000 more that he owes to Lumîr. He knows his father has the money since Ali Habenichts had given it to him that very morning. Turelure is steadfast in his refusal. Instead, he suggests that Louis return to the army and make a career of it; Turelure would help him advance.

Louis is aware of the fact that his father is afraid of death, and that he also fears his son. As a senex figure, he realizes he may be overthrown by him, thereby experiencing a psychological castration, as Cronus had emasculated his father, then becoming sovereign of the world. It all seemed preordained in the name Turelure had chosen for Sichel: sickle, that shearing and cutting instrument that Cronus carried around with him always. So Turelure, like Cronus, will become his son's victim, a patricide.

Tension grows as father and son argue. Suddenly Louis takes out his pistols, shoots at his father and misses. Turelure, however, dies from the shock. Louis rushes over to him, bends over his corpse and removes the 20,000 francs from his pocket.

Act III opens as Louis, the notary, Lumîr, and Sichel are going over Turelure's accounts, discussing his will and his investments. When Louis is alone with Lumîr, he begs for a kiss; she refuses because she sees Turelure in him and is repelled. Louis has accepted guilt: he killed his father. Patricide, overt or covert, symbolizes an adolescent's revolt against the patriarchal principle, a need for liberation.

Heraclitus wrote: "War is the father of all things."[13] For Louis, Turelure was that tension-provoking element, the obstacle which prevented him from reaping the profits of his venture. Louis saw his father as a devouring and destructive force: the divestor of his fortune, the libidinous male who sought to take Lumîr from him. He had to be destroyed in order to free Louis from playing out a perpetually negative role. Whenever Turelure was present or his influence felt, Louis was overwhelmed by a sense of defeat, paralyzed with an inferiority which prevented him from experiencing his own reality. His father's powerful personality eradicated his own.

Turelure, an archetypal image, had been conditioned by cultural values. He represented life focused on material and social gain; his was the road of the *arriviste,* the individual whose ideas fluctuate with the government in power. He stood for order, civilization, as well as revolution. He was the guardian of a certain masculine order. When Louis caused Turelure's death, he was not, however, rejecting the so-called traditional attitudes his father favored—business ventures, industrial enterprises, atheism—which would have been the true hero's course. Unlike the young Turelure, the one-time revolutionary who dreamed of changing the world, Louis has no such intention. He is no hero. He does not want to rebuild, recreate, or renew. He merely wants to tap the resources due him and glide along in life.

The true heroic figure would be the youth who leaves his land, his home, and builds a new way of life. Abraham who followed Jehovah's command: "Get thee out of thy country, and from thy kindred, and from thy father's house, unto a land that I will show thee" (Gen. 12:1). Abraham by destroying the gods of his fathers created a new world religion. Jesus' message was a restatement of a similar *renovatio.* Ideas such as these are repeated during every revolution, every period of birth.[14] They represent an individual's understanding of and rebellion against what had been, along with his desire to bring forth the new, vital, and meaningful.

In certain cases, a father's rejection of a son is that very factor which accounts for his becoming a hero. It arouses resentment in him and compels him to act; it creates incentive, tension, fire: Orestes, Heracles. Otto Rank suggested that to overcome the father is at the root of the hero's act, the basis for his superhuman performance. When Luther, symbolically, murdered the Pope/Father, and Protestants did away with his image and his function, they all abandoned the patriarchal emphasis.

In Louis' case he committed patricide, but was too weak to alter his ways, too feeble to bring forth the new. He did want to return to Algeria, but with Lumîr. He despised the French climate, the rain, the desolation, both inner and outer, and the old house falling to ruin. It was a world forever crying out its hostility to him, symbolizing the harshness of hatred, the antagonism his parents had known for each other, and which had been projected onto him. Even though Louis entreats Lumîr to accompany him, she remains unflinching in her goal. She is strong, powerful, and independent and will not yield to Louis' needs. His plan and life venture is devoid of reality for her. Only by completing her mission—her vision—can she give meaning to her life experience.

Louis and Lumîr are at crossroads: two ways of life, two continents. Lumîr feels no guilt when she refuses to follow Louis. She is free, unfettered, "alone in this vast universe." She has grown in strength. She needs no one. The ties that had once bound her to Louis have been loosened. She will go her way now that she has no father, brother, or lover. Prior to her departure, she confesses to Louis that both pistols had been loaded; she had lied to him. She had wanted him to be caught and punished for his crime so that he would not marry Sichel.

Rather than assume the blame for the patricide, so impulsively committed at the outset of the scene, Louis cries out his desperation, weakly, and angrily: "You made me commit this crime and now you abandon me." He tries to hold on to Lumîr, but she has cut her ties, cleaved relationships, severed feelings. The Sobieski sword she considers already in her possession. Thrust on her own resources, she fights for what she believes. Lumîr will not allow Louis to forget his pact: "patricide," she states emphatically.

After Lumîr's departure, Sichel, accused of being obsessed with money as all Jews reputedly are, tears up the promissory note Turelure had signed in which he stated he owed Ali 300,000 francs. "I returned / Your money and ours. Such is our cupidity." To prove herself worthy of Louis, an indication of the depth of her own feelings of inferiority, she again rejects her past, her father and his money, her ghetto ways, and in so doing confesses: "I steal from my father, I rob him and place myself at your mercy." Rather than evoking Louis' admiration, or inspiring him with esteem for her, she elicits his disgust. Sichel's very act has degraded her still further in Louis' eyes. A person ashamed of her heritage and origins inspires repugnance in others.

Louis killed his father. Sichel rejected hers. They were made for each other. Louis will marry Sichel, despite the fact that such an alliance would create a scandal. He is not afraid to blend Catholic and Jew. It is the only honorable procedure: "you desire me, my name, my future, and my fortune."

Sichel looks upon Louis as her savior, and her joy is complete. She feels unburdened. The future looks bright for one who has cast her people, the Book, and her own dignity to the wind. "I renounce my race and my blood! I execrate the past! I step on it; I dance on it; I spit on it!"

Louis reviles her pusillanimous ways, subservience, and cowed look, which reminds him of a dog: "Jewess, hold still and don't lick my hand this way, so passionately, like those horrible little feverish and affectionate dogs," he says; it is a stunning image, which sums up the very essence of the Jew who seeks to escape his identity—the Jew who attempts to do away with his uniqueness—his soul.

The Humiliated Father

The Humiliated Father is situated in Rome and focuses on a three-year period: 1869–1871. Napoleon III is Emperor of France, a land in which gaiety and glitter reign; it is a period referred to as *la belle époque.* Italy, which concerns us in *The Humiliated Father,* has been a divided land ever since the fall of the Roman Empire (A.D. 395). It was a conglomerate of jealous and warring states, some of which frequently became the pawns of outside forces. The Spanish, Austrian, and French armies fought on Italian soil for many centuries, each vying for power. A desire to unify Italy began in a serious and concrete manner after the Congress of Vienna (1815), when the allies reestablished the old order. Unrest became flagrant.

Adding to the complex nature of Italian politics was the fact that Rome was the seat of the papacy. Since late classical times the Roman Catholic Church owned vast lands throughout Italy. The pope argued that he needed all this land, which brought him wealth and temporal power, to maintain his position as spiritual guide. Yet, such an attitude presented very grave dangers for Italians. If the pope felt his power to be threatened or if he in some way disagreed with one of the monarchs ruling an Italian state, he merely had to call upon another Catholic power in the world to help him impose his ideas or will. Such had been the case on many occasions, when foreign armies were brought into the papal states to fight against Italians. This situation did not inspire contentment or feelings of security among the people. Therefore, leaders came to the fore, such as Giuseppe Mazzini (1805–1872), Camillo Cavour (1810–1861), and Giuseppe Garibaldi (1807–1882), who wanted to liberalize Italy and remove the domination of the pope in Rome. It was a difficult period for Italy and one used as a background by Claudel for *The Humiliated Father*.

Act I: A masked ball is taking place at the Villa Wronsky, an elegant home in the city of Rome. Pensée, the daughter of Louis and Sichel, is disguised as Night; her mother is Autumn, Prince Wronsky is the River Tiber, and Lady U is the city of Rome. That Claudel chose to begin his drama in an atmosphere of masquerade is significant. Masks, which have been used since the beginning of time by the most primitive and sophisticated of peoples, infuse stage happenings with a sense of eternity. The viewer is allowed to penetrate another dimension, that of fantasy, a static image—an archetype. Time, therefore, is no longer eschatological but cyclical: eternal. Actions may take place over and over again, perpetually. Masks also add a sense of mystery to the proceedings. Since they hide the individuals whose faces they cover, they confuse the viewer and inject chaos into the proceedings. In thirteenth-century France, masks were alluded to as "artifices," designed to mislead spectators as well as to terrify them. Claudel's masks may be considered as symbols, visual replicas of amorphous characteristics, revealing unconscious tendencies and sensations within the protagonists. They serve to arrest a temperament, to structure a view, as well as to baffle and confuse. At times they add a sense of malaise and irritation to the play; at other moments they underscore the spectacular beauty of the hidden individual and the poetics uttered.

That Pensée wears the costume of Night serves to exteriorize her inner world; it also defines the role she plays in the drama. Pensée is blind; her world is blackness and shadows. Hesiod wrote that Night was the "Mother of the gods"; yet Night is not only a negative and passive principle, it is also the period which precedes dawn. It is a time in which all possibilities exist in their potential condition, where all is alive, mobile, fertile, ready to be awakened. At night people dream, ideas germinate, anticipation grows, and inner riches exist in a state of virtuality. To experience Night is to participate in an indeterminate domain in which everything moves, bubbles, and acts in an indifferentiated state. Night, similar to the unconscious, is an inner ocean.

Pensée, then, is the dark potential force that spells mystery, a tremulously exciting and sinister entity. As her name indicates, Pensée stands for thought, remembrance, and meditation. Her world is experienced within her being. Her blindness forbids her to look out into the world; she may only indwell. Since ancient times, blindness has been the attribute of seers; it indicates a state of clairvoyance. To be sightless is also a mark of expiation and of sacrifice: Oedipus destroyed his eyes in order to pay for his crime; Samson was also made sightless for having yielded to temptation.[15]

Pensée also means the flower pansy, known for its beauty of shape, coloring, and the smoothness of its five petals; this uneven number indicates an unharmonious state of being, and underscores the imbalance or lack of equilibrium in Pensée. The number five for numerologists, and Claudel studied the mystical implications of numbers as discussed in *Break of Noon*, represents man, that is the earthly aspect of life; for St. John of the Cross, this flower stood for the virtues of the soul, the gathering together of the spiritual perfections; Novalis took the flower to mean a form of love, primordial nature.

All of these attributes are present in Pensée: her delicacy, sensitivity, and gentility; her highly vulnerable nature; her emotionalism and lack of balance. There is also something childlike and innocent about Pensée, as though she, a flower, were still living out her infantile fantasy in an unreal world—in a Garden of Eden. Reminiscent of Persephone, who was ravished by Hades when picking flowers with her girlfriends in Sicily, so Pensée will become the target of her own unredeemed instincts, unavowed feelings, and unconscious.

Pensée is an anima (soul) figure, an archetype of the young virgin, the pure in heart and soul: Sophia or Divine Wisdom. Yet, as an archetype, she also becomes a *complexio oppositorum*: a temptress and a harlot. Poets have been inspired by anima figures such as Dante's Beatrice in the creation of some of their most exquisite works. Once the poet projects upon his anima as maiden, daughter, sister or bride, she becomes the recipient of values, fosters illusions, and sets his imaginative spirit into action. *Esse in anima*, Jung suggests, is to be inspired by the feminine being upon whom one focuses one's unconscious mind; it is to have one's creative instinct triggered by her, and to suffer through or because of her.[16]

From the very first moment that Pensée speaks, audiences know that she lives on a different plane; life is experienced as an inner activity. She is neither bitter nor angered about her blindness; she accepts it and even believes in its positive value: "But perhaps, if I saw I wouldn't hear as well." Indeed, she suggests that she has been chosen to fulfill a very special purpose in life, since she is different, set apart from others.

Hélène Sauvaneix, Jacqueline Morane, Daniel Sarky, and Judith Magre in a scene from *The Humiliated Father*, produced by Bernard Jenny at the Théâtre de Vieux Colombier.
FRENCH CULTURAL SERVICES

When Sichel looks at her daughter's eyes, she comments on their brilliant blue color, which is so pure as to appear black at times. Although they are incapable of seeing, they shine, sparkle, scintillate, shedding light and luster about: "Others receive light but yours give it." Pensée herself compares them to grapes in season, thus associating her eyes with nutritive forces, as well as with sacrifice and mystery. "I am the vine," Christ said; he who drinks of His blood, therefore, undergoes communion, that is, experiences divinity within. Wine is also identified with the Lamb of God, who is depicted in art works, frequently, amidst thorns and bunches of grapes. Pensée's eyes, therefore, reveal multiple functions: they are an agent of sacrifice in that she is blind; they also stand for fertility, since they express so much feeling and light for others. Their blueness in its darkness exudes a sense of immateriality, transparency—a quality inherent in the sky. Purity and truth are theirs. Let us also recall that blue is the traditional color of the Virgin, who wears a blue mantle. Pensée's eyes, in that they reflect the tonalities of water in its limpid liquidity, and sky as well, are cold and impersonal, limitless in their meaning; they are not personal entities, but exist on a transpersonal domain.

Although Pensée is blind her other senses are highly developed. So acute have they become that she feels linked to the world about her. The slightest rustle in the garden or an infinitesimal breath of air makes her face glow, caresses her body; she feels its most minute vibrations and "variations." She knows the meaning of daylight and sunshine, although she has never seen them. The forces of creation are alive for her on this very special night: "Everything speaks to me, everything touches me to the bottom of my heart." Her sense of correspondence with nature allows her to hear voices, even though these timbres are inaudible to others: "He speaks and my soul trembles when I hear him." Pensée shivers as she listens to the voice of the one she loves. She already knows he is destined for her, long before the young man in question ever realizes this. Pensée's sense of hearing, touch, taste, and smell are so acute that the synesthetic experience she is now undergoing nearly dazzles her. She feels those primordial vibrations within her being, perceives a mysterious light, and listens in rapture to a voice she sees in crystal clear sounds: "I heard it: this word alone which spoke."

The word for Jews and Christians is a human form of God's voice. It is within the word that Divinity's will is contained and becomes manifest. In the Old Testament God's voice preexisted the creation. "The Lord gave the word: great was the company of those that published it" (Psalm 68:11). In the New Testament we read: "In the beginning was the Word, and the Word was with God, and the Word was God" (John 1:1).

That Pensée hears the inaudible, perhaps because of her sightlessness, indicates her penetration of another dimension, where she is able to communicate with transpersonal forces, understanding the meaning of Divine Will and Wisdom. Since such meanings penetrate through the ear, it would liken her for some to the Virgin Mary. After the Council of Nicaea (325), the notion that Mary conceived through the air became acceptable: "The Verb entered through Mary's ear." In the Salzburg Missal, it was written: "Rejoice, Virgin, Mother of Christ, who conceived through the ear." The ear, then, represents that site where divinity penetrates, the idea is nurtured, and emotion grows.

Feeling guides Pensée. In this regard she is the antithesis of her mother, who allowed tenderness and sensibility to be arrested by agreeing to give up the piano. In so doing, she cut herself off from her deepest feelings, living, henceforth, peripherally. Pensée's hearing faculties are so well developed, her musicality so profound, that the pitch and harmonics of her beloved's voice inhabit her profoundly. So acute is it, that it makes her grow dizzy; it disorients her. Joy and pain become one; opposites merge. Her mood alters and becomes one of exaltation; her happiness is unbounded, as are her fears. Opposition is expressed in an oxymoron: "Happy shadows which permit me to be so well hidden."

An immense upheaval is taking place in her soul now that love has intruded. She is intoxicated, thus identifying with the earlier image of grapes. The vine and the wine, attributes of both Christ and Dionysus, not only allow for ecstatic visions of a divine nature, but they may also attract cruel and frightening images, such as the Maenads, those

ancient dismemberers who figure so powerfully in
Euripides' *The Bacchae*, or God's grapes of wrath as described in Revelation (14:18–20). Pensée's instincts, dormant until now, erupt with crescendo force; unchanneled
sexual urges break through as the earth principle is
awakened by the voice she hears and the thrill she feels.

Wine, the vine, and grapes are also associated with The
Song of Songs, a work Claudel read and reread. "For thy
love is better than wine" (1:2), the lover said to his beloved,
"let me hear thy voice; for sweet is thy voice" (3:14), thereby
combining spiritual intoxication with earth forces. Pensée
has not rejected Judaism as her mother had. On the contrary, and despite the fact that she was baptized, Claudel
maintains, she identifies with her ancestors. Her mother
even compares her to "La Fiancée de Salomon." (Claudel
is in error here. According to Jewish law, if a Jewish girl
converts or is baptized, she cannot retain her religious
affiliation.) Pensée understands the practical reasons involved in her mother's change of faith, but she does not
follow in her footsteps. On the contrary, she is detached
from both parents, although she honors them and maintains good relations with them. She lives in another order,
sphere, and world. The realm of politics, economics, and
organized religion do not concern her.

Sichel tries to guess the name of Pensée's beloved.
Which of the two brothers has aroused her daughter's passion? Is it Orso de Homodarmes or Orian de Homodarmes?
Both are orphans; both are nephews of the pope. Orso is the
more handsome of the two, but it is Orian, we learn later,
whom Pensée loves. Sichel tries to reason with her daughter. Neither will love a blind girl, she says. Pensée knows
differently. She asks her mother not to mention the fact that
she is blind. They are newly arrived in Rome and no one yet
knows she is sightless. She knows how to get around the

room in which the masquerade is being given; she also knows every corner of the garden outside the villa. Moreover, Pensée senses everything: "My foot alone tells me where I am, a thousand noises, a thousand touches, a thousand tonal differences that you do not hear, a thousand signs as instantaneous as a look." Distances hold no secret for her, since she has second sight, "I am warned inwardly about everything." Her inner world is rich with premonitions, wealthy with feelings, unlimited in sublime notions. Past, present, and future cohabit in her life; time and space are experienced simultaneously in an eternal present.

Orian enters. Pensée has already sensed his presence. Her fantasy has gained dominance over her. Reminiscent of the hero in fairy tales, Orian resembles those beings who fight their way through brambles and boars, to reach the treasure hard to attain—the princess. Orian is dressed as a gardener; a modern prototype of Adam, who cultivated God's garden before the Fall and who has frequently been alluded to in religious and poetic works as a gardener. In The Song of Songs, "A garden inclosed is my sister, my spouse; a spring shut up, a fountain sealed" (4:12). The garden, then, is a place for growth, dreams, anxiety, fear, for the cultivation of inner and vital phenomena. Orian, then, is the guardian of the garden; the preserver of the culture within. Pensée is the flower.

Onomastically, Orian's name may be associated with the word orientation: the process of ordering one's way; channeling one's instincts; becoming aware of one's place in time; gaining insight into one's being. It also indicates a means of viewing a new set of conditions, an altered ideology. To turn eastward, toward the Orient, is to view the rising sun in all of its gemlike brilliance.

Orian is a complex figure. Although he is the gardener[17] who seeks to keep Pensée in line, contained within the garden gates, grounded within the preconceived structure, his name may be euphonically identified with the brilliant constellation Orion, the giant hunter who was placed in the sky after Diana accidentally killed him. Within him exists a complex of opposites: a struggle for containment and at the same time a need to destroy the container.

Orso, Orian's brother, is an engineer. Handsome, ordered in his way, gentle, he enjoys life, accepts its tribulations and responsibilities. Although he loves Pensée, he knows it is Orian whom she loves and will not try to disturb this profound feeling. Unlike Orian, who believes he has a higher cause to fulfill in life, Orso does not suffer from youthful inflation. He enters the festivities at the masquerade ball with mixed emotions: feeling both joy and fear. He understands the law of polarities and of attraction; he is awake and can see into the world.

Claudel introduces two fascinating archetypal figures into the proceedings: Lady U (dressed as the city of Rome) and Prince Wronsky (as the River Tiber). Lady U, reminiscent of the ancient Greek chorus, is involved in the action and yet remains apart from it; she prefigures the climate to be delineated and also replicates a distant past.[18] As the city of Rome, she is feminine, as are so many cities which figure in religious writings: the "harlot" Babylon, the "celestial" Jerusalem, and so forth. According to Medieval thought, man was but a pilgrim on earth, his stay here was a passage from earth to celestial conditions—from one city to another. The city also symbolizes the Mother: protector of her children within the city gates (womblike), or stifler of her offspring, if she prevents change. Romulus and Remus founded the city of Rome. It was over the city that they fought; it was the city which led to Romulus' fratricide. In *The Humiliated Father*, Rome has become a battleground between lay and religious forces. Within the city, conflict and turmoil coexist. Lady U, as the city of Rome, says that she is a good Catholic; she could not and would not destroy the city by war, but she understands the fluidity implicit in life and would not, therefore, be averse to a new age. Rome is Italy; it is unity. Reminiscent at times of the legendary Oracles and Sibyls which used to people the ancient world, so Lady U replicates those transpersonal beings who allow mortals to commune with cosmic forces. She is the spokeswoman for the new order and the container of the old.

Prince Wronsky, as the River Tiber, is also archetypal. The Tiber flows through Rome, thereby dividing the city into the old and the new. An impoverished Pole, whose villa has been bought by rich bourgeois, he must face an uncertain present and feels nostalgia for a glorious past. On the lapel of his jacket he wears a cameo, a sculpture of Lumîr's face. Now that she is dead, he says, she lives only as a memory: the grandeur that was.

When Prince Wronsky sees Lady U, he hardly recognizes her. She is lionesque, he suggests, therefore, energetic, powerful, a sun figure that lights the way. As symbols of wisdom and power and the guardians of mystery, lions were carved on Solomon's throne; they were also a symbol of Christ. It is within Lady U, then, within the city of Rome, that unknown forces are coalescing, powerful entities live inchoate. "All is filled with intrigue, love, conspiracy and music," she tells Prince Wronsky. Rome is a melting pot, a cauldron, a witches' brew, filled with encountering fluids, altering elements, refreshing concepts, and new alloys. It represents the end of the status quo: constriction, autocracy, and theocracy; and the onset of a new and more liberal existential condition—the era of the common man.

Louis Coûfontaine-Turelure, ambassador from France, enters. His function is to protect the pope against Republican forces. Personally, he is antagonistic to the Church, which he considers retrograde and no longer valid in purpose. He senses that something is ending on this night; the twilight of the Gods is coming to pass: Death and Resurrection. Yet, he will do nothing to activate the situation, to add to the dynamics of already strained circumstances: "My name is peace, accord, conciliation, transaction, entente, goodwill, reciprocity," he says.

Lady U looks at Orian and comments on the beauty of his ring. A family jewel, he answers, called "the stone which sees clearly." The stone he wears, then, has visionary powers, perception; it is prophetic. One merely has to close one's eyes to see it clearly: "It is there; it guides you through obscurity." It spells magic and mystery, virtues which stones have always possessed as attested by the ka'ba for the Muslims and "the altar stone" erected by God for the Hebrews (Exodus 20:25; Deut. 27:5). As opposed to sand, for example, the stone represents durability, frangibility; it is a solid form of creative and cosmic rhythms.

Pensée calls the stone in Orian's ring a sapphire; and she is correct. It is the color and luster of Pensée's sightless eyes. Interestingly, the sapphire used to be placed near eyes in Medieval times to cure inflammation; it was also used in the treatment of ophthalmological diseases. Golden rings set with sapphires were placed on the ring finger of a Cardinal's right hand when he was elected pope, symbolizing the fact that "the Church is now his spouse and he must never abandon her." Sapphires adorn God's throne: "And above the firmament that was over their heads was the likeness of a throne, as the appearance of a sapphire stone" (Ezekiel 1:26). Sapphire is the jewel associated with September, a period which Pensée fears.

Orian's sapphire is surrounded with diamonds and set in gold. The diamond (Sanskrit *dyu* meaning "luminous being," "light," and "brilliance") is connected with the Greek word *adamas* (adamantine) defined as "unconquerable." The diamond irradiates moral, spiritual, and intellectual values. It represents the treasure hard to attain: clarity, purity, illumination, and wisdom. To possess a diamond is to be in the process of realizing one's purpose; it denotes a quest which entails extreme difficulty. A diamond, such as the one worn by Orian, is pure in state and perfect in necessity. For Orian to achieve such a spiritual condition requires great strength and fortitude: he must polish his character traits in order to bring out their hidden light and luster, to force out their luminosity which lies buried within the darkest recesses. Only then, when the various stages of the evolutionary process have been completed, will sovereignty and incorruptibility emerge.

The ring itself is a closed circle, reflecting notions of continuity and eternity. It is said that Prometheus was the first to wear a ring set with sapphires; it was given him after he had been reintegrated into the pantheon of gods, following the conclusion of his ordeal. Orian's ring radiates flame, excitement, and passion. It takes on the brilliance of a constellation, whose function is to battle darkness and fight the unredeemed or unconscious elements surrounding it. "And they that be wise shall shine as the brightness of the firmament; and that they turn the many to righteousness as the stars for ever and ever" (Daniel 12:3).

Orian approaches Pensée, and an exquisite love duet ensues: soul and spirit blend with flesh and earth. Pensée takes hold of Orian's ring, places it in front of her at eye level, and uses it to guide her steps through the garden. Orian is unaware of her blindness; to make certain her sightlessness remains a secret, Pensée uses the verb "to see" throughout the dialogue. The ring is a substitute eye; a psychopomp, a guide to the soul, a representative of unity of being. It is the outer manifestation of the eye, with which Plotinus, St. Augustine, and St. Paul indicated heart and mind; the eye of God. As Pensée walks about the stage holding the diamond and sapphire ring, she speaks of the intense joy she is now experiencing, in this, the month of May. Her anguish mounts, however, when pronouncing the word September, which ushers in the winter, when nature will be denuded and virtually lifeless.

Pensée confesses her feelings of pain at what Orian must consider a humiliating experience: her father has purchased Orian's home and garden. Although he is poor, he tells Pensée, he feels happy now that he is free and unencumbered with worldly things. His interests and destiny live elsewhere: with the pope, his Church, and his religion. He is the gardener of the religious structure, the fighter for the status quo. Material entities pass, "The Pope is that which does not pass."

Pensée tells Orian that she knows Orso wants to marry her but that he should not. She considers herself a Jew, and although baptized, still is identified with her people. "You need a lot of water to baptize a Jew!" Centuries of tradition are alive within her: "I feel as if I bear within me all the centuries since the creation of the world." Although Jews have been martyred, persecuted, and exiled, they were placed on earth to fulfill a function, to represent a way of life: they are repositories for divinity: the People of the Book. Moreover, "A soul like mine cannot be baptized with water, but with blood." A blood sacrifice is required in Claudel's drama so that redemption comes to pass; endowing participants with "the grace of inspiration" and eternal life.[19]

Pensée and Orian look at each other with rapture. Both are young and filled with life and the joy of existence. She feels the beauty of a moonlit night with its warmth exuded by the flowers and the coming of dawn. She loves and is loved, and although she cannot see, she compares herself to "The Synagogue," a statue featured on some French Cathedrals of a woman looking downward, whose eyes are covered; she trembles with anticipation and fervor.

Pensée's love for Orian is pure, beautiful, and complete. His feelings, on the other hand, are complex and divided. He cannot marry Pensée because he would betray his cause in life, his obligations to the Church and the pope. "You are made for love, Pensée, and love is not made for me," he tells her. Although he sees his soul engraved in hers, he cannot give himself to love fully. It is at this moment that Orian asks her to raise her eyes and look at him; it is at this instant that she reveals her blindness.

Act II takes place in a Franciscan cloister near Rome. The pope is seated. A veritable senex figure, he is weak, powerless, and depressed. He speaks of his desolation and disenchantment. The political and religious unrest has taken its toll on his well being. He feels he has suffered at the hands of his children; he is no longer omniscient or omnipotent, the ordering principle he once was. The breakdown of the man is a replica of the deterioration of the structure which he serves.

The pope is a stereotypic figure: no longer an inspiration to the masses, he appears on stage as a faltering and doddering man whose lamentations underscore the static condition of his personality and ideations. He stands for degeneration. What he offers the multitude is evidently no longer valid: a tightly structured religious institution, unbending and unyielding, unwilling to take changing times into consideration, opposed to people hungering for freedom. Mazzini, Garibaldi, Cavour and their representatives and followers were fighting hard to do away with the vast papal states. Rome, he realizes, is no longer his; it belongs to the Italians.

A spirit of levity is imposed on the scene with the arrival of Orian and Orso. They are teasing each other; each wants the other to marry Pensée. Orso knows his brother loves Pensée and is loved by her. Gentle, altruistic, Orso wants his brother's happiness more than his own. Moreover, he tells Orian and the pope that he is really a soldier; he will not father a family and, therefore, Orian should marry Pensée.

Neither should wed Pensée, the pope says. He is aghast at their choice. Louis Coûfontaine-Turelure is an enemy of the papacy. To marry a blind girl, whose mother was Jewish, makes matters even more serious, and an alliance such as they propose is impossible. As for loving Pensée, he states categorically, love does not even enter into marriage: "But marriage is not for pleasure, it is the sacrifice of pleasure; it is the study of two souls which, for always, must content themselves with one another for some inexplicable reason." According to the pope, marriage is a religious and legal bond, a sacrament, which helps fulfill a life function: to bring children into the world and to continue religious traditions. Indeed, earthly love is almost a sin; it prevents a spotless, incorruptible, and perfect life experience. To know love and fulfillment on the earthly sphere is to detract from one's obligation to and immersion in divinity.

Orian is also averse to marriage. He cannot give Pensée what she wants. "She asks for my soul, and I absolutely cannot give it to her, / [since I'm] not in possession of it myself." He is correct in his assessment of himself. His soul is not his own; it belongs to God. On an aesthetic plane, it represents poetic imagination, the as yet uncreated, the world of infinite possibilities, a preformal structure; psychologically, it stands for the Self, that is, the entire Psyche and, therefore, Orian is not free to give that which transcends the ego (the conscious personality) and is not his. That Orian desires Pensée is incontestable: as an anima figure, she draws him out of his individual sphere, his temporal existence (his ego), and lures him beyond the sensately real. It is she who spins the reverie. She is temptation!

The pope comments on Orian's inner struggle and the sadness which he feels has engulfed the young lad. Half-jesting, half-mocking, he asks: "Tell me, are these bonds with the earth so strong?" He wants Orian to remain with him, preparing himself for his tribulations, those that await the servants of God. Orian must learn the joy of sacrifice, the pleasures of divesting himself of worldly accouterments, and terrestrial love. He knows that Pensée is "danger, night, fatality!" A feeling of terror grips his heart.

The notion of sacrifice (sexual or otherwise), which has reached chronic proportions in Claudel's dramas, indicates a need to annihilate physical pleasure in an attempt to prove one's devotion to divinity; psychologically, it implies a compulsion to demonstrate one's power over oneself, and in this context, it is an example of hubris. If sacrifice is given for personal reasons, however, it has no value. A sacrifice is valid only when it entails complete giving: the acceptance of its destruction.[20] Abraham's sacrifice of Isaac was complete as was Christ's. Orian, however, knew he could not give himself to Pensée because he did not own himself; he did not understand his needs or his instinct. He was not in possession of himself. His ego had not yet been scrutinized; his ideations had not been consciously contemplated. The meaning and implication of his gift (the sacrifice of his sexuality in marriage) for Church and God was still experienced as an impulse, an adolescent urge. Orian needed time to sort out his feelings and to understand the consequences of his purpose in life.

That the pope and Church demanded such a sacrifice of Orian, indicates their devouring and destructive attitudes: their need to become self-perpetuating, to remain fixed, rigid, immobile. To pursue such a way necessitates the rejection of woman, since the anima figure prefigures archetypal change. Unlike *Golden Head*, in which the *senex* king was killed, it is the *puer* (boy) in *The Humiliated Father* who will be mutilated. The senex figure lives on; it is preserved, at least for the time being.

Act III. The year is 1870. The Revolution is underway in Rome; the Franco-Prussian War has commenced in France. In a week—at the end of September—Orian is scheduled to join the French forces. Pensée wants to see him again before his departure for the front and he acquiesces.

Pensée tells Orian of her feelings of abandonment. If he could tell her he no longer loves her, she would understand and go her way, voluntarily secluding herself. Orian, however, cannot bring himself to utter such an untruth; he cannot, therefore, alleviate her pain. On the contrary, she represents "danger" for him, he tells her; she is an obstacle to his quest, his search for *light*. To seek out divinity requires isolation on his part, purity, and spirituality. Psychologically, he must plumb his own depths. He must define himself, find his essence and equilibrium. A period of soul-searching must come to pass.

Orian cannot function in this new utilitarian age, he implies, with its factories, industries, and technology; it is a world which replaces the brilliantly green fields and gloriously crystal-blue lakes with soot and oily residue. He is glad she cannot see the change taking place. Chaos also inhabits his inner realm, because he admits to her that he thinks of her nightly. She disturbs his peace, his equilibrium. She fills his dreams in his slumber; he hears her voice, which traumatizes him. He considers it a premonition of their separation. Orian struggles against his feelings, against the growing turmoil invading his being. Why was Pensée placed in his path? Why was she tempting him? She was everywhere in his life, his thoughts, his senses. "To see each other, to speak, to listen to the other talk," he believed was sufficient. He repeats: he cannot give her his soul, nor can he give her eternity. These are not his to give.

Orian knows, unconsciously, perhaps, that he will be drawn into her web: the sexual urge is powerful and the act will be perpetrated. As he speaks to her in the most tender terms, as he makes known his love for her, he still fights his instincts, his desire for fulfillment in her. The momentum accelerates: the more he struggles against his need, the more he enjoys the dynamics involved; the irritant and counterirritant, the energy, the friction. A force engulfing his senses, suddenly, dazzles his mind, as madness overtakes him. His sexuality has leaped over the barriers his conscious mind has erected; constriction and morbidly limiting dogma are buried as psychic energy erupts, allowing the archaic and untapped contents of his being to gush forth. The rigidity of his adaptation to life, constructed so slowly and precisely during the course of his early years, has now been disarranged.

Orian, it might be said, lusted after the sin he so desperately sought to annihilate; he savored it, wanted it, was mesmerized by it. Pensée had touched off certain psychic elements within him, which then flooded his being. His ideas concerning the Church and his mission in life were evidently not strong enough to stem the tide: he had been until this time, a "puppet of fate,"[21] of circumstances. Never had he sifted his feelings, analyzed his ideations on a profound level. Rather than integrating the disparate forces within him, he repressed some and totally adapted others. When, therefore, the anima figure presented itself to him in all of her radiance, she was temptation, because she represented that which he had tried to extinguish within himself, those elements lurking about in dark corners ready to burst forth when sparked with energy.

Act IV takes place in January 1871. Pensée is inhaling the perfume from a most exquisite bouquet of flowers. The aroma invades her body, and she utters a little cry. Exultation, ecstasy. She has just felt the first signs of life within her. The breath of a living being, of another soul now inhabiting her world. A force is building within her—a being which she is sustaining with her flesh and blood—a child who will unite the divided in her world and Orian's; multiple attitudes, social classes, and religious ideations. Pensée is no longer the virgin; she is the mother-to-be, no longer the sister, but the beloved. She has taken on the stature of the city of Rome.

Pensée's joy is so intense and complete that she compares herself to a child awakening from slumber "in a closed room," going into "an unknown land." Pensée asks her mother if she is ashamed of her pregnancy. No, Sichel answers, but she has not mentioned it to Pensée's father. No one has yet noticed Pensée's condition. Since she is only four months pregnant, the secret may still be kept. As for Pensée, she sings out her jubilation, her rapture—the happiness at being able to participate in a cosmic act—that of creation.

Pensée's joy, however, is short-lived. Orso arrives. Orian has been killed in battle, he tells her. It was his heart that Orso sent to her in the basket of flowers; the very life force that she inhaled and, in so doing, transferred his energetic principle into that of his child. It was Orian's wish, he informs her, that he marry her. Pensée rejects the idea; she could live with no one but Orian. Orso is aware of this and offers to live with her as brother and sister. Her child would then be given a name and legal status. Pensée agrees: "I shall live for this obscure child who is the legatee of my soul and of his."

Claudel's trilogy, which opened shortly after Napoleon's exile and concluded with the birth of a unified Italy, takes the viewer through a period of religious and political upheaval. It also penetrates the very heart of Claudel's emotional and spiritual problem: his view of sacrifice and his perpetual struggle to maintain some semblance of purity of soul. Claudel's conflict, experienced through his protagonists, revolves around the forces of Good and Evil, or the divine in man as opposed to the world of instinct. What is arresting in his struggle is the intense sensuality implicit in the dialogue he uses to describe undergoing the battle against the sin of the flesh and the committing of the sin. Such friction gives rise to excitement; it engenders fire, which then releases a powerful flow of energy, that is sublimated, finally, in the *scintillae* of inspiration and creation and lived out in the sexual act by the protagonists. Pensée is temptation; she is flesh. She is also anima—soul—that force, luring and alluring the poet, which lives deeply in his unconscious and emerges full-blown in the clash when his spiritual outlook is antipodal to his earth being. Evil and Good are alive and active phenomena in Claudel's world. Pensée is the spokeswoman for his gnosticism: "there is no resigning to evil; there is no resigning to the lie; there is only one thing to do when confronted with evil and that is to destroy it." To destroy Evil/Eve, the Temptress, that dangerous factor which leads the artist astray, irritating his very fiber, is to destroy the essence of his creative urge, his lifeblood as poet.

The trilogy explores more incisively than any of Claudel's dramas his motivations and attitudes in the existential sphere. Unlike his great religious dramas, *Golden Head, Break of Noon, The Tidings Brought to Mary,* the trilogy deals with the realities of life. On the whole it is devoid of poetry. The world he brings forth on stage is not beautiful; the people are sordid and their ways deleterious. Each in his own way is a mirror image of Claudel.

8. THE DIARY OF CHRISTOPHER COLUMBUS: A DEMIURGE JOURNEYS FORTH

The Diary of Christopher Columbus (1927) is unique in Claudelian dramaturgy. This strange and haunting play of a hero figure journeying forth on his global trajectory is a dream fulfilled. *The Diary of Christopher Columbus* not only combines Claudel's poetics, based on powerful imagery, rhythmic and breathing techniques, stylized gestures, religiously oriented themes, and intensely cruel love episodes, but it is also, technically speaking, adventuresome. By combining the eurythmics of Emile Jaques-Dalcroze, the film projection techniques of Erwin Piscator, and by using the vast scenic spaces in spectacularly new ways, as Max Reinhardt had suggested, Claudel succeeded in injecting an outerworldly climate into the play's physical and spiritual realm. That he also applied some of the techniques used in Japanese Bunraku and Noh theatre is understandable, since he had lived in the Orient for so many years.

The Diary of Christopher Columbus is a reworking of Claudel's favorite themes—subsumed in *Golden Head*, the Coûfontaine cycle, *Break of Noon*, and *The Satin*

236

Slipper—that of the adventurer, the discoverer who is mis-understood, rejected, and vilified. Claudel certainly identified with this kind of creative spirit, which he looked upon as the prototype of the poet: a demiurge, whose overwhelming ambition encourages him to break ties with family and friends, as well as with his land. Compelled by a dream, he forges ahead into the unknown, the untraveled, a world of mystery and terror; there, he bares his solitude, living out his sacrificial role and torment.

Claudel had said, repeatedly, that the man Christopher Columbus had "haunted" him for many years. This quasilegendary figure fired his imagination. He saw him as a giant "assembler" and "re-assembler" of disparate earthly factors, of land masses; a man who succeeded in bringing together divergent segments of life and humanity.[1] For Claudel, whose psyche and soma were so divided, Colum-bus represented an ideal, a global force; he sanctified the profane. Claudel's drama may be looked upon as a giant awakening—a gathering together and activation of somno-lent forces—the *naissance* and *co-naissance* of privileged moments, when the poet/adventurer pierces through the mysteries of the yet unborn. Here he thrashes about, up-rooting, dislodging the *prima materia*, bringing forth the treasure—the colossal poem.

Max Reinhardt had commissioned Paul Claudel and Darius Milhaud to write an opera. *The Diary of Christopher Columbus* was the result. It was produced in Berlin at the Grand Opera (1930); it was also performed as an oratorio on several occasions.[2] Claudel looked upon music as a means to accentuate and prolong both lyrical and dramatic mo-ments, emphasizing words, gesture, and the composition of scenic design.[3] This was not the first time Claudel and his long-standing friend, Milhaud, had worked together. The score for *The Tidings Brought to Mary* had also been

Milhaud's. Claudel had used musical accompaniment for *The Woman and Her Shadow*, produced in Tokyo (1923), which called for Japanese music and instrumentalists.

Milhaud's music played a multiple role in *The Diary of Christopher Columbus*. It sustained the action, but it also counteracted it, creating excitement and heightening tension. It injected irritating and brash sonorities into the stage happenings, as well as tremulously moving tones, thereby creating a contrapuntal impression. The periods of protracted silence accentuated the play's fearful and awesome sides, adding to its dimension of sacrality. Music frequently served to build power, to inject the scenes with cumulative force, forming energetic charges, which discharged their violence, leaving audiences and protagonists gasping for breath, as if on the edge of a gaping void.[4] Music blended with the stage happenings and was severed from them: speech, rhythms, moods reacted in consort.[5]

Facts surrounding the lives of heroes are usually scanty and shrouded in mystery. Those concerning Christopher Columbus, the mythic voyager, are no exception. Biographies usually place his birth in Genoa (1451–1506), refer to his father as a weaver by trade, and suggest that he became a seaman at an early age. He grew in this profession, and by the age of thirty-one, became master mariner in port merchant service. His dream, however, which he called "The Enterprise of the Indies," a voyage to the West, was still unrealized. After he had met with some difficulty in finding financing, Ferdinand and Isabella of Spain finally agreed to Columbus' plan. The sailing date was set for Aug. 3, 1492. After experiencing a mutiny, sickness, storms, and virtual starvation, Columbus and his crew finally reached a land he named "Hispaniola." He left some of his men there to found a colony. Upon his return to Spain, he was greeted with fanfare, made an "admiral of the ocean sea," and appointed governor general of the areas he had discovered.

In October 1493, Columbus was again outfitted with a large fleet and set sail for a second time, discovering St. Kitts, the Virgin Islands, Puerto Rico, Jamaica, Cuba, and more. His colonists at Hispaniola, he now realized, were interested in gold, alone; they had become unruly, and when Columbus attempted to maintain order, they complained to Spain. A new governor was appointed (1500) and Columbus was brought back to Spain in chains. Released, he again pursued his dream, sailing to Trinidad and what is Venezuela today. His popularity, however, had vanished. Times had changed. Other navigators—younger, stronger— were sailing the seven seas, among them, Amerigo Vespucci, after whom the new continent would be named. Columbus' zeal, nevertheless, did not flag. He still hoped to find Asia and left on yet another expedition. The hardships experienced this time were harrowing. After being marooned in Jamaica, then rescued, he returned to Spain, where he died, impoverished and alone: a forgotten man.

A movement to canonize Columbus was begun by the archbishop of Burgos and Mexico, as well as by the primate of Bordeaux. They spoke and wrote of his courage, his fortitude; they spoke of him as the spreader of the Gospel, the converter of thousands of souls to Catholicism. Although Pope Pius IX read the documents relating to Columbus, canonization never came to pass. Too little was known about him, it was said. For Claudel, however, Columbus was worthy of sanctification. He was, as his name indicated, Christopher, the Christ-Bearer, and Columbus, the *colombe*, or dove, identified with the Noah legend as well as that of the Holy Ghost.

Although the Diary kept by Columbus during his journeys is no longer extant, fragments of it do remain, thanks to the Dominican Bartolome de Las Casas, who had Fernandez de Navareete copy them. It is upon this work, among others, that Claudel based his play.[6]

Part I of *The Diary of Christopher Columbus*, consisting of eighteen short scenes, opens with a processional. Officers, musketeers, halberdiers march onto the stage; banners of Aragon and Castille are carried about in celebration of the newly unified Spain and its monarchs, Ferdinand and Isabella. A young assistant carries a Book—*The Diary of Christopher Columbus*—which he places with great solemnity on a desk, set on a small platformlike area to the side of the stage. A Chanter walks toward the desk, "pompously," and alone, drawing attention to himself. People, carrying all sorts of objects (books, flowers, bottles of wine, baskets filled with musical scores) make up the Chorus. In a playful mood, they poke each other; they eat apples. The Chanter opens the Book to the accompaniment of trumpet blasts. He speaks out in clear and precise tones: Here is "The Book of the Life and Voyages of Christopher Columbus who discovered America!"[7] He explains that it is Columbus who "reunited the Catholic Land and made of it a single globe beneath the Cross."

The Chanter sets the tone of the scene, dividing the stage between narrator and actor. During the course of the play, frequently, two activities will occur simultaneously. This duality is geared to emphasize man's essential division: soul and flesh, good and evil, as well as the natural multiplicity inherent in the world of contingencies. At times the Chanter reinforces the stage atmosphere by interrogating or inciting the protagonists, remonstrating with them for their ways, repelling or capturing their feelings. At other times the Chanter may remain aloof, cold, and alienated from the proceedings. When the focus is on the protagonists rather than on the Chanter, audiences are made privy to all types of vocalizations: from harsh and throaty screeches to mellifluous modes; from grunts and hiccuping sounds to accented rhythmic beats either in the sonorities called for by the dialogue or in the thumpings of the feet, contrasting or paralleling the narrated sequences.

The Chanter is an important element in Bunraku (Japanese puppet theatre). Along with the Shamisen (accompaniment) and the puppets, he helps create the spectacle. Puppet theatre dates back to the beginning of time in Japan, and Bunraku is one of its forms. Unlike the traditional dolls used throughout antiquity, Bunraku's puppets are larger and manipulated by three people, two of whom are dressed in black capes and hoods. The Chanter (or narrator) speaks on the puppet's behalf, relating events, explaining emotions and situations.[8]

Claudel's Chanter draws attention to himself and to the reality of the Book he is reading. He also manipulates events according to his understanding, scrutinizing actions and peoples, satirizing, commenting upon the activities, whether past, present, or future. He distinguishes between the real Columbus and the legendary figure who lives powerfully in the audience's mind. It is the Chanter, then, who creates illusion and also forces reality to intercede.

In an expository sequence, the Chanter explains the scenes to be enacted. As he speaks in cadenced sentences and rhythmic clauses, the rear of the stage, bathed in blackness, now sparks life, confusion; a conglomeration of hushed murmurs invades the atmosphere. A screen emerges from the depths of the stage, as if from chaos. An "enormous globe" and a "luminous" dove are projected. The audience now concentrates on film, their attention having been drawn away from the Chanter who stands virtually motionless on his platform.

Claudel was not the first dramatist to include filmed sequences in his theatrical works. Erwin Piscator (so popular in the Berlin of the 1920's) used lantern slides, newsreels, and documentaries to underscore his leftist political

ideology. He felt the cinematographic technique im-
plemented his philosophy; it aroused audiences and could
be used effectively for propaganda purposes. The plays
which he directed, such as *Fahnen (Flags)* in 1924, described as "epic drama," consisted of loosely knit scenes,
sketches, films, and declaimed sequences, held together for
the most part by one or several narrators.[9]

Claudel used this same filmic device and for similar
reasons—to point up his religious beliefs—as well as for
aesthetic reasons. Although theatrical purists, such as
Jean-Louis Barrault who produced *The Diary of Christopher Columbus* (1953), were weary of introducing a
mechanical medium into a world swirling with life and
activity, they had to agree to the dramatic advantages of this
procedure. It enlarged objects to be used on stage (such as a
dove) which might otherwise have remained virtually invisible from the back of the orchestra or the balcony; it syn-
thesized, by combining a variety of stage activities in the
screen image, and it also brought simultaneity to what
could have simply become a chaotic hodge-podge.[10]

As the globe, which is projected onto the screen, turns on
its axis, and the "luminous" dove flies to and fro, its
radiance injecting an outerworldly quality into the proceedings, the Chorus declaims the biblical verses of Creation:[11]

> And the earth was without form, and void; and darkness was
> upon the face of the deep. And the Spirit of God moved upon
> the face of the waters *(Gen. 1:2)*.

The Chorus, as used by Claudel, is both observer and
commentator yet intervenes in the drama as the events
progress. Describing these, it frequently sides for or against
the protagonists. The Chorus may also explain the characters' inner lives, responding and corresponding to the poetic
innuendoes and oscillations narrated by the Chanter. The

Chorus' declamatory procedures vary: at times it murmurs; at the other instances it cries out, screeching, wailing, groaning; they speak in sing-song tonalities or delightful cadences, reinforcing either the mystical elements or workaday factors. When reciting biblical verses, the Chorus litanizes, psalmodizes in rhythmic arrangements, fusing or drowning, alienating stage/spectator relationships; it underscores words, sounds, and images, sometimes by drowning them out or by swallowing them.

Claudel's Chorus differs from that of antiquity. It is modeled after the church choirs and represents that sacred link between the parishioner and the priest. A voice was needed, Claudel iterated, to express the Church's official message, its feelings and dictates, to the mute crowd invading the cathedral.[12] The Chorus in *The Diary of Christopher Columbus* is an active participant in the dramatic procedure: it adds, comments, relates, describes, explains, answers, incites, cajoles, intervenes, and unravels the mysteries enacted on stage, on both personal levels. It is a collective force; a "memory," Claudel wrote.[13]

The Chanter interrupts. We are now at Valladolid, Spain, he declares. Christopher Columbus enters. He walks onto a sloping platform which fills the stage area. He is old, dying, poor, and treated as a pariah. Unlike the characters in some of Claudel's previous plays, there is no attempt at psychological analysis in *The Diary of Christopher Columbus*. The protagonists neither grow nor evolve in personality structure. They are not real creatures, flesh and blood beings. Rather they are unidimensional figures, more like marionettes; they are but ambulatory ideas clothed in human garb, airy notions instead of solid forms. As such, they deepen the mystery of their existence and involvement in life's course, thereby strengthening the spell cast by the dramatist.

The Chanter explains that Columbus has few possessions left, among them an old and faithful mule, which he loves above all else, and its harness. He is afraid that they may be taken from him. We watch Columbus unpack the rest of his meager belongings: books, papers, the portrait of a woman, and chains. He looks around, furtively. He hears the Chanter's voice calling him by name. He does not understand. The Chorus explains. They represent posterity. They will stand in judgment of him. Still he does not comprehend. They tell him he has discovered a land without really knowing what he has done. No, Columbus counters. He knew what he was doing: "What I knew was infinitely greater than what I discovered!" Eternity belongs to him; the legend is his, the Chorus declares, not merely the land masses stamped onto a map, delimited by a globe. The Chorus asks him to walk out of the limited world he inhabits, the existence imposed upon him by reality—the earth, circumstances—and join them on that other side, in death. Columbus steps away from his chains and his poverty; he agrees to examine his life, which will now unfold before him, and he will respond in kind to those who are called to evaluate and judge his activities and oppose his views. He will live through his story now, as both actor and objective bystander, involved and alienated from the events, in consort with his present reality as well as imbricated into mythical dimension.

To effect such a dichotomy, Claudel resorted to the technique of *dédoublement*: he created two Columbuses. Christopher Columbus I will live out the events on the proscenium as he experiences them during his early sojourn: as a man driven by a dream, compelled to act, to travel to the ends of the earth by the force of God. Christopher Columbus II is the legendary figure who observes the actor completing his worldly existence. He sees things from another perspective, accepts matters objectively, and enjoys the glory and fame which belong to legend. By using this "double register,"[14] Claudel broke through the space/time continuum, integrating both linear and cyclical time schemes. Time, therefore, is a *complexio oppositorum*: it is active and passive, transposed and fixed, concentrated and diffused, solid and liquid. By the same token, Claudel has divested his work of the usual stage conventions of the well-made play; he also achieves, frequently, the breadth and scope of Aeschylean tragedy, *Prometheus Bound* or *The Suppliant Women*. These Greek dramas, Claudel suggested, were the first to have "detached themselves from the dithyramb," the earliest to have reduced theatre to "a passionate dialogue between protagonist and Chorus."[15]

Claudel's use of the *dédoublement* technique increases the tension between illusion and reality, fact and fiction. It also adds to the fuguelike quality of the multiple activities revolving around a single theme in the drama itself.

Two spheres exist simultaneously as Christopher Columbus II waxes in complacency, enjoying his preordained universe, where events have been determined in advance. He encourages Christopher Columbus I to pursue his course no matter what the difficulties, while also pointing to the fact that if one is to succeed in the world of contingencies, then compromise, mediation, and accommodation are also required. The Platonic world of ideas, perfection, and the myth stand in sharp contrast to the imperfect world in which Columbus I experiences his successive defeats. Chaos and pain fill his world; bitter and ironic vicissitudes exacerbate his spirit. By juxtaposing the two figures, Claudel depicts the imperfect earthly being, weighed down by matter, straining and heaving through life, in contrast to his eternal counterpart, who is relaxed, and seemingly above these trivialities. The finite and the infinite are exposed on stage in a world where time flows forward and backward—is stilled and activated—enveloped in duration.[16]

Affinities exist between Claudel's dual Columbuses and the *shite* character in Noh drama. When the shite first appears on stage in most Noh plays, he wears the mask of a humble person or is the reincarnation of this individual. The action frequently consists of a recalling of past events and is enacted "objectively." When the shite makes his presence known for the second time, he usually enacts the role of a ghost or supernatural being repenting some previous act in a subjective manner. Claudel's Columbuses are also double creatures, mortal and immortal specters, roaming through a constantly erupting and combusting universe. The earthly Columbus is forever attempting to purify his essence, to free himself from the dross and weight of matter, while the celestial Columbus justifies and glories in his legend.

The Chanter again intervenes. What is happening in the Spanish court? he queries, now that Columbus is stricken with poverty and old age. Dancing and music are sounded. Images of America as it existed when Columbus was old are projected onto the screen; land emerging from uterine waters, masses and continents being born. Music encroaches, grows louder. Speech takes on a sing-song quality and, although apparently continuous and parallel, injects a mood of discontinuity and antagonism into the proceedings. Music, here, does not replicate the stage activity; it creates a contrapuntal mood, acting as an irritant, an obstruction. It arouses emotions of anger, pain, and frustration. Four dancing women "superbly plumed" enter the forestage. They represent Envy, Ignorance, Vanity and Avarice (of "the mind and heart"), Claudel adds. As they dance about instilling panic, agitation, fragmentation into the hearts of the onlookers, their

A scene from *The Diary of Christopher Columbus*.
FRENCH CULTURAL SERVICES

rhythmic movements intensify and a mood of suspense-
ful anguish prevails.

Claudel was a strong believer in eurythmics: a technique
which coordinates bodily movements with music, deepening and unifying three artistic experiments: music, movement, rhythm. The inventor of Eurythmics, Emile
Jaques-Dalcroze (1865–1950), the author of *Rhythm,
Music and Education* (1922), exerted a profound influence
on Claudel. The French dramatist went to Hellerau, where
Dalcroze had founded his school, to study the techniques
involved. Dalcroze believed that every gesture, facial
nuance, rhythmic device must serve to exteriorize an inner
voice. The actor must listen to this invisible world, see it,
translate its message into plastic images, mobile moods,
and spatial compositions. Claudel also believed in "com-
posing" a role, by gathering together the disparate parts of
body and mind, and weaving them into a cohesive whole:
internal and external movements must be made to work in
harmony; accessories, like the synecdoche, must enhance

the frame of reference; lighting and sound must illuminate and order the spectacle; scenes must revolve around a specific "phare," and thereby point up an inner architecture. Claudel's "appetite for reality" compelled him to reject impressionism and opt for a synthetic approach to theatre.[17]

The four dancers on stage, then, emphasize the marriage of the arts, and unify the visual and aural elements, creating an emotional climate which inundates goodness and spirituality and centers on man's immorality and sinful nature. Allegorical in focus, these intellectual abstractions, so popular in the Medieval period as attested to by *Everyman* and in modern times in Ibsen's *Peer Gynt*, feed their moral values and religious concepts to spectators.

The four dancing figures in *The Diary of Christopher Columbus* introduce friction. The Prosecutor enters into the melee. He defends the King of Spain who outfitted Columbus with ships, sailors, and food. The Defense retorts, in exchange: Columbus gave his monarch the world. A heated interlude ensues. Columbus II intervenes: "I knew much more than you know." The Prosecutor chides him for deigning to enter into the conversation, for being willing to reach down to earthly levels. Then he accuses Columbus I of being a charlatan, an ignorant man, a dreamer, a slave trader, a liar, a rebellious spirit, a calumniator, a generally incapable boob. The Defense interrupts. To be sure, Columbus I has defects; he did disturb the smoothly organized Spanish world. He did activate Europe's propensity for greed and lust; but his lies, jealousies, cruelty, disdain, were the result of his great love: "Who could judge a man in the throes of love?" The Chorus litanizes now, repeating the name: "Christopher Columbus. . . ." in refrainlike sequences, shedding the mood of excitability.

The stage fills with doves. The characters are chased away. The proscenium has been cleared for the following scene in Isabella's garden in Castille. Since the difficulties involved in the scene changes were so enormous, Barrault, who used live, trained doves in his production, also resorted to another theatrical device. He used a nine-yard-long piece of white cloth to function as a screen, a sail for Columbus' caravels, a rag, a tempest, and more. The sail, Barrault noted, was "the seminal spark around which everything else gravitated" and "it is a living being," as are the protagonists. [18]

Isabella is depicted as a child. She is holding court; the other dignitaries present are also children. The entire scene is reminiscent of canvases of Infantas by Velasquez: soft lightness and gentle airiness invade the surroundings, in sharp contrast to the stiff and sumptuously decorated dresses worn by the princess. Isabella represents all the good qualities implicit in the depiction of an ideal: joy, hope, and purity. The Sultan Miramolin has brought her a gift; a caged dove. She accepts the gift, ties a ring around the dove's leg, and then gives it its freedom.

Isabella is an anima figure. As delineated in the play, Isabella stands for a religious entity: a spiritualized force. It is she who liberates the dove or Holy Spirit, which will make its way into the world, inseminating Columbus, the navigator, the great "assembler." Comparable to the Virgin Mary or to the Gnostic Sophia, Isabella encompasses perfection. She belongs to a higher sphere of woman. Within her is contained all nourishment, happiness, and the beauty of ethereal climes. Isabella functions only as a spiritual principle in Claudel's work—not as a wife or mother. She is inspiration. Her beatific nature grows throughout the play and attains nearly cosmic proportions until she becomes a mediating force between the world of reality and the poetic vision. She is mystery incarnate, as is the dove she liberates. In this connection, she warrants the appellation Solomon gave to his beloved when he called her, "my dove, my undefiled" in The Song of Songs (6:9). The dove is not only identified with the Holy Spirit, which inseminated Mary, but is also related to Noah's story. After forty days and forty nights, the righteous man, Noah, whom God spared from the Flood, sent out a raven, then a dove, to see if land were visible.

The dove in Claudel's play is a religious symbol. It is also a theatrical device linking the court of Spain with Columbus' inner as well as his outer personalities, his mortal and immortal selves. It is Isabella's soul—her anima—which has been sent to Columbus to encourage him in his task, to inspire him in his endeavor, to allow him to see clearly into the vast vision of life.

The Chanter pursues his narration, interrupted now and then by the Prosecutor, the Chorus, or Christopher Columbus I or II. On the screen, meanwhile, we see Columbus as a young boy. He is at home in Genoa. He is reading: The Book of Marco Polo. Images of Asia, camels, the great Khan's palace, vessels sailing forth are flashed onto the screen; they incite the boy's imagination. Columbus' sister steps behind him; she glances over his shoulder at the book. Marco Polo (1254–1324), the Venetian traveler and adventurer, introduces the young lad to a world of fantasy—to the unknown—Persia, Turkmen, the Gobi Desert, China, Tibet, Burma, India.

An interchange between Columbus I and II takes place. The earthly man is dreaming of leaving his home, of sailing off to distant lands, but suffers because he knows his departure will bring pain to his family. His future is uncertain; danger lurks all about. Tension rises. Columbus II intercedes, encouraging the wayfarer to break out of his constrained environment into the new world, as Abraham had left Ur when God called upon him to sacrifice the comfort and security of the known for the harrowing uncertainty of mystery. Columbus must listen to his inner voice, to God, as the poet experiences the soundings and poundings of the visualizations which erupt from his unconscious into his conscious mind. The interchange between the Columbuses and the Chorus, which also intervenes, grows more powerful, increasingly excitable. Cadences increase in choppiness, ejaculate in swift succession, only to grow more lax, passive, diminishing in intensity, to be followed by a halting effect, then a fresh charge, a swift succession of contrapuntal beats, interruptions, alliterations. Suddenly, the Chorus blurts out, mercilessly, repeatedly, stressing the gutturals and velars; pounding the dentals, aggressively, searingly, bloodily: "Quit, quit your mother . . . quit . . . quit . . . quit . . . Christopher! Christopher!"

A dove suddenly appears on the screen. It makes its way into the weaver's home. It has a ring tied to its foot. Isabella's dove has reached its destination: the great inseminator has found its host; the searcher for land, the word, the image, the heartbeat has inspired the poet to begin his work, to pursue his vision. The ring, a link between court and commoner, Church/state and the lowly parishioner/citizen, aids in the completion of the circle, stressing the continuous alliance of seemingly multiple and fragmented elements. The ring binds; it also maintains in bondage. Isabella's destiny is marked, as is Columbus'; their future is intertwined.

The Chanter announces Columbus I's imminent departure, repeating in rhythmically accentuated clauses, as well as in choppy and staccato sequences, the conflicts involved: the intent to leave, the pain experienced by the family. As in the case of most visionaries, heroes, and men of genius, the all-powerful dream annihilates the dangers the rational mind apprehends. Only the realization of life's goal counts. The Chorus echoes and reechoes the emotions involved, taking up each side of the question in contrapuntal arrangements; then, the various steps marking Columbus' voyage are sounded. The Chorus is prophetic; it sees into the future. Columbus will go to Spain: three ships will be put at his disposal and they will make their way through icy and inky waters; blackness will follow them throughout their long course; tempestuous and energetic forces will fight them, impeding their progress, offering them agony and torment. Columbus I will go on to the Azores, where he will see a sailor—nearly dead—bound and tied to the figurehead of a wrecked ship.

Columbus II recalls the scene with utmost objectivity, oblivious to the pain the sailor knows. Nor is compassion to be found in Columbus I, who leans over the sailor, hoping beyond hope he is still alive. Columbus I has only one idea in mind: he wants to learn as much from the sailor as possible. Is there land about? Where has this man traveled? What has he seen? Another world? the West? Land? Columbus I is breathless. He prods the sailor, unwilling to let him succumb. He demands to know more and more. Columbus I is undaunted by the human element. Fire inhabits his breast, nothing more. The Chorus and a half-Chorus intervene: they represent sensitivity, feeling and understanding; they ask Columbus I to comfort a dying man. Passionate in his outlook, with conquest alone in mind, Columbus I looks away, gets up, sustained throughout the scene by his vision alone. Fear and anguish have vanished. The thought of the mystery involved in an unfolding world activates his desires, foments his energies.

In Spain, Columbus I looks wistfully at the sea from the port: "How beautiful is the sea! How wonderful the rounded earth in my arms! How beautiful it is, the path toward the Occident! . . . Ah, how much longer will I delay before

following the call of the sun which invites me to follow it!"
Water is personified, poetized, humanized. Columbus I
longs to possess it, dominate its every wave, its motion, its
lilting and tumultuous soul. He is hounded out of his reverie
by business affairs, by his wife; the world of reality makes
its demands upon him. Chaos invades his home life. "Pay
your debts, Christopher Columbus," the Creditors shout in
strident and structured beats. The Chorus mocks him.
They sneer, snicker, cackle, then in multiple hiccupping
sounds, erupt into laughter. The crowd standing hoots,
shoots, deafens at times; piercing cries emanate from all
corners of the stage; they flagellate the would-be explorer,
castigating and bruising his creative spirit. They trample his
ideal, blacken his luminescent vision. Impractical, unreal,
the man is insane, they say.

According to the Chanter, Columbus I has made his way
to the Spanish Court. Now the most powerful land in the
world, Spain dominates Granada, the Pyrenees. Therefore,
when Columbus I announces that he has something to give
the King of Spain, the courtiers jeer the little Genovese
upstart with his inflated ideas. The room resounds with
angry murmurs. Laughter explodes, Columbus I shows
them his ring. He has been chosen to perform a special
mission, selected by higher forces to pave the way for
the new. A dove is seen flying about on the screen.
Unflinching, the world roamer states: "With this ring I
shall marry the entire earth."

Scientists, scholars, wise men congregate, attempting to
instill fear into Columbus I's heart. Don't tamper with the
unknown, they advise him; don't delve into the mysteries
which belong to God alone. Death will be the outcome of
such an adventurous goal. The earth is flat. To think
otherwise is to counter the laws of Church and God. Columbus I believes otherwise. They refuse him an audience
with the King.

Isabella emerges onto the stage area. She is praying, the

Chanter says. On screen, crowds are visible. Parades and general disorder are rampant as events are enacted helter-skelter. Past and present are fused. Isabella glows because she has "married Castille to Aragon"; the Moors have been driven from her land, and Spain is one. The images on the screen vanish; along with the screen. In its stead, a stained glass window appears, radiant in contrast to the darkened background. It features a gigantic image of St. James of Compostela. A dove flies above his head.

The Chorus calls to Isabella. She is hampering the march of St. James, obstructing him in his work. Patron saint of Spain, Saint James was known for his military prowess, for the establishment of Christianity in Spain. One of the most famous shrines the world over is dedicated to him and is located at Compostela; it is here that miracles galore are said to have taken place, namely, the liberation of Spain from the Moors. As Isabella prays, murmurs resound. Life seems to be awakening from all quarters of the stage. She cannot understand what is happening. She listens to inaudible emanations, confused tonalities, blendings of feeling and sentiment. Slowly the din is patterned, with the sounds evolving into words and the words into ideas. Concomitantly, behind the stained glass window, the vague shadow of a man on horseback and carrying a sword appears. He is a fighter, a mover, an actor. It is St. James of Compostela himself.[19] The Chorus speaks for him: why is Isabella preventing him from carrying out his mission, from riding forth? Isabella is confused. Why is she being accused of hampering St. James' work? Then, she remembers an image in some distant past or present, of a man, a very poor man who had come to ask for money in order to sail the sea; past fuses with present in contemporaneous sequences.

Timelessness is now wedded to spacelessness. The port of

Cadiz is featured on stage: masts, ships, flags, cords, con-struction, sailors mulling about; all is in perpetual flux; tension runs high, particularly as group movements alter-nate on stage; screams, chantings, shouts are exhaled as cargos are being hoisted onto the vessels. The King has agreed to Columbus I's project. Three ships are being outfitted. The journey has begun. The sailors have been chosen; each has his appointed task.

The Chanter evokes new shores, different Gods. The Mexican divinities come to the fore, associated with pyramids, fresco paintings, and races of giants. The feath-ered serpent god, Quetzalcoatl, the rain god, Tlaloc, the warrior god with his long sword, Huitzilopochtli, along with others, emerge from oblivion. Each wears a mask. Each is depicted by Claudel in unfortunate and ugly tones, as anthropophagous evil-doers. One has perverted the compass, another has introduced worms into the salted beef; a third has given the sailors fever, a fourth has brought madness and despair to Columbus I's crew. These gods are ready and waiting for their European visitors.

As depicted by Claudel, the Mexican gods are cold, fearful, and cruel. Their function in the play is to impede Columbus' march into the new world, and to destroy him if possible. They do not want to be bothered with a new religion or anything that would alter their enjoyment of life, their complacent ways. It was Claudel's pejorative view of Mexican deities which irritated Barrault, as did his statements concerning them: "We must only respect the things that we make use of and that we need," Claudel said. Barrault, who had studied and appreciated the Mexican religion, looked upon it, as he did all other divine concepts, with respect. Claudel, however, did not enjoy this open-mindedness in religious matters and considered all reli-gions save his own as propagators of false gods.[20]

What stands out as fascinating in this Mexican interlude, however, is the use Claudel makes of the mask. As in Noh, so the Mexican gods are endowed with expressionless faces: emotions do not register; feelings are concealed; only words, grunts, lamentations or cries are ejaculated. During quieter moments, when their activity diminishes, when movements grow sparser, energy is depleted, their gestures, now effected in slow motion, take on the quality of hiero-glyphics implanted in space.[21]

As mentioned before, masks both hide and reveal, and, therefore, they are essentially ambiguous in nature; emana-tions from an invisible, dark, and illusory domain, they inspire fear. Since earliest times masks have been used in religious ceremonies to represent unreal and inhuman as-pects: gods, demons or animal forces. The masks worn by Claudel's Mexican gods are an expression of mutable di-vinities, modified by the course of civilization, temporary beliefs, erroneous ideations. There is nothing numinous about them; nothing is sacred. On the contrary, they stand for obstructive and destructive elements, demoniacal forces at work. The are semiotic spokesmen for man's anthropoid nature. Elemental in every way, they stand for physical and spiritual ugliness.[22]

The Chanter intrudes. He announces the onset of the great scene. Columbus I and his crew are on the high seas. Murmurs resound, words, anger, threats, supplications; endless water pours in from all sides. Columbus I appears in an admiral's uniform. Officers are about. The crew's dele-gate arrives; complaints are endless: no flour, no wine, no water; the beef has rotted. They want to turn back. Colum-bus I is adamant. Complaints or no complaints, he intends to sail on, to serve his sovereign and his God. He defies all human and inhuman elements, anything that bars his way. As his name indicates—Christopher, the

Christ-bearer—he too will stride forth onto the waters, whether these be turbulent or not; he too will be weighed down with cargo—his mission. Although the burden may be heavy, the dream shall be fulfilled.

Tension rises. The crew's increasing anger is sounded in binary opposition to Columbus I's vision. The poet's voice is heard; he will fight darkness. The crew's delegate voices their request: turn back. No food, no water, no land. Only a void, nothingness. A terrible emptiness engulfs them all; it is the calm before Creation, when elemental existence covers the visible world, when *prima materia* reigns. Columbus I knows that suffering is implicit in the seer's credo, the visionary's dream; the poet's writing. Grief and affliction have a cleansing effect; they water down the layers of encrusted matter, of superfluous detail, of prolixity, elements which serve to diminish the power, the vibrancy of the creative individual's élan—muddy and beclouded—the mystic's central point. Only after a *tabula rasa* has come to pass, when all earthly existence has been pared down to its essentials, does a new orientation emerge, a fresh lifeline come into being. No more earth. Sea alone is visible—nothing more.

The crew's delegate accuses Columbus I of madness—a dreamer, an adventurer, a searcher for an unknown star, for a mysterious force—he will bring destruction upon man. The sailors shudder and tremble with fear. Columbus I answers, prophetically: "But if you knew what I know, you would feel even more fearful." He alone knows the compass is no longer working. The sun remains his only guide. As the lamentations grow more desperate, Columbus I tells his tormentors they may all return; they may all perish. He will proceed, if need be alone. Let him be blamed for the suffering of his crew, for the mishaps involved in his discoveries, for his fortune and misfortune in his apocalyptic vision. Fire inhabits him: incandescence inspires him, compels him to love the earth and to want to embrace it, to possess it as his bride. There is something outerworldly in Columbus I's being: something intangible glows within him, emanating in brilliant clusters, undefinable, incomprehensible: a soul which draws him out, prods him, excites him, thrills him. Unlike the average person who adapts to the workday world, Columbus I sees beyond the phenomenological sphere into the deepest abysses, the very crucible of earth and sea. He usurps power. As master of three vessels, he dictates his way, imperious and oblivious to all else.

A bird appears on the screen. The Chorus sings out:

> And the dove came into him in the evening; and, lo, in her mouth was an olive leaf pluckt off: so Noah knew that the waters were abated from off the earth (*Gen. 8:11*).

The earth is born. It has emerged from the waters, the *prima materia*: the idea from its amorphous substance; structure from fluidity. An undifferentiated mass, water stands for the domain of infinite possibilities, a world *in potentia*. It is the unformed, undeveloped, unrealized germ—the source of all life—the immense reservoir where the integrated has been reintegrated, the baptismal bath purified. "Everything is water," the Hindu text says, "the vast waters had no shores." Water is yin, the feminine, embryonic, abysmal, continuously mobile matter, implicit in initiation rituals. Water is described as wisdom in Proverbs (8:9); as it was in Medieval times for such philosophers as Hugues de Saint-Victor. In performing the benediction, it announces the birth of new life, a new era, according to the prophet Isaiah: "for in the wilderness waters shall break out, and streams in the desert" (35:6). Water indicated spiritual as well as physical life for John (4:14).

America is discovered. The *Te Deum* is voiced. The ship docks.

Part II of *The Diary of Christopher Columbus* is shorter than the first section and consists of only eight sequences. The Creation has come to pass. The idea has been etched. Contours have taken shape. For Claudel, the Creation, whether it be of a play or a poem, is an example of what the Hindu calls Prakriti: matter. In his essay *The Legend of Prakriti*, Claudel wrote of the Creation of the world out of matter—ebullient, fulminating chaos—as it took form from breath, aspiration and inspiration. God speaks and separates chaos, classifies its multiple aspects, bringing into existence a "double time": the visible and invisible, the fixed and the fluid. On stage, the waters surrounding Columbus I's ships boil and brew, agitating in their organic and inorganic states, consolidating and separating, immersing themselves in dry and liquid blendings.[23] Prakriti, the *prima materia*, virginal and untouched, upon which evolution impresses itself, is illuminated, distilled, made phosphorescent and mobile.[24]

The Chanter returns to the *Diary*. He narrates the list of Columbus' achievements and how the world reacted to his discoveries. Were people disturbed now that a new land had come into existence? Had covetousness, greed, disorder blanketed the world? Columbus returns to Spain in triumph. Soon, however, disappointment sets in. The colonists have not found gold, barely a handful of pearls. The men who have sailed to the new world are being massacred by the natives. Columbus brings some Indians back to Spain, reintroducing slave trade.

The King and his advisors (Three Wise Men) talk over the impact of Columbus I's discovery, but only after more important matters are broached: affairs in Italy, Flanders, and Germany. They advise the monarch not to continue helping Columbus. The unknown is disagreeable to many; honest men do not find treasures. On the surface, to be sure, the King must honor Columbus, thus placating man's vanity. Moreover, the people need an idol, the masses long for a figurehead to keep them in check, to keep their desires and passions in line. Columbus I must then be "buried," the Wise Men inform the King, relegated to some innocuous sphere.

The wind begins to blow; a tempest is brewing on the high seas. Rats abound. Columbus I is being brought back to Spain in chains; he is oblivious to what has been happening in his homeland as well as in the colonies. He has been imprisoned in the hold, attached to a pole "in the very bowels of the boat." There in the depths, as Jonah had been in the whale's belly, Columbus I indwells. Darkness prevails. Abyss. The sound of wind vibrates, takes on force, moment, echoing man's fear in rhythmic pantings. There are terrified groans. The boat heaves to and fro. The wooden beams crack. The mast sways. The swelling waters invade, encapsulating the entire stage area; the squall beats in gusts as Claudel's verse throbs with compressed fear. The stage is transformed into a colossal receptacle. The theatrical illusion is completed as music rises in crescendos, agitation reigns. The Cook lunges for Columbus.[25] Then, sudden silence.

Elemental powers have assumed control. Man is impotent against cosmic energy, cosmic rage, which sweeps across the stage in tempestuous gusty statements. Strident laughter is sounded, giving way to sobs and piercing cries which echo and reecho to the blast of cannon balls in spasms, shrieks of pained despair. Shadows grow visible on the screen. Indians are silhouetted as they pass in array before the spectators, mute at times, then frenzied. The Chorus and an orchestration of percussion instruments fade in and out, shedding their cacophonies, blasts in so many spatial eruptions—stripping the entire atmosphere of all cohesion.[26]

Claudel considered the tempest scene the most important in the play. It represented the gathering together of volcanic forces, the grouping of unleashed emotions.[27] Vibrant, piercing, irritating matter eructates, dispersing all that lives inchoate within the dimmer recesses of both the earth's and man's being. Tempests, with which man attempts to cope, whether on a physical, spiritual, or psychological sphere, disrupt, disorder, and frequently destroy. So inordinate is the charge that in many religions a storm is considered a theophany, a manifestation of God's power, a revelation or a punishment. Whether in Judeo-Christian literature, Scandinavian, Babylonian, Assyrian, Greek or Roman mythologies, high winds, cyclones, tornados are held to have a sacred quality about them. They descend from heaven to man bringing torment and trouble in their wake; they inspire fear, uproot worn and staid formulae. They also fecundate, inspire, energize.

For Claudel, the storm represented Columbus I's agony: his catharsis. Still holding onto the mast, to his idea, he listens to the Commander's words: "As long as you hold on to the mast, all the furies of Chaos will not succeed against you, and our boat will find a sure path through this gutted universe." Howling breaks into the atmosphere, along with images of water, smoke, thunder, lightning, each pounding its way onto the proscenium platform. The ship vanishes. Blackness engulfs the earth: "In the beginning was the Word," Columbus I states, "and the Word was with God, and the Word was God" (John 1:1).

The Cook, the Chorus, and the half-Chorus, announce Columbus I's ordeal. It is not over yet; despair, rejection, destruction ensue. "Is it you who will remake heaven and earth?" the Cook questions sarcastically. No, his task is to "discover" the world and not to remake it, he answers.

The icy winds are stilled. The backdrop is "cold green," Claudel writes.[28] Angular, elongated beings invade the stage: masked men wearing black cowls, carrying lit candles. Fanaticism prevails, religious zeal, passionate faith. Women complain, bursting into sobs, rage, anguish; emotions of all types—tenderness, love, and consolation—also invade the atmosphere. Stillness grasps the protagonists. Their countenances are immobile; a mood of isolation prevails. Thoughts and feelings are interiorized. The eye of the cyclone has come upon them: perception, illumination, introspection. Reminiscent of El Greco's "The Scourging of Christ," these elongated forms move about in a chiaroscuro which now fills the stage. They seem incorporeal, underscoring the outerworldliness of the scene: eyes observing, eyes peering into a sphere beyond reality. The Cook informs the spectators that they are in Columbus I's inner world, his conscience, his invisible domain.

It is significant that the Cook should be the one to tell the audience that the area depicted is "the inside of your conscience." A mixer of elements, a transformer from raw to cooked state, from primitive to civilized cultures, the Cook, a magician of sorts, will help Columbus I to penetrate his depths, to counter his accusers, assess his worth. Blamed for having introduced slavery, Columbus I justifies his act: he had found no gold, he needed money, as did Spain. Men, traded and sold, like animals throughout the world—a cargo of "human flesh" was the outcome of lust for lucre. The screen is flooded with the shadows of human beings moving about in eerie configurations, frightening groupings. Columbus I is accused of egoism and having abandoned his mother and his family. His conscience is haunting and taunting him. Youth is rash and brash, furious and aggressive, as it seeks to pave its way in life. Old age, more thoughtful, sensitive and pensive, examines acts more thoroughly to determine their value. Pity overwhelms Columbus I; his self-centeredness encroaches and his guilt weighs heavily upon him. What did he really discover? What had he added to man's knowledge?

A globe is again flashed onto the screen. A land mass is viewed, linked to another continent through the isthmus of Panama, America: Balboa's discoveries, Magellan's findings, Amerigo Vespucci's fame—new islands, peoples, customs—a fresh universe.

Columbus I is no longer enchained, the Chanter explains. The ship has reached Spain. Columbus I's ordeal is nearly over. The Queen has arrived. In parallel scenes, we see Columbus yielding his chains to the inn-keeper at Valladolid in lieu of money. He wants to keep his mule. The proprietor demands more payment. He is an exile, he tells his persecutor, wretched, a pariah. The Queen's Messenger arrives. She understands the impact and depth of his discovery: he has given her New Indies and she accepts his gift. She murmurs his name ceaselessly. Columbus I knows no greater joy. His suffering, isolation and torment, even the chains of injustice which weighed so heavily upon him, have now been accepted.

The Chanter announces the near end of Columbus' *Diary*. The innkeeper demands Columbus I's mule. The old man, barely able to move, begs him to leave it. It is his only friend, his servant and faithful companion. A dialogue now ensues between Columbus I and II. The earthly figure accuses his celestial counterpart of having abandoned him, of being pitiless, and hard. He should help him confront his poverty and age. Columbus II asks Columbus I to join him—to cross over that giant step from life to death—from mortality to immortality.

"It is over," the Chanter says. The curtain falls. Suddenly, someone comes out from behind the curtain. There is really one more scene to be played, one more page to the *Diary*. It takes place in the "Paradise of the Idea," an area which is crystal and white, silvery and phosphorescent. It features an exotic landscape having no depth of vision, no perspective. A voice is heard asking the Chanter whether a mistake has not been made. Certainly, the scene has already been played; the decor is the same used when Queen Isabella had placed the ring on the dove's foot. Perhaps the Chanter has mistaken the last for the first page. No. He has not. He explains: "All begins again in light and understanding. . . . "

Queen Isabella is once again young and beautiful, filled with life and spirit. The Sultan Miramolin brings her two great keys on a cushion: those of Granada and those of another realm. She reminisces about the day on which he had brought her the white dove. She longs for the return of her ring. How will she enter heaven without it, she wonders. Her servants assure her that they are looking for the ring throughout the world. In a parallel scene, they arrive at Valladolid; there they find Columbus I. He is dying, but still refuses to return the ring. Instead, he will give his Queen his faithful and true companion—his mule. Scandalized by the paltry nature of his gifts, the servants recoil in shame and anger. The Queen, however, accepts the gift: the greatest and most meaningful of all of her treasures.

Night falls. Blueness invades the stage area; an oblique image of the two Americas appears. Saint James is delineated against a blue backdrop, colossal in his pilgrim's costume, carrying his staff and scallop shell.[29] The constellation Orion emerges from blackness; then the gates of Hercules appear. The cosmos vibrates as it invades the acting area in the whiteness of a flowing sail, in the palpitating and rapturous spasms, in the glaring whiteness of an as yet unborn day. The heavens open up; the stars activate, shine, burn, pointing the way to future voyages; in the background emerges the image of the Virgin holding a child.

Isabella has arrived. She alights from the mule she has been riding. She kneels, as do the other protagonists, including the mule, and then enters the Holy Gates, praying for Columbus I, while he takes his decisive step—from his world to the great Abyss. A Halleluja Chorus is intoned. On the screen, a globe rotating on its axis becomes visible; a dove emerges from the depths of the black stage and crosses the proscenium. All is effaced. The dove alone remains visible against a backdrop which now features a giant pontiff covered with a gold stole and a chasuble.

The Diary of Christopher Columbus is a colossal awakening; it is an integration of poetry and dramaturgy, an unforgettable theatrical experience. Claudel's use of the Chanter—borrowed from Bunraku—the Chorus—from the Church—the two Columbuses—from Noh drama —enabled him to break out of the conventional space/time continuum and to inject global and cosmic dimension into his work. His use of the cinematographic medium permitted him to emphasize active synchronistic factors. The doves accentuated the symbolic as well as the realistic overtones his work called into play. The music added to the luster and excitement of the spectacle. Two worlds are in collision in *The Diary of Christopher Columbus*, confronting, agitating, sparking one another in rhythmic patterns, alternating with spasmodic repartees and moments of repose and silence.

To dramatize the life of a conqueror, a discoverer, had been on Claudel's mind from his early youth, when he used to climb to the highest area in his hometown, giving him access to unlimited horizons: it was as if he saw the entire earth unfolding at his feet, and it was his task in life to *reassemble* all that was disparate, to conquer what was beyond his reach.[30] For Claudel, *The Diary of Christopher Columbus* was the "culmination" of *The Satin Slipper*; it had been a lifetime preoccupation; the work of a Demiurge, a Re-assembler.

An immensely complex work to produce because of the technical difficulties and the breadth and scope of the religious and philosophical ideas, *The Diary of Christopher Columbus* was nevertheless a success whenever and wherever produced. It is a work charged with energy and activity, comparable in many respects to *Golden Head*, Claudel's first play. The latter deals with the conqueror on land, while this play deals with the conqueror on water. It is a fitting conclusion because it completes the circle for Claudel's own poetic forays, his own imagistic projections, his own flights of fantasy and spiritual hunger.

EPILOGUE

Action in Claudel's theatre, whether it be in *Golden Head, The City, Break of Noon, The Tidings Brought to Mary,* or the *"Trilogy,"* follows a pattern: the situation is descanted at the very outset in slow, architecturally balanced scenes; gesture and attitude are not only paced in a rhythmic flow intensifying the emotional climate, but they are also simplified to the extreme, shorn of any extraneous elements. The bare necessities are projected upon, elaborated, and then descanted. Expressed in a glance, a turn of the wrist, an arched hand, a sigh, a moan or giggle, each gesture indicates a mood and sets the tone for the protagonists' lowly or superior spiritual encounter. The characters in Claudel's more complicated dramas such as *The Satin Slipper* and *The Diary of Christopher Columbus* are comparable to mirror images; they are paradigms of greater forces in the process of living out their workaday and spiritual existences in contrapuntal blocks. Frequently Claudel's characters are featured as doubles (the sisters in *The Tidings Brought to Mary*) or as terrestrial and celestial aspects of the same characters (as in *The Diary of Christopher Columbus*). As such each echoes and responds to the other, ushering in clusters of feelings, sensations, analogies. These are made all the more powerful because of Claudel's special use of stichomythia: a form of dialogue used in ancient Greek theatre in which alternating lines, frequently of antithetical nature, point up the divisiveness of the characters on stage, thus emphasizing anxiety and heightening emotion. Universal antitheses are fashioned by Claudel in this manner—signs are revealed more mysteriously and imperiously—with cosmic repercussions.

The trajectory of Claudel's characters is cyclical, beginning with a crime and concluding with a punishment. The protagonist, at least one in each play, is drawn, instinctually, toward a mate and commits the sin of concupiscence. Claudel, quoting Saint Augustine's famous *etiam peccata*, also believes that sin serves a purpose. Once the protagonist bathes in sin he seeks punishment, whether it be in ascetic practices, in flagellation, deprivation, or prayer. Redemption and forgiveness are then earned. The notion of sacrifice lies at the heart of Claudel's theatre: his last acts are always "bloody," he writes in *Reflections on Poetry*, but "always magnificent" for "Religion not only placed drama in daily life, but also at its end, in Death, the highest form of drama which, for all true disciples of our Divine Master, is *sacrifice*."

Had Claudel not invested himself with some kind of armature, a restrictive and containing device, his inner world might have flowed forth unchanneled and taken on destructive dimensions. The Church helped him maintain his equilibrium, at least outwardly and, as such, Claudel was able to enjoy a career as writer and government official (attaché, diplomat, ambassador), which allowed him to travel around the globe to China, Japan, Europe, and the United States. Active, dynamic, he was forever writing, and on all topics, such as literature, philosophy, commentaries on the Bible and on the Patristic fathers, and art criticism. Poetry and plays flowed from his pen as did numerous letters to his directors (Lugné-Poë, Copeau, Barrault), to composers who wrote musical scores for his works (Milhaud, Honegger), and to friends such as Mallarmé,

Valéry, Gide, Jammes, to mention only a scattering. Claudel's creative output was immense. His energy was boundless, his curiosity insatiable. Excitement generated in all of his acts; mind and body pulsated as sensations stretched and tensed toward the new, unlived, and untried. Yet, had Claudel been free of a containing device, he might not have longed so desperately for its opposite—freedom. The Church served Claudel in an ambivalent fashion: it helped him leap from a constraining domain into a primitive earth sphere, which nourished him viscerally, while quenching his thirst for orgiastic pleasures, at least momentarily. Only after enthrallment, when satisfied and thoroughly gorged, did awareness come upon him; he balanced his return with a retreat into the cloistered realm of the religious fathers. There, he felt purified, expurgated, expunged of the "tainted" elements overwhelming his soul.

Repression and suppression have their price. Attempting to still the chaotic, to drive inward what gushes forth, to annihilate that aspect or aspects of the individual which may not conform to the image one has in mind, is to castrate a personality, to dismember a psyche. The cost to Claudel? Continuous conflict, perpetual struggle, unhappiness, shattering pain, and feelings of corrosive guilt forever in need of being assuaged. Penitence, spiritual flagellation, suffering are all potent forces in his writings, in the way of his protagonists. This duality plagued and tortured him, eroded his flesh, destroyed the harmony for which he so desperately longed. Claudel was a man at odds with himself. He yearned for serenity, which he might have experienced in flashes during moments of grace or in the very act of his literary creations; but at most other times, his appetite for the visceral and lust for the sensual left him distraught, dissatisfied, and with irretrievable feelings of sinfulness.

Claudel's theatre encapsulates saint and sinner, penitentials and flesh-ridden beings, the sick in heart and soul and the virginal creature whose life is unlived. Impurity cohabits with purity, murderous desires with feelings of beatitude, jealousy, anger, revenge or deception, along with an insatiable need for God. Creator of a very personal theatre, Claudel lives out his own dramas in projection, combining excoriating guilt with a need for punishment in what could be called a sado-masochistic round. Adultery must be paid for by the man of the earth who seeks spiritual tranquility. Feeding on the heaving pulsations of the body, purification is required; it is distilled in Claudel's dramas, which are works of art.

Claudel's plays are modern renditions of ancient mystery practices enacted formerly by the Greeks at Dodona, Eleusis, and Delphi in the depths of grottoes or in forested areas, and by the Egyptians within the Pyramid. In these somber areas the seed germinates and *renovatio* comes into being. Impulses toward life are experienced in all of their boisterous grandeur, their savory sensations; an exploding sunset; a sea fired by the broiling heat of the sun; the onset of a detonating love affair. As in Rubens or Jordaens painting, so Claudel's prose breathes, celebrating a woman's flesh, or nature in its multiple and radiant tonalties. It knows also subdued lighting tones, as in the moist rays of a moonlit night or the chiaroscuro of a Georges de la Tour canvas: here Claudel's passions melt, blend, suffuse. Rembrandt tonalities are subsumed by Claudel as he creates multiple emotional nuances, while asceticism follows in his El Greco—like figures: elongated, floating, stretching and distending limbs and muscles. Zurbarán's martyrs are present in Claudel's dramas: their stares fixed, eyes glaring pleadingly and unendingly toward heaven. Bloodied forms, reminiscent of Soutine's visions, expose man's innards as they heave the last time before the great flagellation and dismemberment as in an *imitatio Christi*.

It is through the word that Claudel distills raw pain, humanizes matter, or descants brutalities, until subtle correspondences radiate in structured sequences, in blocks, placed one upon the other, and en masse, assuming the power and stature of a cathedral, its foundations dug deep into the subsoil and its spires soaring toward divinity. Claudel's theatre is a *complexio oppositorum:* it contains the seed of both beauty and ugliness, happiness and despair, good and evil. The protagonists are all tainted with their opposites, bearing within their realms the spark of Divine as well as Luciferian Light and Delight!

NOTES

1. Introduction

1. Paul Claudel, *Mémoires improvisés*, pp. 13—15.
2. *Ibid.*, p. 20.
3. *Ibid.*, p. 27.
4. *Ibid.*, p. 30.
5. Paul Claudel, *Oeuvre en prose*, p. 1469.
6. *Ibid.*, p. 1010.
7. *Cahiers Paul Claudel*, I. *Correspondance Paul Claudel—Stéphane Mallarmé*, p. 25.
8. *Ibid.*, p. 128.
9. *Mémoires improvisés*, pp. 48, 75.
10. *Ibid.*, p. 85.
11. Paul Claudel et André Gide, *Correspondance. 1899—1926*, p. 54.
12. *Mémoires improvisés*, p. 116.
13. Paul Claudel, *Théâtre*, I, p. 27.
14. *Cahiers* I, p. 20.
15. *Mémoires improvisés*, p. 271.
16. *Ibid.*, p. 153.
17. Paul Claudel, *Oeuvre poétique*, p. 90.
18. *Claudel-Gide Correspondance*, p. 81.
19. *Mémoires improvisés*, p. 79.
20. *Ibid.*, p. 151.
21. Jacques Madaule, *Le Drame de Paul Claudel*, p. 139.
22. Harold A. Waters, "Claudel's Partage Desacralized," *L'Esprit Créateur*, Spring, 1973.
23. *Claudel-Gide Correspondance*, p. 152.
24. *Mémoires improvisés*, p. 200.
25. *Ibid.*, pp. 229—31.

26. Claudel-Gide *Correspondance*, p. 60.
27. Paul-André Lesort, *Paul Claudel par lui-même*, p. 80.
28. *Mémoires improvisés*, p. 302.
29. Paul Claudel, *Oeuvre en prose*, p. 387.
   Translation: *Claudel On Theatre*, pp. 44–45.
30. Maurice Pinguet, "Paul Claudel Exegète du Japon," p. 11.
31. *Oeuvre en prose*, pp. 961–963.
32. *Ibid.*, p. 33.
33. *Claudel on Theatre*, p. 18.
34. Claudel-Gide *Correspondance*, p. 84.

2. GOLDEN HEAD

1. Paul Claudel, "Connaissance de l'Est," *Oeuvre poétique*, p. 67.
2. Paul Claudel, "Les Mots ont une âme," *Positions et propositions*. *Oeuvre en prose*, p. 91.
   All quotes from *Tête d'Or* come from the Mercure de France edition (1959).
3. C. G. Jung, *Psychology and Religion: West and East*, p. 346.
4. The Latin noun for tree is masculine; its ending and gender are feminine. See C. G. Jung, *Symbols of Transformation*, p. 232.
5. Edward Edinger, *Ego and Archetype*, p. 232.
6. *Ibid.*
7. *Cahiers Paul Claudel*, I. p. 140.
8. C. G. Jung, Psychology and Religion, p. 209.
9. Mircea Eliade, *Myths, Dreams and Mysteries*, p. 116.
10. George Ferguson, *Signs and Symbols in Christian Art*, p. 48.
11. Jung, *Symbols of Transformation*, p. 359.
12. Jung, *Psychology and Religion*, p. 115.
13. *Ibid.*, p. 205.
14. *Ibid.*, p. 212.
15. *Ibid.*, p. 77.
16. Jung, *Symbols of Transformation*, p. 360.
17. Paul Claudel, *Réflexions sur la poésie*, p. 184.

3. THE CITY

1. Paul Claudel, *Mémoires improvisés*, p. 84.
   All quotes of *La Ville* come from vol. I. of the Pléiade edition of Claudel's *Théâtre* (1947).
2. *Mémoires improvisés*, p. 89.
3. *Ibid.*, p. 93.
4. Claudel will flesh out this idea in his *Poetic Art*.

4. Break of Noon

1. All references to *Partage de Midi* come from Gallimard, 1949 edition. For further references to the sun, see *Oeuvres poétiques*, p. 68.
2. George Ferguson, *Signs and Symbols in Christian Art*, p. 178.
3. Paul Claudel, *Mémoires improvisés*, p. 225.
4. C. G. Jung, *Aion*, pp. 50–1.
5. Paul Claudel, *Oeuvres poétiques*, p. 54.
6. Oeuvres poétiques, p. 100.
7. John Read, *Prelude to Chemistry*, p. 206.

5. The Satin Slipper

1. Paul Claudel, *Oeuvre en prose*, "L'oeil écoute," p. 221.
All quotations from *Le Soulier de Satin* come from the Gallimard edition (1953).
2. Paul Claudel, *Mémoires improvisés*, p. 341.
3. *Oeuvre en prose*, p. 353.
4. Paul Claudel, *Journal*, Cahiers IV, p. 793.
5. *Mémoires improvisés*, p. 353.
6. Lyn Cowan, "On Masochism," *Spring*, 1979, pp. 42–51.
7. Maurice Blanchot, *Les Critiques de notre temps et Claudel*, "L'Autre Claudel," pp. 23–29.

6. The Tidings Brought to Mary

1. *The Tidings Brought to Mary* was a revision of *The Young Girl Violaine*, which Claudel had first written in 1892.
The edition used here of *L'Annonce faite à Marie* was published by Gallimard in 1940.
2. Serge Hutin, *Les Sociétés secrètes*, p. 10.
3. Mircea Eliade, *Patterns in Comparative Religion*, p. 228.
4. George Ferguson, *Signs and Symbols in Christian Art*, p. 40.
5. Eliade, *Patterns in Comparative Religion*, p. 371.
6. Claudel frequently took liberties with history. Charles VII was crowned in July, not at Christmas. *Mémoires improvisés*, p. 272.
7. Eliade, *Patterns in Comparative Religion*, p. 4.
8. C. G. Jung, *Vision Seminars*, I, pp, 123–27.
9. Marie Louise von Franz, *The Feminine in Fairy Tales*, pp. 85–90.
10. Claudel, *Mémoires improvisés*, p. 269.
Claudel had been inspired to include the rebirth miracle in his play

by his readings of German Medieval literature. He had heard of a mystic who had been able to suckle a babe though she had never been pregnant. It was also said that St. Bernard had been suckled by the Virgin herself.

Medically speaking, a woman of childbearing years can produce milk if constantly suckled—even without having a baby. It stimulates the necessary hormones.

11. *Ibid.*, p. 270.

7. The Trilogy

1. Paul Claudel, *Mémoires improvisés*, pp. 278–86.
2. Georges Cattaui, *Claudel*, pp. 106–7.
3. H. G. Baynes, *Mythology of the Soul*, p. 879. Quoted from Blake's *The Marriage of Heaven and Hell*.
4. C. G. Jung, *Psychology and Alchemy*, p. 204.
5. *Ibid.*
6. Norman Cohn, *The Pursuit of the Millenium*, pp. 127–47.
7. Lyn Cowan, "On Masochism," pp. 42–52.
8. André Gide, *Journal*, (Nov. 2, 1930).
9. Paul Claudel, *Correspondance* (Gide) p. 239.
10. John Garraty and Peter Gay, eds., *The New Columbia History of the World*, pp. 803–820.
11. Claudel, *Mémoires improvisés*, p. 280.
12. Arthur Herzberg, *The French Enlightenment and the Jews*, p. 1. See also Léon Poliakov, *Histoire de l'Antisémitisme de Voltaire à Wagner*, pp. 351–71.
13. C. G. Jung, *The Structure and Dynamics of the Psyche*, p. 53.
14. Erich Neumann, *The Origins and History of Consciousness*, p. 174.
15. In the Apocryphal work, the Book of Tobit, we learn that Tobit, a righteous man, was blinded in his sleep and his son, obeying the angel Raphael's orders, was able to restore his sight. Suffering, then, is experienced by good people; in Tobit's case it gave way to the birth of a new and fuller happiness.
16. C. G. Jung, *Alchemical Studies*, pp. 77–8. James Hillmann, "Anima" (II), pp. 113–140.
17. Allah, too, was a gardener in Islam.
18. See Rimbaud's poem "Voyelles" and the line "*U, cycles, vibrements divines des mers virids.*"
19. Esther Harding, *Psychic Energy*, p. 173.
20. C. G. Jung, *Psychology and Religion: West and East*, p. 256.
21. Harding, p. 280.

8. The Diaries of Christopher Columbus

1. Paul Claudel, *Mémoires improvisés*, p. 353.
2. Jean-Louis Barrault, *The Theatre of Jean-Louis Barrault*, p. 202.
3. *Cahiers Paul Claudel*, III. *Correspondance Paul Claudel–Darius Milhaud* (1912–1953), p. 16.
4. *Ibid.*, p. 84.
5. *Ibid.*, p. 293.
6. *Magazine Littéraire*, Novembre 1979.
7. Paul Claudel, *Théâtre* II, Pléiade edition will be the edition from which the quotes are taken, p. 1057.
8. Tsuro Ando, *Bunraku*, pp. 4–10.
9. Martin Esselin, *Brecht*, pp. 23–24.
10. Jean-Louis Barrault, p. 228.
11. *Ibid.*, p. 204. To express the vastness and awesome nature of the Creation scene, Barrault resorted to an ingenious stage device which he describes as follows. "The shapeless and naked earth was fresh mud spread on a large tin tray. By pouring over it a chemical substance it fermented and produced gas which bubbled up and broke through the bubbling surface. The layers of vapour which were supposed to hover over this first surface of the earth were obtained by using tetrachlorine of titane, and the Spirit of God became the Finger of God, for which I humbly lent my hand. I can still see myself lying on a scaffolding, my arm hanging above the tray covered with mud. The fumes caused by the tetrachlorine of titane tickled my throat and every now and then 'God's Finger' was shaken by bouts of coughing which made filming impossible. While God's hand was moulding the earth, God was above shedding floods of tears as if he had been engaged in peeling onions."
12. *Cahiers Paul Claudel*, III, p. 306.
13. Paul Claudel, *Oeuvre en Prose*, p. 1170.
14. Jacques Madaule, *Le Drame de Paul Claudel*, p. 369.
15. Paul Claudel, *Oeuvres complètes*, XIV, p. 258 (May 12, 1935).
16. Madaule, p. 372.
17. *Cahiers Paul Claudel*, V, *Correspondance Paul Claudel–Lugné-Poë*, pp. 63–67.
18. Barrault, pp. 207–08.
19. George Ferguson, *Signs and Symbols in Christian Art*, p. 123.
20. Barrault, p. 204.
21. Ando, pp. 4–10.
22. Paul Claudel, *Oeuvre en Prose*, "Bounrakou," p. 1181.
23. *Ibid.*, "La Légende de Prakriti," pp. 945–961.
24. Heinrich Zimmer, *Philosophies of India*, p. 325.
25. *Cahiers Paul Claudel*, III, p. 79.

26. *Ibid.*, p. 99.
27. *Ibid.*, p. 88.
28. *Ibid.*, p. 99.
29. Ferguson, p. 24.
30. *Mémoires improvisés*, p. 355.

BIBLIOGRAPHY

PRIMARY SOURCES

Théâtre. I. Paris: Pléiade, 1947.
Théâtre. II. Paris: Pléiade, 1948.
Tête d'Or. Paris: Mercure de France, 1959.
Partage de midi. Paris: Gallimard, 1949.
Le Soulier de Satin. Paris: Gallimard, 1953.
L'Otage. Le Pain dur. Le Père humilié. Paris: Gallimard, 1956.
L'Annonce faite à Marie. Paris: Gallimard, 1940.
Oeuvre en prose. Paris: Pléiade, 1965.
Oeuvre poétique. Paris: Pléiade, 1967.
Mémoires improvisés. Paris: Gallimard, 1969.
Cahiers Paul Claudel. Paris: Gallimard I, 1959; II, 1960; III, 1961; V, 1964; VI, 1966; VII, 1968.
Journal. Paris: Pléiade, I. 1968.
Paul Claudel et André Gide Correspondance (1899–1928). Paris: Gallimard, 1969.

TRANSLATIONS OF SOME OF CLAUDEL'S PLAYS

Tête d'Or. Tr. John Strong Newberry. New Haven: Yale University Press, 1919.
The City. Tr. by John Strong Newberry. New Haven: Yale University Press, 1920.
The Book of Christopher Columbus. Tr. by Paul Claudel with the help of Agnes Meyer. New Haven: Yale University Press, 1930.
The Hostage. Crusts. The Humiliation of the Father. Tr. by Reverend Father John O'Connor. Boston: John W. Luce, 1944.

The Satin Slipper. Tr. by Reverend Father John O'Connor. New York: Sheed and Ward, 1955.

The Tidings Brought to Mary. Tr. by Wallace Fowlie. Chicago: H. Regnery Company, 1960.

Break of Noon. Tr. by Wallace Fowlie. Chicago: H. Regnery Company, 1960.

SECONDARY SOURCES

Alter, André. *Paul Claudel.* Paris: Seghers, 1968.

Barjon, Louis. *Paul Claudel.* Paris: Editions universitaires, 1953.

Barrault, Jean-Louis. *The Theatre of Jean-Louis Barrault.* Translated by Joseph Chiari. New York: Hill and Wang, 1961.

Baynes, H. G. *Mythology of the Soul.* London: Rider and Co., 1969.

Béguin. Albert. "Grandeur de Claudel," *Poésie de la présence.* Neuchâtel: La Baconnière, 1957.

Brady, Valentini Papadopoulou, "The Archetypal Structure of Claudel's *Tête d'Or. Romanic Review.* May 3, 1976 (vol. LXVII).

——————, "Mimesis, Artifice, Disbelief, and the Problem of the Supernatural: Paul Claudel's Le Soulier de Satin." *L'Esprit Créateur.* Summer 1978. (vol. XVIII).

Burckhardt, Titus. *Alchemy.* Baltimore, Maryland: Penguin Books, 1971.

Cattauï, Georges and Jacques Madaule, eds. *Entretiens sur Paul Claudel.* Paris: Mouton, 1968.

——————, *Claudel.* Paris: Desclée de Brouwer, 1968.

Cowan, Lyn, "On Masochism," *Spring,* 1979.

Edinger, Edward. *Ego and Archetype.* New York: G. P. Putnam's Sons, 1972.

Eliade, Mircea. *Patterns in Comparative Religion.* New York: New American Library, 1974.

——————, *Myths, Dreams and Mysteries.* New York: Harper Torchbook, 1967.

Esslin, Martin. *Brecht.* New York: Anchor Books, 1961.

Fowlie, Wallace. *Paul Claudel.* London: Bowes and Bowes, 1957.

Ferguson, George. *Signs and Symbols in Christian Art.* New York: Oxford University Press.

Franz, Marie Louise von. *The Feminine in Fairy Tales.* Zürich, Switzerland: Spring, 1972.

Garraty, John, A. and Peter Gay, eds. *New Columbia History of the World.* New York: Harper and Row, 1972.

Griffiths, Richard, ed. *Claudel: A Reappraisal.* London: Rapp and Whiting, 1968.

Guillemin, Henri. *Le "Converti" Paul Claudel.* Paris: Gallimard, 1968.

Harding, Esther. *Psychic Energy*. Princeton: Princeton Univ. Press, 1973.

Herzberg, Arthur. *The French Enlightenment and the Jews*. New York: Schocken Books, 1968.

Hutin, Serge. *L'Alchimie*. Paris: Presses universitaires de France, 1971.

Jung, C. G. *Collected Works*. 5. New York: Pantheon Books, 1956.

_____, *C. W.* 8. Princeton: Princeton University Press, 1969.

_____, *C. W.* 9, ii. Princeton: Princeton University Press, 1968.

_____, *C. W.* 11. New York: Pantheon Books, 1963.

_____, *C. W.* 12. London: Routledge and Kegan Paul, 1953.

_____, *Vision Seminars*. I. Zürich, Switzerland: Spring, 1976.

Knapp, Bettina. *Dream and Image*. Troy, N.Y.: The Whitston Press, 1977.

Lesort, Paul-André. *Paul Claudel par lui-même*. Paris: Seuil, 1963.

Les Critiques de notre temps. Paris: Editions Garnier, 1970.

Lioure, Michel. *L'Esthétique dramatique de Paul Claudel*. Paris: Armand Colin, 1971.

Madaule, Jacques. *Le Drame de Paul Claudel*. Paris: Desclée de Brouwer, 1964.

Marcel, Gabriel. *Regards sur le théâtre de Paul Claudel*. Paris: Beauchesne, 1964.

Micklem, Niel. "The Intolerable Image," *Spring*, 1979.

Mondor, Henri. *Claudel plus intime*. Paris: Gallimard, 1960.

Neumann, Erich, *The Origins and History of Consciousness*. New York: Pantheon Books, 1954.

Parkes, James, *Anti-Semitism*. Chicago: a Quadrangle Paperback, 1963.

Petit, Jacques and Jean-Pierre Kempf. *Claudel on the Theatre*. Coral Gables, Florida: University of Miami Press, 1972.

Peyre, Henri. "The Drama of Paul Claudel," *Thought*, Summer 1952 (vol. XXVIII).

Pinguet, Maurice. "Paul Claudel exégète du Japon," *Etudes de langue et littérature française*, March 1969 (no. 14).

Poliakov, Léon, *Histoire de l'antisémitisme de Voltaire à Wagner*. Paris: Calmann-Lévy, 1968.

Poulet, Georges. *The Metamorphoses of the Circle*. Tr. by Carley Dawson and Elliott Coleman. Baltimore: The Johns Hopkins Press, 1966.

Silberer, Herbert. *Hidden Symbolism of Alchemy and the Occult Arts*. New York: Dover Publications, 1971.

Stillman, John. M. *The Story of Alchemy and Early Chemistry*. New York: Dover Publications, 1970.

Tsuruo, Ando. *Bunraku*. New York: Walker/Weatherhill, 1970.

Vachon, André. *Le Temps et l'espace dans l'oeuvre de Paul Claudel*. Paris: Seuil, 1965.

Watson, Harold. *Claudel's Immortal Heroes*. New Brunswick, New Jersey: Rutgers University Press, 1971.

Zimmer, Heinrich. *Philosophies of India*. Princeton: Princeton University Press, 1974.

INDEX

842

Knapp, Bettina Lie-
bowitz

Paul Claudel

842
Knapp, Bettina Liebowitz
Paul Claudel.

$14.50

AUG 15
NOV 10

S A   1 4 4

SA 3136